RAILWAYS
AN ANTHOLOGY

RAILWAYS

AN ANTHOLOGY

Compiled by
JACK SIMMONS

COLLINS
London · 1991

William Collins Sons & Co. Ltd
London · Glasgow · Sydney · Auckland
Toronto · Johannesburg

First published 1991

BRITISH LIBRARY CATALOGUING IN PUBLICATION DATA

Railways: an anthology.
1. Prose in English. Special subjects: Railways.
Anthologies
I. Simmons, Jack 1915–
828.08

ISBN 0 00 215656 3

Typeset in Linotron Sabon
by Rowland Phototypesetting Ltd
Bury St Edmunds, Suffolk
Printed and bound in Great Britain by
William Collins Sons and Co. Ltd, Glasgow

TO
JOHN AND BETTY DALRYMPLE

CONTENTS

ACKNOWLEDGEMENTS

The compiler is most grateful for comments and suggestions to A. L. Rowse, Michael Robbins, and Alfred Heinimann; and, at Collins, to Carol O'Brien, Vera Brice and Tracy Lamb.

The publishers gratefully acknowledge the following for permission to reproduce copyright extracts in this book.

Ian Allan Ltd for extracts from *Locomotive Panorama* by E. S. Cox; and *Tales of the Glasgow & South Western Railway* by David L. Smith;

Blackstaff Press Ltd for an extract from *The Golden Years of the Great Northern Railway* by R. S. Arnold;

The Bodley Head for an extract from *The Jenguing Pennings* by Paul Jennings;

J. M. Bourne for his piece entitled *Who Cares?*;

British Railways Board and TrainLines of Britain (TLB/90/2409) for extracts from *British Railways Board: The Reshaping of British Railways* by Dr Richard Beeching; and from *Time Table for Victory* by E. John;

Ivor Bulmer-Thomas for an extract from his book *Top Sawyer*;

Cambridge University Press for extracts from *British Railways 1948–73* by T. R. Gourvish; from *Victorian Lincoln* by Sir Francis Hill; and from *Correspondence of Charles Darwin* by J. D. Hooker to Darwin;

Jonathan Cape Ltd for extracts from *Autobiography* by Eric Gill; from *London: the Unique City* by S. E. Rasmussen; and from *The National Trust Book of Bridges* by Sir James Richards;

Frank Cass & Co Ltd for an extract from *Victorian Railwaymen* by P. W. Kingsford;

The Charter Trustees of Burton upon Trent for an extract by H. Edwards from *County Borough: the History of Burton upon Trent* by D. Stuart;

Curtis Brown, London on behalf of John Wain for an extract from his book *The Smaller Sky*, © John Wain, 1967, published by Macmillan;

David & Charles Publishers for extracts from *The Man Who Built London Transport* by Christian Barman; from *The Railway Navvy* by David Brooke; two extracts from *The Northern Counties Railway* by J. R. L. Currie; from *Regional History of the Railways of Great Britain: South Wales* by D. S. M. Barrie; and from *Red for Danger* by L. T. C. Rolt;

Duckworth and Company Ltd for an extract from *Zuleika Dobson* by Sir Max Beerbohm;

Edward Arnold for an extract from *The Age of Peel* by Norman Gash;

Faber and Faber Limited for 'Night Mail' from *Collected Shorter Poems* by W. H. Auden; for an extract from *Manchester Made Them* by Katharine Chorley; for 'Skimbleshanks: The Railway Cat' from *Old Possum's Book of Cats* by T. S. Eliot; for 'Restaurant Car' from *Collected Poems* by Louis MacNiece, edited by E. R. Dodds; for an extract from *The Railway Workers* by Frank McKenna; for an extract from *Without Knowing Mr Walkley* by Edith Olivier; and for an extract from *Period Piece* by Gwen Raverat;

Grafton Books for three extracts from *Notes from Overground* by Tiresias (Roger Green);

Harrap Publishing Group Ltd for an extract from *The Nineteenth Century and After* by Michael Sadleir;

Brian Harrison for an extract from his book *Drink and the Victorians* published by Faber and Faber Ltd;

David Higham Associates, on behalf of Michael Robbins for an extract from his book *Points and Signals* published by Unwin Hyman Ltd; and on behalf of Sir Osbert Sitwell for extracts from *Left Hand, Right Hand*; and *Penny Foolish* published by Macmillan and *Queen Mary and Others* published by Michael Joseph Ltd;

The Historical Model Railway Society for an extract from *Midland Style* by George Dow;

Hodder & Stoughton Publishers Ltd for an extract from *A Norfolk Diary* by B. J. Armstrong;

The Irish Railway Record Society for an extract from a manuscript in the National Library of Ireland which was reproduced in the *Journal of the Irish Railway Record Society*; and for an extract from *The Great Southern & Western Railway* by K. A. Murray and D. B. McNeill;

David Jeffreys for his translation of 'The Tay Bridge' by Theodore Fontane;

The Journal of Renaissance and Modern Studies for a statement by Francis Strelley in proceedings before the Court of Chancery;

Leicestershire Museums Arts and Record Services for an extract from a piece by Sir Gordon Russell in preface to Ernest Gimson exhibition catalogue;

Leicester University Press for two extracts from *British Transport: an Economic Survey from the Seventeenth Century to the Twentieth* by A. J. Dyos and D. H. Aldcroft;

London Regional Transport for an extract from *A History of London Transport* by T. C. Barker and M. Robbins;

Macmillan, London and Basingstoke for extracts from *Henry Ponsonby* by A. Ponsonby; and from *The Life of Thomas Hardy* by Florence Emily Hardy;

John Murray (Publishers) Ltd for the poems 'The Metropolitan Railway' from *A Few Late Chrysanthemums*; and 'Summoned by Bells' by Sir John Betjeman; and for an extract from *Munby: Man of Two Worlds* by Derek Hudson;

Thomas Nelson and Sons Ltd for an extract from *How I Became An Engine Driver* by Norman McKillop;

Nigel Nicolson for an extract from *Some People* by Harold Nicolson;

Northamptonshire Record Office for an extract from *Northampton Vindicated* by Joan Wake;

The Oakwood Press for extracts from *The Barry Railway* by D. S. Barrie; and from *The Great Northern Railway of Ireland* by E. M. Patterson;

Oxford University Press for an extract of a letter from Oscar Wilde to Lord Alfred Douglas taken from *Selected Letters of Oscar Wilde* edited by Rupert Hart-Davis (1979), © Vyvyan Holland 1962;

Peters Fraser and Dunlop Group Ltd on behalf of Evelyn Waugh for an extract from his book *Scoop* published by Chapman and Hall Ltd;

Mrs Eva Reichmann for extracts from *Seven Men and Two Others*; and *Zuleika Dobson* by Sir Max Beerbohm;

Dr C. J. A. Robertson for two extracts from his book *The Origins of the Scottish Railway System 1722–1844*;

Mrs L. T. C. Rolt for an extract from *Railway Adventure* by L. T. C. Rolt, published by Pan Books Limited;

Routledge for extracts from *The Impact of Railways on Victorian Cities* by J. R. Kellett; and from *Early Wooden Railways* by M. J. T. Lewis;

A. L. Rowse for 'Home-Coming to Cornwall' from his book *Poems Chiefly Cornish* published by Faber and Faber Ltd;

George Sassoon for 'A Local Train of Thought' from *Collected Poems, 1908–56* and 'Morning Express' from *Collected Poems* by Siegfried Sassoon, published by Faber and Faber Ltd;

Alan Sutton Publishing for an extract from *Life in a Railway Factory* by Alfred Williams;

Professor Thompson of the Institute of Historical Research for an extract from *Victorian England: the Horse-Drawn Society* by F. M. L. Thompson;

University of Toronto Press for an extract from *Collected Works* by John Stuart Mill;

The University of Wales Press for an extract from *The Golden Valley Railway* by C. L. Mowat;

Unwin Hyman Ltd for extracts from *An Economic History of Transport in Britain* by T. C. Barker and C. I. Savage; from *Britain's Railways in World War I* by J. A. B. Hamilton; and from *J. R. R. Tolkien: a Biography* by Humphrey Carpenter;

Frederick Warne Publishers & Co for an extract from *The Journal of Beatrix Potter 1881–1897* edited by Leslie Linder, copyright © Frederick Warne & Co., 1966, 1989;

Waterstones Booksellers on behalf of Bowes and Bowes Publishers for an extract from *Papers from Lilliput* by J. B. Priestley;

A. P. Watt on behalf of J. I. M. Steward (Michael Innes) for an extract from his book *Appleby's End*;

Dorothy Wise and the St Marylebone Society for an extract from the *Diary of William Taylor* edited by D. Wise;

The Estate of P. G. Wodehouse and Hutchinson (Publishers) for an extract from *Uncle Fred in the Springtime* by P. G. Wodehouse;

Every effort has been made to contact the copyright holders of extracts included in this book. In the instances where this has proved impossible, we offer our apologies to those concerned.

NOTE ON THE ILLUSTRATIONS

The vignettes used to illustrate this book are from the following sources:

title-page, The approach to Leeds (New) station from the east; from *Illustrated London News*, 30 May 1868;

p. 7, The Penrhyn Railway, from *Repertory of Arts and Manufactures*, 2nd series, vol. 3;

p. 11, sketch by John Bourne of men at work on the Great Western Railway, *c.*1839 (Ironbridge Gorge Museum, AE185.128);

p. 38, satirical sketch directed against the Eastern Counties Railway in a fly-sheet by G. W. Ancell, 1856–7;

p. 52, opening of the Canterbury & Whitstable Railway, lithograph by C. J. Hullmandel, 1830;

p. 61, 'The Pleasures of the Rail Road Showing the Inconvenience of a Blow Up' by Hugh Hughes, 1831. (Elton Collection, Ironbridge Gorge Museum, AE502);

p. 73, title page vignette from *Our Iron Roads* by Frederick S. Williams (4th ed., 1883);

p. 90, drawing by Fougasse, from *Punch*, 202 (1942) 327;

p. 125, Didcot station, from G. Measom, *Illustrated Guide to the Great Western Railway* (1852), p. 34;

p. 146, seals of two companies, from W. W. Tomlinson, *The North Eastern Railway* [1915], 106, 353, together with British Rail's logo;

p. 166, signal-box at Charing Cross, from J. Pendleton, *Our Railways* (1896), ii. 284;

p. 191, from *Punch*, 8 (1845) 101;

p. 225, illustration to chap. 3 of Lewis Carroll's *Through the Looking-Glass*, by John Tenniel (1871);

p. 260, 'Dead End', from F. S. Williams, *Our Iron Roads* (7th ed., 1888), 511.

INTRODUCTION

This book brings together some 320 comments that have been passed on railways in Great Britain and Ireland, ranging in length from three words to six printed pages, and in time from 1615 to 1989. That the collection should be limited to the British Isles may seem insular, but anyone who thinks so must recognise that railways have forged a literature across the world. To illuminate them all alike – themselves and their work and the experience they have occasioned – would demand an enormous book. Wolfgang Minaty combed German literature to make his excellent anthology *Die Eisenbahn* in 1984. In *Le Train dans la littérature française* Marc Baroli charted the course of the railway through the wonderfully productive literature of France. As for the United States, the American railroad ballads – to take them alone – would make a book very much larger than this one. A world-wide anthology of railways, in say five volumes prepared by a committee, would seem readable to ten devoted students, no more. And how much joy would that bring?

But if the comments presented here all relate to the British Isles, some of them come from sharp-eyed foreigners: from the Dane S. E. Rasmussen (173);[1] from two highly intelligent German engineers (32) and from Theodor Fontane (20, 81); from Taine and de Franqueville (97, 138); from Nathaniel Hawthorne (95) and the expatriate Henry James (67, 139, 285c).

What was it that such writers as these, whether foreigners or natives, were looking at? Some were only trying to describe operations they saw – though even that might be an exacting task, for several of them were barely literate (11, 19). Some were moved to plain admiration, or to affectionate laughter; others to denigration or fear or intense dislike. As railways grew to be a normal, accepted part of life, familiar to most people, they came to provide a natural setting for imaginative works, in a train or at a station or on the line; but it was a setting different from any other, offering its own opportunities, imposing restrictions. These observers were not required to invent, however. Some of the best did no more than record, needing only a pair of good eyes, a pencil and a scrap of paper or a sound memory. For the railway is unconsciously self-revealing. It has become an institution, to some of those who run it a way of life (208), governed by strict rules, codes of practice and conduct, influenced now and then by something thought of rather vaguely as "public relations"; a craft the railways seldom mastered

---

[1] The numbers in brackets refer to the passages printed in this book.

(see 26, however, 168, 173) and for which they often display no feeling whatever in our time (178).

The literature of railways is not confined to literary works. One may come upon it in odd places: scribbled up in a disused station (285g); proclaimed on gravestones and memorial tablets (205), in a legal judgment (59) or in evidence given to Parliamentary committees (22, 35, 154). Even when the comment is made by a well-known writer it may have been published in an unlikely place. What some people may find one of the best pieces of prose here comes from a letter addressed to a Manchester newspaper in 1884 (268).

The railway cannot properly be thought of as a work of engineering, an economic and administrative device, alone. It was forged and maintained by human beings, for the service of other human beings. This book is not concerned primarily with the railways' technical equipment or their complicated operations, with pounds and pence or with management, though all those important things find a place here. The human beings are the heart of it: those who used the railways, admired or denounced them, the men who built them and made them work. It deals very largely with the people who travelled on the railways themselves or watched them carrying passengers, and with the effects that their work seemed to produce. In that it reflects the literature itself, for most of those who have written about railways in such a way as to interest us now were concerned with them as instruments of human life and effort, and as agents of change. The eyes and minds of some of them reached out in pursuit of that change, delighted by the new facilities, the release the railways afforded (87, 91, 96) through their services and the security and regularity they offered, to a degree never known before (272). But others viewed them much less favourably, pointing to the social miseries and injustice often entailed by their construction (236, 245), to the dangers involved in their working – spelt out carefully in the inspecting officers' reports on accidents (see for instance 80, 83, 84, 160) – and the damage they might cause to the landscape they traversed (58, 219, 268).

Now and then this observation, at its most refined, concentrates itself not on human beings in general or on the community a railway served but on one person, who speaks of it and its arrangements as they affected a single life. People who remember the old Euston station thirty years ago, before it disappeared, will if they are candid be bound to agree that it had become a sad, dreary muddle. Yet it was a place entered and left by millions of human beings, and to many of them its physical shortcomings mattered very little. To some, intent on the meetings to which it opened the way, it personified happiness and love. One of them expressed this feeling in a haunting elegy on the old station (279).

That was the work of a woman. Only twenty-four pieces in this book are due to women writers. Railways may not be, in any special sense, their subject. Yet they all travel on them, and they can comment on their journeys quite as well as men. Some people (I am certainly among them) feel they owe what is the most richly comic account of a railway journey made anywhere in the British Isles to two Irish ladies (117). Emily Dickinson wrote one of the most delightful of all tributes to a locomotive, "I like to see it lap the miles", but alas it has had to be excluded here according to the rules of the book, for it relates to New England, not to Old. (Those rules have also required the omission of Kipling's splendid poem "The King".) Patricia Beer illuminates the character and conduct of a little line in East Devon (her father was a railwayman there) and muses on its closing (55). Confronted with a railway Beatrix Potter's eyes, as usual, missed nothing (260d, 273).

Looked at all together, these writers make up an interesting company. Among the professionals four Victorians stand out, as one might expect: Dickens, Ruskin, Trollope, and Hardy, each with several pieces in the book. Three politicians who were, or became, Prime Ministers figure here; two Poets Laureate; three clergymen. Railway men, of different types, show us something of their own business. We come here face to face with George Stephenson in the early days and with Brunel, the most articulate of railway engineers. Then in 1889 we can observe George Findlay, who was the first officer of an English company to set out with the deliberate intention of describing and interpreting the practices of railway management to the public; a public that had shown itself strongly critical of that management for more than twenty years before he wrote. His book was a pioneer, a deft and intelligent exercise in public relations. At the same time too a much younger man, W. M. Acworth, published his observations on the railways of England. He wrote in a way that was intelligible and highly attractive to the general reader. These two men's success in their widely different tasks can be proved, for five editions of each of their books were called for in 1889–1900.

Acworth has had no successor in the twentieth century. No writer equally expert has appeared, commanding the same respect both in the railway and in the academic worlds, and at the same time communicating easily and plainly with laymen. On the other hand the range of opportunities for recording well-informed comment on railway matters was greatly enlarged in his time by the multiplication of journals and other vehicles for publishing, and a new interest in railways showed itself among imaginative writers who had no connection with railways at all, which has carried on into our own time. Arnold Bennett and Max Beerbohm, Sassoon and Eliot and Wodehouse and Betjeman all figure in this book; Osbert Sitwell too, damning trains as "slums on wheels" (286g).

He wrote, as usual, with a satirist's exaggeration, tongue in cheek. But his dislike of railways has come to be widely shared in the twentieth century; notably by those who support and make use of other means of transport, though not by them alone. Politicians have treated them with undisguised cynicism, as a public service to be favoured or disadvantaged not in accordance with any long-term strategy of social or economic development but as passing opportunity might seem to them and their advisers to dictate, and with no regard whatever to the morale of the service itself, which ought to have been among their cares (256). High technology has been accompanied on the British railways by low reliability. The timetables they issue twice a year contain a great deal of inaccurate or carelessly-presented information. The computer is a great new public servant, but it needs a direction that British Rail seems unable to supply.

Yet at the same time something of just the opposite tendency has emerged. The contraction of the railway system, in the face of improving transport on the roads and in the air, moved slowly in the 1930s, quickened as a consequence of Hitler's war, and then gathered speed rapidly in the 1950s and 1960s. This was seen by many people to be a weakening of the vital services they relied on; services, moreover, to which Great Britain had just owed a debt in war-time that was beyond adequate acknowledgement (204–5). It represented the loss of a lifelong acquaintance, an old companion, or at least a tool of life that seemed to be there for good. The displacement of the steam engine, carried through at what some well-qualified observers thought a brash and injudicious speed (48), symbolised the whole process, and it provoked an extraordinary demonstration of regret and resentment. Much of this was futile, an attempt to resist changes that were demonstrably required. Dr Beeching, who enunciated the "reshaping of British railways", was held up – to my surprise, he is still held up in some quarters thirty years later – as a figure of evil. Most unjustly: for he was a public servant, making a case for what had to be done to relieve the railways of part of the burden they carried, and making it cogently (175). But the emotion was there, and it would express itself; sometimes after a very dignified fashion, rather in the spirit of what Cromwell called "cruel necessity", and – though very rarely – enjoying the luck to be recorded by an eye-witness who could do justice to both the necessity and the sadness (54, 55).

This reaction against public policy went further than demonstrations of mourning as lines were shut down and steam engines taken out of service. It set out positively to find the means of keeping some of what had been condemned, or of resurrecting it after it had been killed. The way to success in this effort was shown when the Talyllyn Railway was prevented from closing and put immediately on to its feet, by a society formed for the purpose, in 1950–1 (56). This successful operation was quickly matched by others. Today there are some fifty "preserved" railways in the British Isles, running passenger services in summer over nearly 200 miles of line.

None of these enterprises was ever expected to make a true profit. The work has called for much professional expertise, in engineering, management, and finance. But though some of that has of course had to be paid

4

for, the whole is essentially an achievement of amateurs. Most of them are amateurs in the fullest sense of the word: they are lovers of railways. Similar things have been done all over the world during the past forty years, some of them on a considerably larger scale. But the example was set on that Welsh railway, and Wales has reaped the reward it deserved. Its "Great Little Trains" have drawn many visitors there, to look at them and enjoy travelling on them through a remarkable landscape, and the money they have spent has aided the economy of a tract of the British Isles that has never been rich.

It is right to end the consideration of the things that have gone into this book by dwelling on the affectionate attitude towards railways displayed in Britain. The mechanically-worked railway was set going there on a path of its own; a path that proved to be different from that laid down in other countries, different in management, in engineering, and in operation. The British government played no part at all in determining the system (210, 217), and though there were those who thought, at various times, that it should assert itself and take them over (236), that policy did not prevail until 1947. A British railway came to be immediately recognisable, even on a casual inspection, as something different from one that was to be seen anywhere else: its carriages smaller and divided into compartments, which most North Americans disliked (104); its engines smaller too (for running in small islands), neat and trim, concealing many of their moving parts (50, 274); adorned with a spare and telling precision and painted in a striking variety of colours – green, red, blue, brown, black.

Those liveries, worn by engines and carriages alike (46), personified the British railways' competitive system. For all the discomfort, and some-times the strong hostility, that railways might arouse in Britain, the general affection for them lasted, and is apparent still. It derives ultimately from a certain pride, in the fact – clear beyond argument – that Britain pioneered the mechanically-worked railway. As an American put it, looking back to the opening of the Liverpool & Manchester line in 1830: "Its advent was in the highest degree dramatic. It was even more so than the discovery of America" (7).

*

A little needs to be said about the distribution of the pieces printed here.

The first section of the book brings together a small number of passages illustrating the early emergence of the railway in Britain. The next two are concerned with the building of the lines, the machinery used in working them, and the speed the service attained – one of the most evident and undeniable advantages it enjoyed in competition with any other form of long-distance public transport until the middle of the twentieth century. Section 4 considers the opening of lines and, in our own time, examples of their closing and revival. In spite of what they offered, they had to face opposition and strong public criticism (Section 5), exacerbated by misfortunes they encountered and by much that was evidently wrong with their operation (Section 6).

Section 7 opens out the whole act of travelling by train, the opportunities, the pleasures and unhappiness to which it might give rise. In Section 8 stations are treated on their own; the chief interface between railways and their public. The next two sections illustrate the working of the railways: their organisation (Section 9), the men of all kinds who built and ran them (Section 10).

Section 11 looks at the part the railways came to play in the life of the community of these islands as a whole. And finally, Section 12 tries to draw together something of the total experience that arose from railways and their working, to consider the impression they have made on the minds and eyes, the imagination of those who saw and used them.

The date in diamond brackets at the end of each piece gives the date (or approximate date) that the piece refers to. The order of the pieces within each section is usually chronological (except where a number of short ones on a single subject have been grouped together).

This book is in no sense a history of railways. But it is a commentary on that history, largely in the words of men and women who observed it themselves but also, at some points, in those of historians who have looked back and reflected on it since.

Leicester   J.S.
September 1990

1

Prehistory

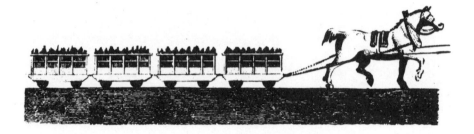

1. ORIGINS

The first clear references to what we now call "railways" in Britain relate to the years 1603–5, with traction by horses and men. Here is a brief account of one in use, at Wollaton in Nottinghamshire in 1615. The words "railway" and "railroad" have been traced first in Staffordshire and Shropshire in 1681–1702.

The said Huntingdon Beaumont hath used new and extraordinary inventions and practices for the speedy and easy conveyance of the said coals, and especially by breaking the soil for laying of rails to carry the same upon with great ease and expedition the length of two miles or thereabouts, and by drawing of certain carrylaggs [carriages] laden with coals upon the same rails. ⟨1615⟩   Statement by Francis Strelley in proceedings before the Court of Chancery, 1615: Richard S. Smith in *Renaissance and Modern Studies* (1960), 123

2. WIND-POWER AT NEATH

His [Sir Humphry Mackworth's] new sailing-waggons, for the cheap carriage of his coal to the water-side (*whereby one horse does the work of ten at all times*; but when any wind is stirring, which is seldom wanting near the sea, *one man and a small sail does the work of twenty*) . . . do sufficiently show what his genius is capable of in matters of that nature. And I believe he is the first gentleman, in this part of the world, that hath set up *sailing-engines on land, driven by the wind*, not for any curiosity or vain applause, but for real profit. ⟨1698⟩

> William Waller, *An Essay on the Mines, late of Sir Carbery Price* (1698), preface

3. THE TANFIELD WAGGONWAY

We are so accustomed nowadays to the achievements of engineering that it takes some imagination to understand the contemporary astonishment at these works [the Causey Arch in Co. Durham and the great embankment near by], which would be a mere flea-bite to a nineteenth-century railway engineer. But in the 1720s nothing had been built on this scale since Roman times, as Bowes realised when he compared his waggonway with the greatest Roman road of Italy. Small wonder, then, that people came from far and wide to gaze open-mouthed at man's mastery over Nature in the cause of trade and industry. Though they did not know it, they stood on the threshold of the Industrial Revolution. Romans apart, there had been few precedents for a work of this magnitude: the French canals of the seventeenth century, a number of docks and harbours, but little else. It might be said that it was on the Tanfield waggonway that British civil engineering on a grand scale first saw the light of day; while at the same time mechanical power, in the shape of Newcomen's steam engine, was wheezing into life. ⟨1720s⟩

> M. J. T. Lewis, *Early Wooden Railways* (1970), 150

4. THE FIRST KNOWN ACCOUNT OF A RAILWAY JOURNEY

I never spent an afternoon with more delight than the former one [2 August 1808], in exploring the peculiarly romantic scenery of Oystermouth. I was conveyed there in a carriage of a singular construction, built for the conveniency of parties, who go hence [from Swansea] to Oystermouth to spend the day.

This car contains twelve persons and is constructed chiefly of iron, its four wheels run on an iron railway by the aid of one horse, and is an easy and light vehicle. ⟨1808⟩

> Elizabeth Isabella Spence, *Summer Excursions through Parts of Oxfordshire . . . and South Wales* (2nd ed., 1809), ii. 98

5. GEORGE STEPHENSON AGREES TO TAKE A PUPIL

I will engage to take your son to give him instruction in my profession for the term of five, six, or seven years. My fee is 200 guineas at the signing of the indentures; his board and lodging to be paid by his friends, until I can receive such a sum for his labour as will pay for it. He will be boarded in my house for £1 per week, exclusive of washing, or in any other house if he prefers it.

When travelling with me on business his expenses will be paid him.

Your son will have a full opportunity of learning the various parts of surveying and taking levels, and making plans and sections of the same. Also bridge-building, steam engine building, and the various branches of mining engineering. (Signed) George Stephenson ⟨1827⟩

> George Stephenson to W. T. Salvin, Croxdale, near Durham, 25 June 1827: Durham Record Office, D/Sa/6, 139.2

6. A NOBLE SALUTE

We see, in this magnificent invention, the well-spring of intellectual, moral, and political benefits, beyond all measurement and all price – the source of a better physical distribution of our population – a check to the alarming growth of cities, especially of manufacturing towns, and of this Babylon in which we write – and the source, above all, of such a diffusion of intelligence over the whole country as those statesmen who think the most worthily of human nature will be the least afraid to contemplate. ⟨1830⟩

> *Quarterly Review*, 42 (1830), 404

7.   THE RAILWAY BURSTS ON THE WORLD

The great peculiarity of the locomotive engine and its sequence, the railroad, as compared with other and far more important inventions, was that it burst rather than stole or crept upon the world. Its advent was in the highest degree dramatic. It was even more so than the discovery of America. . . .

It was this element of spontaneity, therefore – the instantaneous and dramatic recognition of success, which gave a peculiar interest to everything connected with the Manchester & Liverpool railroad. The whole world was looking at it, with a full realising sense that something great and momentous was impending. Every day people watched the gradual development of the thing, and actually took part in it. In doing so they had sensations, and those sensations they have described. There is consequently an element of human nature surrounding it. The complete ignoring of this element by both Smiles and Jeaffreson is a defect in their narratives. They describe the scene from a standpoint of forty years later. Others described it as they saw it at the time. To their descriptions time has only lent a new freshness. They are full of honest wonder.

⟨1830⟩   Charles Francis Adams, jr., *Railroads: their Origin and Problems* (1886 ed.), 3–5

2

Construction

mixing mortar

8. STEAMBOATS, VIADUCTS, AND RAILWAYS

Motions and Means, on land and sea at war
With old poetic feeling, not for this
Shall ye, by Poets even, be judged amiss!
Nor shall your presence, howsoe'er it mar
The loveliness of Nature, prove a bar
To the Mind's gaining that prophetic sense
Of future change, that point of vision, whence
May be discovered what in soul ye are.
In spite of all that beauty may disown
In your harsh features, Nature doth embrace
Her lawful aspect in Man's art; and Time,
Pleased with your triumphs o'er his brother Space,
Accepts from your bold hands the proffered crown
Of hope, and smiles on you with cheer sublime.

⟨1833⟩ William Wordsworth: *Shorter Poems*
(Everyman ed.), 573

9. HOW TO DEAL WITH THE RAILWAYS

One form of business which was beginning to breed just then was the construction of railways. A projected line was to run through Lowick parish where the cattle had hitherto grazed in a peace unbroken by astonishment. . . .

The submarine railway may have its difficulties; but the bed of the sea is not divided among various landed proprietors with claims for damages not only measurable but sentimental. In the hundred to which Middlemarch belonged railways were as exciting a topic as the Reform Bill or the imminent horrors of Cholera, and those who held the most decided views on the subject were women and landholders. Women both old and young regarded travelling by steam as presumptuous and dangerous, and argued against it by saying that nothing should induce them to get into a railway carriage; while proprietors, differing from each other in their arguments as much as Mr Solomon Featherstone differed from Lord Medlicote, were yet unanimous in the opinion that in selling land, whether to the Enemy of mankind or to a company obliged to purchase, these pernicious agencies must be made to pay a very high price to landowners for permission to injure mankind.

But the slower wits, such as Mr Solomon and Mrs Waule, who both occupied land of their own, took a long time to arrive at this conclusion, their minds halting at the vivid conception of what it would be to cut the Big Pasture in two, and turn it into three-cornered bits, which would be "nohow"; while accommodation-bridges and high payments were remote and incredible.

"The cows will all cast their calves, Brother", said Mrs Waule, in a tone of deep melancholy, "if the railway comes across the Near Close; and I shouldn't wonder at the mare too, if she was in foal. It's a poor tale if a widow's property is to be spaded away, and the law say nothing to it. What's to hinder 'em from cutting right and left if they begin? It's well known, *I* can't fight."

"The best way would be to say nothing, and set somebody on to send 'em away with a flea in their ear, when they came spying and measuring", said Solomon. "Folks did that about Brassing, by what I can understand. It's all a pretence, if the truth was known, about their being forced to take one way. Let 'em go cutting in another parish. And I don't believe in any pay to make amends for bringing a lot of ruffians to trample your crops. Where's a company's pocket?"

"Brother Peter, God forgive him, got money out of a company", said Mrs Waule. "But that was for the manganese. That wasn't for railways to blow you to pieces right and left."

"Well, there's this to be said, Jane", Mr Solomon concluded, lowering his voice in a cautious manner – "the more spokes we put in their wheel, the more they'll pay us to let 'em go on, if they must come whether or not".....

He set about acting on his views in a thoroughly diplomatic manner, by stimulating suspicion. His side of Lowick was the most remote from the village, and the houses of the labouring people were either lone cottages or were collected in a hamlet called Frick, where a water-mill and some stone-pits made a little centre of slow, heavy-shouldered industry.

In the absence of any precise idea as to what railways were, public opinion in Frick was against them; for the human mind in that grassy corner had not the proverbial tendency to admire the unknown, holding rather that it was likely to be against the poor man, and that suspicion was the only wise attitude with regard to it.

Thus the mind of Frick was exactly of the sort for Mr Solomon Featherstone to work upon, he having more plenteous ideas of the same order, with a suspicion of heaven and earth which was better fed and more entirely at leisure. Solomon was overseer of the roads at that time, and on his slow-paced cob often took his rounds by Frick to look at the workmen getting the stones there, pausing with a mysterious deliberation, which might have misled you into supposing that he had some other reason for staying than the mere want of impulse to move. After looking for a long while at any work that was going on, he would raise his eyes a little and look at the horizon; finally he would shake his bridle, touch his horse with the whip, and get it to move slowly onward. The hour-hand of a clock was quick by comparison with Mr Solomon, who had an agreeable sense that he could afford to be slow. He was in the habit of pausing for a cautious, vaguely-designing chat with every hedger or ditcher on his way, and was especially willing to listen even to news which he had heard before, feeling himself at an advantage over all narrators in partially disbelieving them. One day, however, he got into a dialogue with Hiram Ford, a waggoner, in which he himself contributed information. He wished to know whether Hiram had seen fellows with staves and instruments spying about: they called themselves railroad people, but there was no telling what they were, or what they meant to do. The least they pretended was that they were going to cut Lowick Parish into sixes and sevens.

"Why, there'll be no stirrin' from one pla-ace to another", said Hiram, thinking of his waggon and horses.

"Not a bit", said Mr Solomon. "And cutting up fine land such as this parish! Let 'em go into Tipton, say I. But there's no knowing what there is at the bottom of it. Traffick is what they put for'ard; but it's to do harm to the land and the poor man in the long run."

"Why, they're Lunnon chaps, I reckon", said Hiram, who had a dim notion of London as a centre of hostility to the country.

"Ay, to be sure. And in some parts against Brassing, by what I've heard say, the folks fell on 'em when they were spying and broke their peep-holes as they carry, and drove 'em away, so as they knew better than come again."

"It was good foon, I'd be bound", said Hiram, whose fun was much restricted by circumstances.

"Well, I wouldn't meddle with 'em myself", said Solomon. "But some say this country's seen its best days, and the sign is, as it's being overrun with these fellows trampling right and left, and wanting to cut it up into railways; and all for the big traffic to swallow up the little, so as there shan't be a team left on the land, nor a whip to crack."

"I'll crack my whip about their ear'n, afore they bring it to that, though", said Hiram, while Mr Solomon, shaking his bridle, moved onwards. ⟨c.1835⟩   George Eliot, *Middlemarch* (Penguin ed. 1871), 597–600

10. STAGGS'S GARDENS

(a)

This euphonious locality was situated in a suburb, known by the inhabitants of Staggs's Gardens by the name of Camberling Town; a designation which the Stranger's Map of London . . . condenses, with some show of reason, into Camden Town. . . .

The first shock of a great earthquake had, just at that period, rent the whole neighbourhood to its centre. Traces of its course were visible on every side. Houses were knocked down; streets broken through and stopped; deep pits and trenches dug in the ground; enormous heaps of earth and clay thrown up; buildings that were undermined and shaking, propped by great beams of wood. Here, a chaos of carts, overthrown and jumbled together, lay topsy-turvy at the bottom of a steep unnatural hill; there, confused treasures of iron soaked and rusted in something that had accidentally become a pond. Everywhere were bridges that led nowhere; thoroughfares that were wholly impassable; Babel towers of chimneys, wanting half their height; temporary wooden houses and enclosures, in the most unlikely situations; carcases of ragged tenements, and fragments of unfinished walls and arches, and piles of scaffolding, and wildernesses of bricks, and giant forms of cranes, and tripods straddling above nothing. There were a hundred thousand shapes and substances of incompleteness, wildly mingled out of their places, upside down, burrowing in the earth, aspiring in the air, mouldering in the water, and unintelligible as any dream. Hot springs and fiery eruptions, the usual attendants upon earthquakes, lent their contributions of confusion to the scene. Boiling water hissed and heaved within dilapidated walls; whence, also, the glare and roar of flames came issuing forth; and mounds of ashes blocked up rights of way, and wholly changed the law and custom of the neighbourhood.

In short, the yet unfinished and unopened Railroad was in progress; and, from the very core of all this dire disorder, trailed smoothly away, upon its mighty course of civilisation and improvement.

But as yet, the neighbourhood was shy to own the Railroad. One or two bold speculators had projected streets; and one had built a little, but had stopped among the mud and ashes to consider further of it. A bran-new Tavern, redolent of fresh mortar and size, and fronting nothing at all, had taken for its sign The Railway Arms; but that might be rash enterprise – and then it hoped to sell drink to the workmen. So, the Excavators' House of Call had sprung up from a beer-shop; and the old-established Ham and Beef Shop had become the Railway Eating House, with a roast leg of pork daily, through interested motives of a similar immediate and popular description. Lodging-house keepers were favourable in like manner; and for the like reasons were not to be trusted. The general belief was very slow. There were frowzy fields, and cow-houses, and dunghills, and dustheaps, and ditches, and gardens, and summer-houses, and carpet-beating grounds, at the very door of the Railway. Little tumuli of oyster shells in the oyster season, and of lobster shells in the lobster season, and of broken crockery and faded cabbage leaves in all seasons, encroached upon its high places. Posts, and rails, and old cautions to trespassers, and backs of mean houses, and patches of wretched vegetation, stared it out of countenance. Nothing was the better for it, or thought of being so. If the miserable waste ground lying near it could have laughed, it would have laughed it to scorn, like many of the miserable neighbours.

(b)

There was no such place as Staggs's Gardens. It had vanished from the earth. Where the old rotten summer-houses once had stood, palaces now reared their heads, and granite columns of gigantic girth opened a vista to the railway world beyond. The miserable waste ground, where the refuse-matter had been heaped of yore, was swallowed up and gone; and in its frowsy stead were tiers of warehouses, crammed with rich goods and costly merchandise. The old by-streets now swarmed with passengers and vehicles of every kind; the new streets that had stopped disheartened in the mud and waggon-ruts, formed towns within themselves, originating wholesome comforts and conveniences belonging to themselves, and never tried nor thought of until they sprung into existence. Bridges that had led to nothing, led to villas, gardens, churches, healthy public walks. The carcases of houses, and beginnings of new thoroughfares, had started off upon the line at steam's new speed, and shot away into the country in a monster train.

As to the neighbourhood which had hesitated to acknowledge the railroads in its straggling days, that had grown wise and penitent, as any

Christian might in such a case, and now boasted of its powerful and prosperous relation. There were railway patterns in its drapers' shops, and railway journals in the windows of its newsmen. There were railway hotels, office-houses, lodging-houses, boarding-houses; railway plans, maps, views, wrappers, bottles, sandwich-boxes, and timetables; railway hackney coach and cab stands; railway omnibuses, railway streets and buildings, railway hangers-on and parasites, and flatterers out of all calculation. There was even railway time observed in clocks, as if the sun itself had given in. Among the vanquished was the master chimney-sweeper, whilome incredulous at Staggs's Gardens, who now lived in a stuccoed house three stories high, and gave himself out, with golden flourishes upon a varnished board, as contractor for the cleansing of railway chimneys by machinery.

To and from the heart of this great change, all day and night, throbbing currents rushed and returned incessantly like its life's blood. Crowds of people and mountains of goods, departing and arriving scores and scores of times in every four-and-twenty hours, produced a fermentation in the place that was always in action. The very houses seemed disposed to pack up and take trips. Wonderful Members of Parliament, who, little more than twenty years before, had made themselves merry with the wild railroad theories of engineers, and given them the liveliest rubs in cross-examination, went down into the north with their watches in their hands, and sent on messages before by the electric telegraph, to say that they were coming. Night and day the conquering engines rumbled at their distant work, or, advancing smoothly to their journey's end, and gliding like tame dragons into the allotted corners grooved out to the inch for their reception, stood bubbling and trembling there, making the walls quake, as if they were dilating with the secret knowledge of great powers yet unsuspected in them, and strong purposes not yet achieved.

But Staggs's Gardens had been cut up root and branch. Oh woe the day when "not a rood of English ground" – laid out in Staggs's Gardens – is secure! ⟨1836–8⟩   Charles Dickens, *Dombey and Son* (1846–7), chaps 6, 15

11.   THE POWER OF STEAM

William Tayler, a London footman, kept a diary in 1837, in which he recorded a number of visits made to see railways at work or under construction.

21 Sept. Went to see the Birmingham railroad. Saw the steam carriage start with about thirty more fastened to it. All these thirty was full of people. The steam engine is something like a very large barel on four wheels. It's

wonderful how such a small thing can drag so many carriages after it with such a wait [weight]. It's a proof what a strong thing steam is. ⟨1837⟩

Diary of William Tayler, ed. D. Wise (1962), 51

12. GENERAL PASLEY INSPECTS A TUNNEL

The tunnel at Higham, east of Gravesend, had been built for a canal and was now adapted to serve a railway as well.

The attention of the Government inspectors had been specially called to the tunnel, not only on account of the novelty of the wooden viaduct, but by reason of the fact that it was only lined with masonry for a short distance from either end, and through a few intermediate lengths, where the material was apparently less firm than for the great length of the bore. It was cut through solid chalk, which for the most part showed a fair and regular section. But in some places slips had occurred during the original construction, and lofty domes and galleries ran far above the ordinary level of the crown of the arch. To test the stability of these portions, General Pasley adopted the original, and strictly military, expedient, of firing wooden plugs at the roof. A corporal and small party of sappers and miners, with a mortar and ammunition, awaited the inspecting party at the mouth of the tunnel. A large barge had been prepared, on which a sort of pulpit had been constructed for the inspector, by standing on which he could, with a small mahogany-handled pick, also provided for the occasion, tap the crown of the tunnel as he advanced. The barge was towed by a party of men, furnished with torches. The battery was placed in the forepart of the barge, and Bengal lights were fired from time to time, which brought out into strong shadow each irregularity of the masonry or excavation. On arriving at the first dome-like cavern, the General began to shout, and then in a moment to swear. "Stop, stop! How can I tell what is going on here? Stop, I say!" The engineer in charge was prepared for the emergency. He had constructed the platform on which the General was stationed so as to slide upwards when necessary. "Now, boys", he shouted, "hoist up the General." Up shot the platform, with the officer still in the height of his wrath. But finding himself thus unexpectedly in motion, and brought up to the lofty top of the rift, while the whole scene was suddenly illumined by a Bengal light, the old soldier laughed so heartily as to shake the barge itself. He was greatly delighted with the joke, or rather with the well-adapted nature of the expedient, and specially referred to it in his report to Government. He satisfied himself by firing three discharges in different parts of the tunnel and arrived in high glee at the eastern terminus, no results except a deafening roar having attended his military test.

"How shall I go back, General?" said the engineer in charge of the works, after the last station had been walked over. The inspector, who had made his way down partly on foot and partly on the footboard of the locomotive, stepped quietly into a first-class carriage for the return. "Go?" said he. "How? Go like the devil." It was a rude test for the tunnel viaduct, but none too rude. A snug *parti carré* at the fish dinner concluded the inspection, to the satisfaction of all parties. ⟨1844⟩

F. R. Conder, *Personal Recollections of English Engineers,*
republished as *The Men Who Built Railways* (1983),
154–6

13. SURVEYING IN WALES

While at Leicester I had been altogether out of the business world and do not remember even looking at a newspaper, or I might have heard something of the great railway mania which that year reached its culmination. I now first heard rumours of it, and some one told me of a civil engineer in Swansea who wanted all the surveyors he could get, and that they all had two guineas a day, and often more. This I could hardly credit, but I wrote to the gentleman, who soon after called on me, and asked me if I could do levelling. I told him I could, and had a very good level and levelling staves. After some little conversation he told me he wanted a line of levels up the Vale of Neath to Merthyr Tydfil for a proposed railway, with cross levels at frequent intervals, and that he would give me two guineas a day, and all expenses of chain and staff men, hotels, etc. He gave me all necessary instructions, and said he would send a surveyor to map the route at the same time. This was, I think, about midsummer, and I was hard at work till the autumn, and enjoyed myself immensely. It took me up the south-east side of the valley, of which I knew very little, along pleasant lanes and paths through woods and by streams, and up one of the wildest and most picturesque little glens I have ever explored. Here we had to climb over huge rocks as big as houses, ascend cascades, and take cross-levels up steep banks and precipices all densely wooded. It was surveying under difficulties, and excessively interesting. After the first rough levels were taken and the survey made, the engineers were able to mark out the line provisionally, and I then went over the actual line to enable the sections to be drawn as required by the Parliamentary Standing Orders.

In this year of wild speculation it is said that plans and sections for 1263 new railways were duly deposited, having a proposed capital of £563,000,000, and the sum required to be deposited at the Board of Trade was so much larger than the total amount of gold in the Bank of England and notes in circulation at the time, that the public got frightened, a panic ensued, shares in the new lines which had been at a high premium fell almost to nothing, and even the established lines were greatly depreciated. Many of the lines were proposed merely for speculation, or to be bought off by opposing lines which had a better chance of success. The line we were at work on was a branch of the Great Western and South Wales Railway then making, and was for the purpose of bringing the coal and iron of Merthyr Tydfil and the surrounding district to Swansea, then the chief port of South Wales. ⟨1845⟩

Alfred Russel Wallace, *My Life* (1908 ed.), 131–3

14. RAPID RAILWAY BUILDING

The line between York and Scarborough was opened only a week after an Act had been passed authorising a deviation near York.

After the royal assent to the Act had been obtained on Monday, notice to quit was given on Tuesday to certain landowners with whom the company had not been able to make an arrangement; forcible possession was taken on Wednesday; the rails were laid on Thursday; and Major-General Sir Charles Pasley [Inspector-General of Railways] surveyed the line on Friday. . . . The line was opened on Monday last. ⟨1845⟩

Liverpool Mail, 12 July 1845

15. LEVEL CROSSINGS

When railways wished to cross roads on the level their passage called for careful regulation. In 1839 they were statutorily required to provide adequate gates to close their traffic off from that on the roads, attended by "good and proper persons". Such crossings might prove troublesome over the years, as rail traffic grew. They were adopted at Lincoln (a) and Lostwithiel (b) after careful consideration; yet both of these had, in later years, to be expensively replaced. Most of the persons appointed to look after them did indeed prove good and proper. When they were not, their negligence might have to be supplied by any responsible citizen (c).

(a)

The prospect of two crossings [over Lincoln High Street] 200 yards apart caused dismay. . . . The most urgent representations were made, and the Town Clerk was sent to London to pursue them. There he was assured that the city's representations were exaggerated, and he was advised to go to Canterbury to form a judgment upon the degree of inconvenience caused by a level crossing over a street. There the Mayor and a bench of magistrates affirmed to him that the crossing of their High Street caused not the slightest inconvenience; it had not nearly so great an effect as a turnpike gate would cause in the same situation, and they would as lief it were there as not. His own impressions confirmed this opinion; eighteen trains a day, each taking two minutes to cross, was a tolerable burden. So reassured, the City Council took no further action, with results that afflict the city to this day. ⟨1845⟩   Sir Francis Hill, *Victorian Lincoln* (1974), 114

(b)

The case of the road crossing at Lostwithiel is a very difficult one – I have quite as strong an objection to level crossings as anybody can have and they are a source of constant expense to the railway company, but there are cases in which it is almost impossible to avoid them and in which even if possible the remedy would be more inconvenient to the public than the original evil – and this is one of those cases. The present road is low and the ground liable to be flooded, we are obliged therefore to keep the railway a little above the present level of the road, so that if the latter was carried over the railway it would be raised nearly 22ft, but the line of railway is unavoidably carried close to the present river bridge – about 20 to 25 yards only between the two and the nature of the ground and the course of the river determine this, without remedy. If the road were raised 22ft over the railway therefore it would be nearly 15ft above the present river bridge – which of course would be impracticable and involve a much greater inconvenience to the public than the level crossing. With regard to level crossings, without pretending to advocate their use yet the result of experience proves that they are really attended with no danger and very little inconvenience to the public, particularly near a station, as this will be. ⟨1854⟩   I. K. Brunel to W. H. Bond, 23 March 1854: printed in *Journal of Transport History* 3 (1957–8), 204

(c)

Chapel Row crossing was on the other side of Laurencetown station [Co. Down]. One morning as the first train approached, the gateman apparently remained asleep, despite repeated whistles from the 0-6-0. At the last minute a priest appeared in full regalia from Tullylish chapel a few yards away and proceeded to open the gates like a man who had been doing it all his life. ⟨?1930s⟩   R. S. Arnold, *The Golden Years of the Great Northern Railway* (1983 ed.), i, 4

16. ROUGH TRACK

Perhaps the most interesting feature of the old days [on the Great Southern & Western Railway of Ireland] was the original permanent way, which was laid throughout in 1846 with ∩-shaped iron bridge rails, weighing no less than 90lb per yard, and spiked to cross sleepers. There were no fish-plates, but specially wide sleepers were placed beneath the rail joints. The spikes were of a strong hook-shaped pattern. The permanent way was intended to last, and so much faith did the Irishmen place in its lasting qualities that they forgot to repair it properly, a neglect probably also due to lack of money. Between 1870 and 1875 it had become almost the worst permanent way in the kingdom; the iron rails were constantly breaking, and the effect on the engine springs was shattering. Although by 1880 many miles had been relaid with steel rails in chairs, each engine always carried a spare leading spring in case of emergencies. The emergency generally came off, and but few engines returned to Inchicore [the company's works, outside Dublin] with the same complete set of springs as that with which they had started, in spite of the fact that the leading springs were made specially strong to resist breakage. As for tyres of the old iron or the later soft Bessemer steel variety, though they were there today they were gone tomorrow. Alexander McDonnell, chief locomotive engineer from 1864 to 1881, replaced the old tyres with very hard crucible steel ones, but the engineer's department was so fond of the old rails that it did not like to part with them, so that even in the late seventies it was considered particularly fortunate if an express engine got through from Dublin to Cork without breaking a spring. . . .

When the old rails on the main line had been broken into a sufficient number of pieces, they were used to fill up odd gaps on the branch lines, where lengths of 7, 6, and even 3ft were abundant. The passenger had to stand the jolting and survive. ⟨1846–80⟩

E. L. Ahrons, *Locomotive and Train Working in the*
Latter Part of the Nineteenth Century (1951–4), vi. 2–3

17. AN IRISH RAILWAY INSPECTED

Richard Osborne, engineer of the Waterford & Limerick Railway, recalls the inspection of the line before its opening, in reminiscences written many years afterwards. The inspector later became Sir John Lintorn Simmons, Field Marshal and Colonel Commandant of the Royal Engineers.

Captain Simmons, in his tours of inspection of Irish railways during this year, had not found one in the complete condition required by

Government to enable him to permit it to be opened for travel, without giving each some months to make good the deficiency and obliging him to pay a second visit of inspection. He did not look for any other result on the Waterford & Limerick Railway, especially as Sir John Macneill had said that the iron bridges were very defective and could not stand up under rapid heavy travel. This had reached the ears of shareholders. Captain Simmons entered the train at the Tipperary station on his route of inspection to Limerick. The train consisted of a long American passenger car[1] and a new baggage car of the same type. The Captain's first remark was: "I am surprised and pleased to see the American car at last introduced on our roads. I have been trying for years to get them adopted, and could find no company bold enough to do so".

I said: "the prejudice is because they are not English". A large table in the car had all the plans, profiles, and good drawings of my iron Howe bridges. I particularly called his attention to the latter, as engineers spoke very disparagingly of them and I had erected at each bridge a convenient platform with a means of measuring the deflection of the span, and had two of our heaviest locomotives to pass in any way he directed over each bridge, in order that he might conveniently get the data for his opinion of their capabilities.

The inspector examined the plans. We stopped at each bridge and made close examination, using the locomotives every way and at different speeds, and in the afternoon closed our work. . . .

I informed Captain Simmons that the railway company's meeting was being held in Waterford, and I had hoped to get his permission to leave this evening to attend it. He replied: "You have fully met all my requirements, and I am happy that I can give you my certificate as government inspector, permitting you to open to public traffic the Waterford & Limerick Railway from the city of Limerick to the town of Tipperary". I accordingly left with the certificate in my pocket, in time for the meeting next afternoon. ⟨1848⟩

Journal of the Irish Railway Record Society
(1978), 327–9

18. JOHN FOWLER

Among Fowler's outstanding qualities as an engineer was his dauntless determination: well illustrated in the construction of the Metropolitan Railway, the first underground line ever built anywhere.

[1] i.e. a vehicle mounted on two four-wheeled bogie trucks and open from end to end, not divided into compartments.

Engineers of eminence assured [the directors] that they could never make the railway, that if they made it they could not work it, and if they worked it nobody would travel by it. Such a catalogue of impossibilities was enough to appal anyone, and often faith in the enterprise fell to a low ebb. At such times the directors would say to Mr Fowler, "We depend on you, and as long as you tell us you have confidence we shall go on". It was a heavy load to put on the shoulders of a man who had already sufficient to attend to in combating the physical difficulties of the affair. Yet Mr Fowler never flinched. He had made up his mind that the railway could be constructed, and that it would answer its purpose. ⟨1853–63⟩

Proceedings of the Institution of Civil Engineers, 135 (1899), 329–30

19. WATCHING THE EMERGENCE OF A RAILWAY

John Ostle, farmer, of New Town, Silloth, comments in his diary on the progress of the Carlisle & Silloth Bay Railway.

In the year 1855 about the latter part of the year they commenced making the rail-road to Silloth Bay and the building of houses there is now . . . four farm houses that is all there is at Silloth, but now they are building both lodging houses and Tommy shop Smith shop, joiner do. and now a large hotel. They commenced making jetties, but the sturdy waves of briny levelled them to the ground they drove the piles with their battering rams and now they are making a breakwater or sort of coffer dam now in 1856 Brotherton & Rigg are the contractors for the Rally Road. They built a bridge with two arches over the line and while filling it up it fell to the ground, no person either killed or wounded yet. June 12th 1856 they brought a steam engine to Silloth Bay from Kirkbride. The engine and tender took about 26 horses they landed at Causeway Head in the evening and she did start to travail the next day the first engine that ran to Silloth. I was there two or three days after I saw the sod huts [of the navvies] and families in them slated with tarpoling [tarpaulin]. . . . There are two inns selling one ale and porter the other grog likewise and another fast preparing, but they have not got licence none of them yet. . . .

August 28th there was a cheap trip from Carlisle to Silloth Bay the line was opened I think all the manufacturers and cotton spinners tobacconists and what not was there all the upper cru[st?] chaps. . . . Two bands of music polka dancing that is collar and elbow or the height of impudence. . . .

Silloth Bay is a very wild place in dry windy weather the sand blows very little short of the deserts of Arabia there is a splendid railway but no dock yet. . . . There is a very bad road on the Bank now September 19th they have not got it made yet over the bridge but they [are] hard at work banking this being Carlisle latter fair a great number of passengers went by rail from Silloth there is a splendid little station here and two public houses and one Tom & Harry.[1] Several other dwelling houses and sod huts for ever. ⟨1855–6⟩   Cumbria Record Office, DX/408/1, ff. 11–15

20.   THE APPROACH TO LIVERPOOL

The last quarter or possibly half mile before Liverpool is a giant tunnel through which the train is pulled by means of a stationary steam machine instead of the locomotive. After passing through this one goes straight into the station; only an open space some fifty paces long and wide lies between the two. This whole part is extraordinarily picturesque and gives a splendid impression. Standing in the hall one looks back at the mouth of the tunnel through which one has just passed. The space which lies between it and us is like a basin hewn out of the rock, a stone quarry whose walls stand to right and left, and the whole is easily recognisable for what it is meant to be, a kind of window aperture to provide light from above. The sky peers down into the basin across the bottom of which the rails run, and as we look up to return its greeting we see on the summit of the hill through which the tunnel goes a lovely Gothic church built of brown sandstone gazing down with its tower and windows at the depths where the trains ceaselessly come and go. When we were returning at six o'clock in the evening the bells were ringing to prayer and we turned into the yawning tunnel to the sound of their solemn chiming. ⟨1857⟩

Theodor Fontane, *Journeys to England*, trans. D. Harrison (1939), 138–9

21.   RAILWAY ARCHITECTURE

By utilitarian architecture is meant such as not only answers its purpose most perfectly, but does so in the most natural manner, and derives its character from its uses; . . . and these good looks are derived from a natural and rational manner of decorating the forms which its uses suggest. That all this can be said of the majority of railway buildings will, I think, be hardly asserted. There is, in fact, no general character among them at all. Some are profusely decorated Elizabethan, some are very bad Gothic; others are in the Italian palatial style; others, again, miserable travesties of the Crystal Palace; a large class rejoice in all the luxuries of

[1] Joseph Wright's *English Dialect Dictionary* records "Tom and Jerry" as a Cumbrian phrase for a pub, but not "Tom and Harry".

compo and sham, and another grovels in unmitigated meanness. To make, then, any statement which applies to all would be impossible, but we may safely assert that *all* cannot be right, nor *all* good utilitarian architecture. After all, however, there is a remainder to which this praise may fairly be applied.

As instances, I will mention the two great engine-houses at Camden Town – one oblong, the other circular. These could hardly be better; and though what mouldings they have are Roman, their whole aspect is that of Gothic buildings. Many of the great sheds are also far from unpleasing. An iron roof in its most normal condition is too spider-like a structure to be handsome, but with a very little attention this defect is obviated. The most wonderful specimen, probably, is that at the great Birmingham station; the handsomest, though certainly somewhat abnormal, that at the terminus of the Strasburg station in Paris. The last-mentioned would be perfectly suitable to a Gothic hall. The most contemptible of railway sheds is, probably, that at *Dover*; indeed, if anything could make an Englishman ashamed of his country, it would be his disgust at finding himself under that meanest of roofs on his return from a Continental tour; a feeling in no degree mitigated by the contrast between the South Eastern English and the Northern French railway carriages!

There are some simple country stations between Lancaster and Carlisle which have always struck me as the best stations of the smaller kind I have seen in England. They are perfectly plain and unpretending, and in the style of the old cottages in stone districts. I do not know whether the great station at Carlisle was designed by the same hand:[1] if so, it is a notable instance of a person who succeeds well in small things failing in large ones. I must except, however, the refreshment room, which is like an old dining hall on a small scale, and is itself quite refreshing – contrasting most pleasantly with those close, stuffy cabins at Crewe and elsewhere which symbolise anything rather than refreshment. ⟨1857⟩

George Gilbert Scott, *Remarks on Secular and Domestic Architecture* (1857), 217–19

22.   THE DESIGN OF RAILWAY BRIDGES

A great deal has been said about and some attempts have been made to do something for what is called the aesthetics of railways, or the architectural designs with reference to bridges, and so forth. I should like to explain the difficulties in which we are placed with regard to that question. I have here the photographs of two bridges of different ages. This is a photograph of a bridge which was erected thirty years ago, when young engineers took great pains with regard to what is called architectural effect. That bridge is

---

[1] It was. All these stations were designed by Tite.

erected over the Lancashire & Yorkshire Railway at Wakefield. The bridge is a very handsome structure. Every pains was taken with it that could be taken. That bridge having been built, then came the question of danger to the travellers, and the result of that was that we were compelled to put up a screen, which is shown on that photograph. It utterly destroys the architectural effect. The other photograph which I have here is of a bridge made ten years later, from designs by myself. At that time Parliament, having discovered what was necessary for the protection of the public, compelled me to make the bottom a straight line, with sides a certain number of feet high. Care was taken with the architecture of that bridge. The Committee will see its fate has been to be made an advertising medium. With regard to the Charing Cross line, I have made some bridges which I must say are ugly enough. But the law says that these bridges shall spring from the shop front on the one side to the shop front on the other without intermediate supports, and at an uniform height above the street. Then the requirements of the public with regard to preventing horses being frightened and people being killed give you another line ten feet above that. Those are the conditions you have to work upon. As far as my opinion goes, I do not see how you are to produce architectural effect with such conditions. I think all attempts would be abortive, and therefore I have given it up. I have been asked by gentlemen, "Why don't you do something?" I have said, "What would you do?" They have said, "Make them open". Then they say, "Put panels upon them"; but the panels appear to me to make matters worse. A girder so restricted cannot be made architecturally beautiful. Charing Cross terminus will be a handsome thing. But girders cannot be adorned with any advantage. ⟨1863⟩

John Hawkshaw, in evidence before the Select Committee on Metropolitan Railway Communication, 1863: *Parliamentary Papers*, 1863, viii. 149.

23.   THE MAN WITH TWO HEADS

Thomas Hardy becomes involved in the construction of the line into St Pancras Station.

Mr Blomfield (afterwards Sir Arthur), being the son of a late bishop of London, was considered a right and proper man for supervising the removal of human bodies in cases where railways had obtained a faculty for making cuttings through the city churchyards, so that it should be done decently and in order. A case occurred in which this function on the bishop's behalf was considered to be duly carried out. But afterwards Mr Blomfield came to Hardy and informed him with a look of concern that he had just returned from visiting the site on which all the removed bodies were said by the company to be reinterred; but there appeared to be nothing deposited, the surface of the ground lying quite level as before. Also that there were rumours of mysterious full bags of something that rattled, and cartage to bone-mills. He much feared that he had not exercised a sufficiently sharp supervision, and that the railway company had got over him somehow. "I believe these people are all ground up!" said Blomfield grimly.

Soon there was to occur a similar proceeding on a much larger scale by another company; the carrying of a cutting by the Midland Railway through Old St Pancras Churchyard, which would necessitate the removal of many hundreds of coffins, and bones in huge quantities. In this business Mr Blomfield was to represent the Bishop as before. The architect said that now there should be no mistake about his thoroughly carrying out the superintendence. Accordingly, he set a clerk-of-works in the churchyard, who was never to leave during working hours; and as the removals were effected by night, and the clerk-of-works might be lax or late, he deputed Hardy to go on evenings at uncertain hours, to see that the clerk-of-works was performing his duties; while Hardy's chief was himself to drop in at unexpected moments during the week, presumably to see that neither his assistant nor the clerk-of-works was a defaulter.

The plan succeeded excellently, and throughout the late autumn and early winter . . . Hardy attended at the churchyard – each evening between five and six, as well as sometimes at other hours. There after nightfall, within a high hoarding that could not be overlooked, and by the light of flare-lamps, the exhumation went on continuously of the coffins that had been recovered during the day, new coffins being provided for those that came apart in lifting, and for loose skeletons; and those that held together being carried to the new ground on a board merely; Hardy supervising these mournful processions when present, with what thoughts may be imagined, and Blomfield sometimes meeting him there. In one coffin that fell apart was a skeleton and two skulls. He used to tell that when, after some fifteen years of separation, he met Arthur Blomfield again and their friendship was fully renewed, among the latter's first words were: "Do you remember how we found the man with two heads at St Pancras?" ⟨1866⟩   Florence Emily Hardy, *The Life of Thomas Hardy*, (1933), i. 57–9

24. THE RATIONALE OF THE ST PANCRAS TRAIN-SHED

The engineer, W. H. Barlow, explains it himself:

The approach to this station land was crossed by the Regent's Canal, at a distance of about 45 chains north of the Euston Road; and in order to secure good gradients and suitable levels for stations at Camden Road, Kentish Town, and Haverstock Hill, the main passenger line was carried over the canal. It resulted from this arrangement that the level of the St Pancras station was from 12 feet to 17 feet higher than that of the adjoining roads.

The St Pancras branch, on the other hand, for effecting a junction with the Metropolitan Railway, was taken at a lower level, crossing under the Regent's Canal, as well as under a considerable length of the main line and its works, including the passenger station.

In consequence of the height of the rails above the ground level, a large space extending over the whole area beneath the station was available. The original design was to fill this space with the material excavated from the tunnel of the St Pancras branch, and it was contemplated to make the roof of the passenger station either in two or in three spans. But the station being bounded on the south by the Euston Road, on the east by the old St Pancras Road, and on the west by Brewer Street, and the difference of level being such as to admit of the construction of a lower floor with direct access to these streets, the position was deemed so valuable that it was determined by the directors to devote the whole area to traffic purposes, communication being made with the rails by means of hydraulic lifts. The special purpose for which this lower floor has been arranged is for Burton beer traffic; and in order to economise the space to the utmost it was determined to use columns and girders instead of brick piers and arches, making the distances between the columns the same as those of the warehouses, which were expressly arranged for the beer traffic. Thus, in point of fact, the length of a beer barrel became the unit of measure upon which all the arrangements of this floor were based.

This decision led to a reconsideration of the question of roofing the station. It became obvious that, if intermediate columns were employed, they must be carried down through the lower floor, be about 60 feet in length, and of much larger diameter than the rest of the columns under the station. This would have necessitated the employment of different patterns in the girders, cross girders, and in the plating of the lower floor, and have increased the price per ton for that portion of the ironwork, besides interfering with the economical distribution of the space. Moreover, these columns must have carried large areas of roofing in addition to the flooring, involving a greatly increased weight on the foundations, which must have been enlarged accordingly; and as some of them would necessarily have been placed on the tunnel of the St Pancras branch, special means and increased expense would have been required to carry the imposed weight at those places.

On the other hand, it was seen that the floor girders across the station formed a ready-made tie sufficient for an arched roof crossing the station in one span; all that was required to obtain a roof of this construction being the arch or upper member of the truss, of which the floor girders would form the lower member. There was a third feature in the case. In iron roofs as usually constructed, the depth of the principal is about one-fifth of the span; but here, by adopting one arch extending across the station, the height from the tie beneath the rails to the crown of the arch became the effective depth of the truss; and this height being about two-fifths of the span, all the horizontal strains arising from the dead weight of the roof, its covering, and accumulations of snow, etc., would be about the same in the arch of 240 feet span, with an effective depth of truss of 100 feet, as in an ordinary truss of 120 feet span with a depth of 24 feet. . . . There were several other advantages belonging to the arch – one being that as the weight of the roof was carried at the floor line, and did not rest on the tops of the walls, there was no necessity to make the side walls thicker, for not only was the weight on the tops of the walls avoided, but also the racking motion from the expansion and contraction of an ordinary roof, which, though it may be mitigated, is not prevented by the use of roller-frames at the feet of the principals, and appliances of a like nature. It was also apparent that the arch might be made of rivetted plate ironwork like that of an ordinary railway bridge, and that the expense attending the use of forged and wrought work as in ordinary roofs would be avoided, including the screw-cutting, gibs and cotters, welding, and similar costly workmanship. Again, as to the question of the expansion and contraction of the arched roof, the ties being beneath the ballast, the temperature would vary so little that no provision would be necessary; and for the arched part of the roof, which would alone be subject to appreciable change, the only effect would be a slight rise or fall in the crown.

All the arrangements of roller-frames or slings, required in ordinary roofs to provide for the effect of variations of temperature, would there-fore be avoided by the adoption of the arch; and lastly, the adoption of the single arch would not only save the cost of the columns and their foundations, but also that of the longitudinal girder required to connect them at their upper extremities, with a valley drain between the roofs, and vertical drain-pipes and other provisions for taking off the water from the area between the centre lines of the two roofs, which would have been about two acres.

All these circumstances tending to favour the idea of one arch across the station, the remaining question was, what depth and form of rib, and what additional material, must be employed to make an arch sufficient to retain its form under all conditions of stress arising from its own weight, from snow, and from heavy gales of wind. . . .

The probable additional cost of principals so constructed, of 240 feet span, as compared with principals of two spans of 120 feet and their columns, was estimated at about £6000. Notwithstanding this, the im-portance attached by the directors and the general manager to obtaining perfect freedom in the use of the whole area of the station for traffic purposes, unembarrassed by columns or other impediments, was such that instructions were given for an arch in one clear span. ⟨1870⟩

Proceedings of the Institution of Civil Engineers,
30 (1870), 79–81, 90

25.   A NEW SUBURBAN RAILWAY

For nearly a decade before its first sod was turned a railway through Winchmore Hill had been spoken of as a future contingency. "When the railway comes" and "if ever the railway comes" were phrases to be heard again and again. Various plans were discussed, but nothing came of them, and most people felt that they should not believe in it till they saw it. . . .

In the summer of 1869, rather to the astonishment of the village, there arrived a load of barrows, shovels, and tip trucks, and the Winchmore Hill section of the Enfield branch was begun by the turning of sods in a large field in Vicarsmoor Lane, near the present goods station. In a few days rows of wooden huts arose, mushroom-like, and groups of navvies were soon in full possession. The work was begun also at the Enfield and Wood Green ends. . . .

The great business was the spanning of the deep valley between the village and the hills to the north. The summer was one of heat and drought, the stream was nearly dry, and the engineers took an entirely erroneous view of its capabilities; they did not realise the extent of the watershed from the hills on either side, and when the inhabitants described "lakes of flood water, and bridges washed away and piled one upon another" they were listened to in polite disbelief. . . .

After men and horses had laboured for some time a working engine was brought down called the *Fox*.

The excavations were beautiful in colour, the London clay being a bright cobalt blue when first cut through, and changing with exposure to orange. There were strata of black and white flints and yellow gravel; the men's white slops and the red heaps of burnt ballast made vivid effects of light and shade and colour against the cloudless sky of that excessively hot summer. There were also dark wooden planks and shorings to add neutral tints, and when the engine came the glitter of brass and clouds of steam were added to the landscape. On Sundays and holidays the men were, many of them, resplendent in scarlet or yellow or blue plush waistcoats and knee breeches. . . .

There had been much fear in the village of annoyance from the hordes of Yorkshire and Lincolnshire railway men brought into the village by Firbank, the contractor; but on the whole their conduct was very orderly. . . . A noticeable figure was "Dandy" Ganger, a big north countryman, decorated with many large mother-of-pearl buttons and a big silver watch chain. He instantly checked all bad language in the neighbour-hood of the Doctor's garden. Many of the navvies brought their food or their tea cans to be heated on the great kitchen range, and never once made themselves objectionable.

It had been intended to complete the line in 1870; and that date may be seen on the girders of the bridge, beneath Winchmore Hill station, but many difficulties were met with in the five miles of line; there was a culvert for the great stream in the valley, which looked as if it would carry anything possible, but when the water rose in the winter it sapped the foundations and the arch cracked badly; the treacherous clay, "blue slipper", sank lower and lower, till what had been meant for a level line became a steep gradient; long after the line was opened the "slip", as it was called, was so dangerous that every train slowed down to pass it, and many persons were afraid to travel by rail to Enfield. . . .

The working engines had each a voice of its own, so that it was easy to tell by ear which of them was passing with its load of trucks. *Fox* informed the world that there was "such a hurry, such a hurry". *Hunslet,* a tank engine that arrived much later on the scene, was particularly clear in her enunciation, informing all the world of her huffy temper, though I never heard she was ill to deal with as a worker – "I'm in a huff, I'm in a huff!" she puffed in her way along the line. *Progress,* who laboured at the Wood Green end, proclaimed continually the name of the chief engineer – "Mr Claringbull, Mr Claringbull" she shouted with a strong accent on the last syllable. *Ferret* seldom left the Enfield portion of roadmaking, perhaps because everything was "such a heavy load, such a heavy load". . . .

Five men were killed by accident in making the five miles of railway. A man who sleeps on a ballast heap on a cold night never wakes, the fumes are as poisonous as those of a charcoal brazier, and this fatality occurred more than once, besides other mischances.

All through 1870 the navvies worked; clay and gravel were excavated, and tip trucks filled the valley at Bowes and the much deeper one below the Enfield hills. A viaduct was built over Dog Kennel Lane, and the roadway itself raised 20ft, the streams were imprisoned in culverts, bridge after bridge was built, either to carry rail over road or road over rail, the five-arch bridge at Warren House Lane being really picturesque till it became surrounded by houses. A huge sustaining wall supported the Grove Lodge garden. . . . A foretaste of the convenience of a railway was gained now and then by the wild delight of a rush home on the *Fox.* Once a lurid night-ride from Palmer's Green seemed faster than the *Flying Dutch-man* itself, as the little engine bucketed along over the roughly laid lines, with no weight of trucks behind to steady it. . . .

It was the night of the 31st of March, 1871, the permanent way was completed, the station was finished and smelt strongly of fresh paint, everything was ready. It was late in the evening, all was very quiet, the familiar sound of the working engine and attendant trucks attracted no attention, but suddenly the village was startled by a loud explosion, a perfect volley of explosions!

Many people ran down to the bridge expecting to find some unlooked-for accident had occurred. It was the navvies celebrating their departure with the last train of trucks by a fusillade of fog-signals under the bridge and railway station!

And on All Fools' Day 1871 the first passenger train came through Winchmore Hill, and the little village developed into a Suburb of London Town. ⟨1869–71⟩   Henrietta Cresswell, *Winchmore Hill* (2nd ed., 1912), 110–15

26.   AN EMERGENCY MET

A notable illustration of what can be done in an emergency by a company like the London & North Western, possessing great resources, occurred when, in the great storm of Sunday, the 17th August, 1879, the Llandulas viaduct, on the main line of the Chester & Holyhead Railway, was undermined by flood, and washed completely away, interrupting, for the time being, the traffic between England and Ireland. For two days, until the flood subsided, nothing could be done, but within the space of five days afterwards the railway was deviated for about half-a-mile so as to strike the river at the narrowest point, and a temporary trestle bridge was erected, over which the first train passed at 2 p.m. on the 24th August, exactly seven days after the mishap occurred. The line was cut in the slope of the embankment leading to the old viaduct, and was everywhere placed upon solid ground, or upon stacks of old sleepers, so that there might be no settlement, and the line might be fit for the heaviest traffic immediately it was completed. The gradients were 1 in 23, dipping down to the river, and rising on the opposite side, and everything was finished off in the most substantial and careful manner; but of course great skill and attention were necessary on the part of the engine drivers, and the difficulty of working long and heavy trains, some of which required three engines, over these severe and changing gradients, without breaking the couplings, or heavily bumping the carriages together, can hardly be exaggerated, yet no mishap occurred, and the passengers in the trains were scarcely aware that they were travelling under unusual conditions.

The new permanent viaduct was meanwhile rapidly constructed, and was actually completed and opened for traffic on the 14th September, less than one month after the mishap. Its length is 224 feet, divided into seven spans of thirty-two feet each, and its height is fifty feet. Forty-two girders, each thirty-two feet in length, were required, and the plates and angles for each girder were rolled in one length. All these were made in the

Company's own steel works at Crewe, and the whole of the material was turned out and ready for erection within seven days, the steel having been manufactured, rolled, and worked, within that short space of time. ⟨1879⟩   Sir George Findlay, *The Working and Management of an English Railway* (6th ed., 1899), 114–15

27. A TUNNEL

Somerset looked down on the mouth of the tunnel. The popular commonplace that science, steam, and travel must always be unromantic and hideous was not proven at this spot. On either slope of the deep cutting, green with long grass, grew drooping young trees of ash, beech, and other flexible varieties, their foliage almost concealing the actual railway which ran along the bottom, its thin steel rails gleaming like silvery threads in the depths. The vertical front of the tunnel, faced with brick that had once been red, was now weather-stained, lichened, and mossed over in harmonious rusty-browns, pearly greys, and neutral greens, at the very base appearing a little blue-black spot like a mouse-hole – the tunnel's mouth. . . .

Down Somerset plunged through the long grass, bushes, late summer flowers, moths, and caterpillars, vexed with himself that he had come there, since Paula was so inscrutable, and humming the notes of some song he did not know. The tunnel that had seemed so small from the surface was a vast archway when he reached its mouth, which emitted, as a contrast to the sultry heat on the slopes of the cutting, a cool breeze, that had travelled a mile underground from the other end. Far away in the darkness of this silent subterranean corridor he could see that other end as a mere speck of light.

When he had conscientiously admired the construction of the massive archivault, and the majesty of its nude ungarnished walls, he looked up the slope at the carriage; it was so small to the eye that it might have been made for a performance by canaries; Paula's face being still smaller, as she leaned back in her seat, idly looking down at him. There seemed something roguish in her attitude of criticism, and to be no longer the subject of her contemplation he entered the tunnel out of her sight.

In the middle of the speck of light before him appeared a speck of black; and then a shrill whistle, dulled by millions of tons of earth, reached his ears from thence. It was what he had been on his guard against all the time – a passing train; and instead of taking the trouble to come out of the tunnel he stepped into a recess, till the train had rattled past, and vanished onward round a curve. ⟨1881⟩

Thomas Hardy, *A Laodicean* (New Wessex ed.), 120–2

28.   A NARROW ESCAPE FROM DEATH

The consequences of a tidal wave, during a late stage in the construction of the Severn Tunnel.

At 7 p.m. on the 17th October, the night shift, consisting of about ninety men, had descended the Marsh Pit, to proceed with their work.

About 450 yards of tunnel were completed at the bottom of this pit, and two break-ups were being worked and were in various stages of progress west of it.

It will be remembered that the gradient of the tunnel at this point rose 1 in 90 to the west.

A perfect storm of wind was blowing at the time from the south-west, and it was known that one of the highest tides of the year would occur that night, but no tide had ever been known to come so high as the works at this shaft.

Between the shaft and the river itself, in a south-westerly direction, were a number of small cottages, built by the men employed upon the works, of stone and timber; and there were also several brick cottages, owned by the firm who carried on the Tinplate Works, and inhabited by their men.

Suddenly, in the darkness, a great tidal wave burst over the whole of the low-lying ground between the shaft and the river. It must have come on as a solid wall of water, 5 or 6ft high. It entered all the houses, most of which were only of one storey, and rose above the beds on which the children were asleep. The children were saved by being placed upon high tables, or even on shelves. . . .

The tidal wave passing beyond the houses reached first the boilers that worked the winding and pumping engines at the shaft, extinguishing the fires, and then flowed down the pit with a fall of 100ft. There was a ladder-way from the top to the bottom of the shaft, and by it, when the first force of the water had passed, one or two men who were in the bottom managed to make their escape; one unfortunate man, after climbing the ladder for about half the height, was thrown back by the force of the water and killed.

Eighty-three men were imprisoned in the tunnel at the bottom of the shaft. As the water rose, they retreated before it up the gradient.

In the darkness, and with the whole of the shaft surrounded by water, it was extremely difficult for the two or three who were on the top to communicate with the works at Sudbrook; but at last one man made his way through the water and gave the alarm. The principal foreman of the works, with his brother and one or two of the assistant engineers and other employees, reached the shaft not without difficulty. . . . On reaching the pit-head, where by this time the tide was of course lower than it had been at the first rush of the wave, everything that could be gathered, waterproof clothing, sacks, timber, and suchlike things were used to try to form a dam round the top of the shaft to stop back the water.

In spite of all that could be done, the water rose in the tunnel at the bottom of the shaft, to within 8ft of the crown of the arch. Then the tide going back, and the dam at the top being more effectually made, preparations were made to rescue the men who were imprisoned below. The whole of the bottom of the tunnel and heading was under water, and the men had retreated to a stage in one of the break-ups, where they sat not knowing what their fate would be.

The men who by this time gathered round the top of the pit were sent for a small boat, which was lowered down the pit and launched on the water in the tunnel, a few men with lights getting into the boat pushed up the tunnel to rescue their comrades; but after going a short distance they came to timbers placed across the tunnel from side to side, which blocked their progress. Returning to the shaft they obtained a cross-cut saw, and commenced to cut away the timbers. They had been at work but a short time when the saw dropped overboard, and they had to wait until another was procured; but at last the men were all rescued, and brought safely to bank on the morning of the 18th. ⟨1883⟩

> T. A. Walker, *The Severn Tunnel: its Construction and Difficulties* (1888), 131–4. Walker was the contractor for the tunnel.

29. STABILITY AND FINISH

The feature of the English railroad system which most forcibly strikes an American observer is its stability. . . . The mere traveller sees it in the massive stone bridges, the tunnels and viaducts, the station accommodation, and a thousand details of less importance which combine to produce an impression of solidity and finish, entirely wanting in the majority of American railroads. ⟨1886⟩

> A. T. Hadley, *Railroad Transportation* (1886), 146

30. RUNWAY CROSSES RAILWAY

The aerodromes near the sea coast east of Lough Foyle were built very near to the railway track. . . . Ballykelly had been designed for medium-sized craft, but became a base for heavier and heavier bombers. The short runways had to be progressively lengthened, until one of them reached the railway track at an angle of 45 degrees. It was still too short. It was continued right over the lines. Solid concrete covered the sleepers and left only slits in which the wheel flanges could run. Bewildered and slightly anxious passengers wondered what was to happen when the passing of an aeroplane coincided with that of a train.

The line was far too important to be closed. The aerodrome could not confine the launching, still less the return of its bombers to any daily timetable. Wind, and not trains, must dictate the course of operations. A special signal-box had been erected at the point of intersection. It was linked with the Flying Control which issued warnings when an aeroplane was ready to take off or (perhaps more urgently) needing to descend. If the signalman had accepted no train for the section, he sent back the message "Runway Clear", . . . [which was] a warning for closure of the railway track. It could only be sent if the signals were already at danger. The sending of it automatically locked them in that position. The result (though fools are not allowed in signal-boxes) was fool-proof safety, proof too against darkness or misunderstanding. There were naturally delays to the passage of trains, but these, by friendly co-operation with the R.A.F., were reduced to a minimum. The pathway of the Liberators and the railway trains continued to intersect without mishap. ⟨1939–45⟩

E. John, *Time Table for Victory* [1947], 170–1

31.   FOOTBRIDGES AT STATIONS

There is one further category of railway bridge, contrasting in scale with the viaduct, that still has to be described: the footbridge by which passengers are instructed to cross the line at stations. For some reason station footbridges have been less fully recorded than other kinds of railway bridge although many are quite elegantly designed. They have not however such a long history because in the early days of railways it was not forbidden to step over the lines at the end of the platform. Most footbridges were therefore additions to stations already built. Their construction became general in the 1860s following Board of Trade inquiries into accidents that occurred as the speed and frequency of trains increased. In the 1870s the Board of Trade made it compulsory for all new stations to have either bridges or subways by which passengers could cross the line safely. This requirement did not apply to existing stations and many continued without either, as some small country stations do to this day. . . .

Most of the major railway companies had their own designs for footbridges, some of their standard designs being also adaptable for carrying footpaths over the line and for lineside use by railway maintenance staff; they had then to be built three feet higher than station footbridges since they did not start from platform level. The designs . . . were normally the work of the companies' own engineers, sometimes in conjunction with an ironworks contractor, or of one of the engineer's architectural assistants, except when the footbridges formed part of new stations. Then they were designed by the architect or engineer responsible, who might or might not have been a member of the company's staff.

The first station footbridges were of wood or cast iron – there is a surviving wooden footbridge at Darlington North Road station – and thereafter, as in the case of other railway bridges, successively of wrought iron, steel, and concrete as these materials in turn superseded the earlier ones. In most iron or steel bridges the parapets were also the main girders. Stairs were generally of wood on steel stringers. There is a spectacular open lattice example, supported on circular cast-iron columns, just north west of Rugby. Footbridges were generally unroofed except when they were an integral part of the station buildings. Then they were frequently provided with the additional comfort of glazed windows. When roofs were added they were most often of corrugated iron. Early footbridges of the cast-iron lattice-girder type with wooden flooring can still be seen on the old Great Northern and Midland lines. The North Eastern employed a particularly graceful arched lattice design, as did the Midland and various Scottish lines. The London & South Western used flanged steel-plate girders to replace their first wooden footbridges. The group of lines that merged to become the Southern Railway replaced many of their footbridges with a standard precast concrete pattern around 1930. ⟨1984⟩

Sir James Richards, *The National Trust Book of Bridges* (1984), 115–17

3

Traction and Speed

32.   INCLINED PLANES

*An account of those installed on the hilly western section of the Stockton
& Darlington Railway, given by two visiting engineers from Germany.*

The inclined planes at Greenfield and Brusselton are generally constructed
with as uniform a slope as possible. This cannot be maintained exactly, but
the variation is unimportant. It is more important to lessen the slope
gradually at the lower end, and to allow it to run into the horizontal gently.
It is equally important to lay the railway horizontally on a suitable stretch
on the top of the ridge between the two inclined planes. Therefore, where
the two steam engines [i.e. stationary engines] stand, the railway is
horizontal for a length of about 300 to 360ft, and it is laid double in order
to facilitate the exchange of wagons.

On the inclined planes themselves there is only a single line, as on them
there is only one-way traffic.

The lines on the inclined planes are not straight, but make several turns, as the local conditions necessitate. The rope by which the wagons are drawn up or let down runs over guiding sheaves by which any desired turn may be negotiated with ease, provided that it is not too abrupt.

The guiding sheaves stand in the middle of the track about 24ft apart, and the number of them on the long inclined planes is therefore considerable.

The shortest of the inclined planes is 825yd, and the longest 2185yd. In order to indicate to the stationary-engine attendant at these considerable distances when the train ought to start, a tall signal post is used, at the top of which a disc is turned in an appointed direction. As it is difficult to see these signals at so great a distance, a telescope, continually pointed towards them, is placed beside the seat of the engine attendant, and through this he must look from time to time. When it is not possible to see the signals from the engine house, then long pulling-wires must be employed, but this presents no difficulty. ⟨1826–7⟩

> C. von Oeynhausen and H. von Dechen, *Railways in England 1826 and 1827*, translated by E. A. Forward (1971), 12

33.   PROPHET WITHOUT HONOUR

I sincerely congratulate you on the appointment [as engineer of the Stanhope & Tyne Railway] and more particularly as you will be instrumental in extending the beautiful locomotive line from Shields, and now that I am about to leave Newcastle I am glad in leaving a locomotive engine advocate behind. It is not a little remarkable that in a neighbourhood where this class of engines had their birth enemies to them can be found on every side. ⟨1833⟩

> Robert Stephenson to T. E. Harrison, 13 December 1833: Public Record Office, RAIL 1148/1, no. 15

34.   THE RAILWAYS' USE OF HORSES

Horse-drawn transport had its drawbacks and limitations. But until a substitute became available – and the demonstration that motors were something more useful and reliable than mere playthings of the eccentric rich dates almost precisely from the year of Victoria's death – horse-drawn transport was quite indispensable. . . .

Without carriages and carts the railways would have been like stranded whales, giants unable to use their strength, for these were the only means of getting people and goods right to the doors, of houses, warehouses, markets, and factories, where they wanted to be. All the railway companies kept their own establishments of horses and assorted wagons and vans for goods collection and delivery, and it is in railway records that one may find the best series of prices of van-horses and horse-fodder covering the whole Victorian age. A firm like Pickfords, which had grown up as canal carriers of inter-city through traffic, soon adapted itself to the new railway situation and flourished as never before, as a distributor from railheads; the 4000 horses which this firm had maintained in the 1820s to run its canal fly-boats between London and Birmingham were before long insufficient to cope with the new local town traffic generated by the London & Birmingham Railway. No wonder that a big railway terminus came to require about as much space for stabling as it did for locomotive sheds. . . . The railway age was in fact the greatest age of the horse, albeit in terms of its total contribution to the economy rather than in terms of any heroic qualities in its unaided achievements. The threat of redundancy because of technological change, in other words, turned out to be as unreal for horses as it has often been for men, and given adaptation to new or modified tasks the new technology did not diminish, but substantially increased, the demand for horse-labour. ⟨1837–1901⟩

> F. M. L. Thompson, *Victorian England: the Horse-Drawn Society* (1970), 13–14

35. AMERICAN ENGINES NOT WANTED

Edward Bury, the well-known builder of locomotives at Liverpool, was examined by the Commons Committee on Railways in 1839.

Do you know anything of an experimental engine that was sent over from America, with a view of going upon the incline from Birmingham to Gloucester?[1]

Bury. – Yes, I saw it start.

What was your opinion of the result?

Bury. – That there was no occasion to send to America for engines. ⟨1839⟩   *Parliamentary Papers*, 1839, x. 783

---

[1] The incline rises in the other direction, from Gloucester to Birmingham.

36. MRS GAMP ON THE STEAM ENGINE

"Them confugion steamers", said Mrs Gamp, shaking her umbrella again, "has done more to throw us out of our reg'lar work and bring ewents on at times when nobody counted on 'em (especially them screeching railroad ones), than all the other frights that ever was took. I have heerd of one young man, a guard upon a railway, only three years opened – well does Mrs Harris know him, which indeed he is her own relation by her sister's marriage with a master sawyer – as is godfather at this present time to six-and-twenty blessed little strangers, equally unexpected, and all on 'um named after the Ingeins as was the cause." ⟨1844⟩

Charles Dickens, *Martin Chuzzlewit* (1844), chap. 43

37. A NOOMBOOG

The atmospheric railway was one operated by a combination of suction pumps (powered by stationary steam engines) and the pressure of the atmosphere, applied to a piston beneath the train. The system was tried on three railways in the British Isles from 1843 onwards, in the end without success. Lear heard this conversation himself.

Prince Albert: "Mr Hudson, what is your opinion of the Atmospheric Railway?" Hudson: "Please your rile iness, I think it is a Noomboog". H.R.H. – turning to Lord Farnham: "Explain to me what is a Noomboog?" ⟨1845⟩

Edward Lear to Lord Carlingford, 21 December 1884: *Later Letters of Edward Lear*, ed. Lady Strachey (1911), 324

38. HIGH SPEED OVER A GREAT DISTANCE

The narrator here is James Allport, at this time manager of the Newcastle & Darlington Junction Railway. In 1853–7 and 1860–80 he was the bold and innovative manager of the great Midland Railway.

When the battle of the gauges was being vigorously carried on, I wished to show what the narrow gauge could do. It was, of course, before the days of telegraphs. The election of George Hudson, as Member for Sunderland, had that day taken place, and I availed myself of the event to see how quickly I could get the information up to London, have it printed in the *Times* newspaper, and brought back to Sunderland. The election was over at four o'clock in the afternoon, and by about five o'clock the returns of the voting for every half-hour during the poll were collected from the different booths, and copies were handed to me. I had ordered a series of trains to be in readiness for the journey, and I at once started from Sunderland to York. Another train was in waiting at York to take me to Normanton, and others in their turn to Derby, to Rugby, to Wolverton, and to Euston. Thence I drove to the *Times* office, and handed my manuscript to Mr Delane, who, according to an arrangement I had previously made with him, had it immediately set up in type, a leader written, both inserted, and a lot of impressions taken. Two hours were thus spent in London, and then I set off on my return journey, and arrived in Sunderland next morning at about ten o'clock, before the announcement of the poll. I there handed over copies I had brought with me of that day's *Times* newspaper, containing the returns of what had happened in Sunderland the afternoon before. Between five o'clock in the evening and ten that morning I had travelled 600 miles, besides spending two hours in London – a clear run of 40 miles an hour. ⟨1845⟩   F. S. Williams, *Our Iron Roads* (5th ed., 1888), 332–3

39.   SPEED AND POWER

The ordinary rate of speed is per second, of a man walking, four feet; of a good horse in harness, twelve; of a reindeer in a sledge on the ice, twenty-six; of an English race-horse, forty-three. A railway, travelling at the rate of thirty miles an hour, performs forty-four feet per second, which is eleven times the speed of the man walking, nearly four times that of the good horse, and twice that of the reindeer. But man, horse, and reindeer all soon become exhausted, while the engine is as fresh and strong at the end of a long journey as at first starting; miles to it are but as paces to animated nature. Again, a racer doing one mile in two minutes, and no more, can but carry a featherweight for that brief time and distance, while the locomotive could draw the Grand Stand, and half the sporting world along with it, from Doncaster to Newmarket, and from Newmarket to Ascot, all in one day. ⟨1856⟩   G. Measom, *Guide to the London & South Western Railway* [1856], 2–3

40.   MECHANICAL FITNESS

From an obituary appreciation of William Stroudley, Locomotive Super-intendent of the London Brighton & South Coast Railway.

He succeeded in raising himself to the very front rank of English mechanical engineers. . . . Beyond most men he possessed a special power of not only doing the right thing in mechanical engineering, but of doing it in the right way. He wanted to know the reason for everything, and was always ready to give a reason for what he did. . . . [He had] an intense and truly refined sense of mechanical fitness. On him a faulty, ill-designed, or unmeaning detail had the same effect as a discord on a musician. . . . Nothing did "well enough" for Mr Stroudley. ⟨1870–89⟩

Proceedings of the Institution of Civil Engineers,
99 (1890), 38–9

41. AN AMERICAN ENGINEER PRAISES THE BRITISH BLOCK SYSTEM

It is astonishing to see the blind faith the English engine-driver places in his block signals. In dense fogs, where he cannot see one hundred feet ahead, or dark nights, when his vision is also very limited, for his headlight is only an ordinary lantern, useless for illuminating the track and only used as a signal, the same as the tail light, or frequently where he has both the dark night and dense fog to run through, yet he runs at full speed and generally on schedule time, feeling sure that he is perfectly safe because his block signals have told him so, and they cannot make a mistake or lie.

The underground railroad in London and the London suburban roads afford a fine illustration of this system. Notwithstanding the proverbial London fogs, these roads run their trains, probably several thousand daily, upon schedule time, and with a headway varying from three to three and a half minutes. And this is done without accident or delay.

If it had been in use, the accident two or three years ago in the Harlem tunnel and also that at Spuyten Duyvil, in which Senator Wagner and others were killed, could not have occurred.

The English Government, through the Board of Trade, obliges all English railroads to adopt the block system, and run their trains by it, and we should follow their example. ⟨1885⟩

E. B. Dorsey, *English and American Railroads Compared*
(2nd ed., 1887), 13

42. EXPRESS TRAIN

Conceive what it means to run a train all day long at an average speed little short of a mile a minute. We may take it for granted that permanent way, engines, and rolling stock will all be as perfect as money and skill can make them. Even so, upon how many individuals does sometimes the safety, and always the punctuality, of a single train depend. There are a thousand platelayers – ordinary working men of £1 or 30s a week – on the road from London to Edinburgh, and each of them must do his part, must watch the line from day to day, and almost from hour to hour, and mark that here a key wants wedging in, there a trenail is working loose, or a fish-bolt needs screwing up. There are two or three hundred signalmen, and each must be on the alert to receive and acknowledge the "Be ready" signal, and to pass it on at once to the box in front. The humblest carriage-greaser may bring the "Flying Scot" to an ignominious halt at a roadside station because he has allowed a pinch of dirt to get into his grease-box. These men, however, are to some extent under the eye of superior officers. But what shall we say of the driver and his fireman? Once the train has got away from the station, for the next two hours they are monarchs of all they survey. There are people who think that a driver is a man who pulls a handle to turn on steam, and then stands and looks at the result till it is time to turn it off again, and that a fireman has only to shovel on coal with no more intelligence than is displayed by the domestic footman. They would know better if they had ever been on the footplate of an engine that was booked to run for two or three hours without a stop.

Mark the infinite solicitude with which the driver looks over his engine before he starts, lest a split-pin should be likely to shake out, or the wicks in his oil cups should be too tight and prevent the oil from flowing, or too loose and let the oil run out, leaving the cups empty before half the journey is accomplished. As the train moves off, the utmost skill is required to give the engine just as much steam as she can take; with too much, she would start slipping, and not to use enough is to waste time where every moment may be precious. No sooner are they under weigh than the engineman and his mate have to solve the problem of the scientific application of force. They have got plenty of coal on board, no doubt, but if they are to run from London to Nottingham, or from Newcastle to Edinburgh, they will have to burn 25 or 30 cwt, and to evaporate, even in the most favourable circumstances, nearer 3000 than 2000 gallons of water, to get there. And the tender holds at the outside but 3500 gallons; so there is need of forethought on a rough day or with greasy rails, if the train is not to stop *en route* for a fresh supply of water. Nor must the coal be pitched higgledy-piggledy into the firebox. A lump here, and a shovelful there, little and often, is the fireman's motto; otherwise he might choke his fire, and would certainly waste his fuel, and so spoil his engine's position on the weekly coal sheet. Meanwhile the driver's ear is keen to listen to the regular beat of the engine, to know that all is working smoothly; and his eye is strained forward to catch the first glimpse of each signal as it comes into view, and ever and anon cast back to see that all is right with the following train; and his mind is on the alert to question whether any of the signals that show "line clear" may perchance be delivering a lying message, and only calling him and his passengers forward to destruction. And so the time passes, broken only as at intervals a train flashes past on the opposite metals, and the driver signs with his hand to his comrade that all is well.

And then the train slackens down into Nottingham or Grantham, and five minutes later the tale is taken up afresh by a new engine and a new driver. And so it goes on, day after day and night after night, but when some extra spurt of rivalry leads to performances even more splendid than ordinary, and some of us desire to applaud, we are bidden by the superior persons to stand aside and be silent, for, after all, there is nothing to be proud of in the fact that nowhere but in England can such feats be performed. Nay, we are even invited to pity the poor drivers, who "having gone along the engine to oil a valve, become paralysed with fear, so as to be unable to move forward or backward". Who shall say, after this, that modern travellers' tales cannot match themselves for imagination against the "moving accidents of flood and field" of an olden time? If the tale be true, it is certainly startling to think what a number of express trains must be careering over the country at this moment in charge of paralysed drivers, with their passengers all unconscious of the risk that they run. But, when it comes to pitying the driver, one feels inclined to ask whether anyone ever condoled with Archer, as he came in the winner by a head of a great race at Epsom, because he might have hurt his leg as he shaved round Tattenham Corner with his foot just drawn a hair's breadth clear of the posts. Certainly those who, like the writer, accompanied the *Marmion* as she slowed down through Rugby on her way to Crewe on August 6th,[1] will be able to testify that pity was not the emotion depicted on the countenances of the enginemen who watched her passage all down the long line of engines in the Rugby yard. ⟨1889⟩

W. M. Acworth, *The Railways of England* (1889), 210–13

43. THE RACE TO ABERDEEN

The East and West Coast companies ran trains that "raced" one another from London to Edinburgh in 1888 and from London to Aberdeen seven years later. Both contests aroused much excitement. They challenged the resourcefulness of the managers, and they were severe tests of the endurance of the train crews. The first competition led to a permanent acceleration of the service to Edinburgh. The second had no comparable effect on that to Aberdeen. Here is a judicious verdict on the Races of 1895.

Much remains to be written on certain aspects of the race concerning which the most extraordinary mistakes have been made by correspondents

[1] During the first series of races to Scotland in 1888.

of the daily press. There is, too, some reason to believe that a section of the general public has regarded the race as a dangerous and almost criminal transaction. Mr John Burns, MP, has excelled himself in wild denunciation of the railway companies, and has drawn a lurid picture of the perils and sufferings of drivers and firemen, which only needed a small substratum of truth to be a really pathetic piece of oratory. It seems that Mr Burns has been riding on an engine in the United States and found it hard work, and a little alarming. We are not surprised. The experience of any man who rides on the footplate of an express locomotive for the first time is rather startling, but it is not necessary that as a result he should rush into print. But Mr Burns is by no means alone. Many other worthy people seem to regard with dread an attempt to accelerate communications with Scotland. It is just possible that a few words from us may tend to reassure and comfort these gentlemen. No lady correspondent of the daily press has yet expressed her fears. Possibly the racing spirit that induced the old lady to give her cargo of hams to the captain of a Mississippi boat to enable him to make more steam and beat a rival still beats in the female breast in this country. We have been repeatedly told that the race to Scotland is dangerous; that the men in charge of the train are overworked; that the speed is so tremendous that the passengers' health must suffer; that there is no time to avoid collisions; that the risks of running off the line, breaking the rails, bursting up the engine, breaking bridges, and so on are simply enormous. All this is an admirable and instructive example of the way in which history repeats itself. We can almost see some of the correspondents of the daily press copying their letters from old newspapers and reviews. In 1830, and in one or two succeeding years, anything that has been written during the past couple of weeks was written and printed. The modern terrorist has nothing new to say on the subject. All the fine old crusted arguments have been trotted out. ⟨1895⟩

Leading article in the *Engineer*, 30 August 1895

44.   COMFORT AND SPEED

Few people would mind being an hour or so longer going to Paris from London, if the railway travelling was neither rackety, cramped, nor tedious. One could be patient enough if one was neither being jarred, deafened, cut into slices by draughts, and continually more densely caked in a filthy dust of coal; if one could write smoothly and easily at a steady table, read papers, have one's hair cut, and dine in comfort – none of which things are possible at present, and none of which require any new inventions, or indeed anything but an intelligent application of existing resources and known principles. Our rage for fast trains, so far as long-distance travel is concerned, is largely a passion to end the extreme discomfort involved. It is in the daily journey, on the suburban train, that daily tax of time, that speed is in itself so eminently desirable, and it is just here that the conditions of railway travel most hopelessly fail. ⟨1902⟩

H. G. Wells, *Anticipations* (1902), 19–21

45. GHOSTS

About twelve years ago, in course of my railway wanderings, I found myself "Somewhere on the North-East Coast", in a locality which need not be specified more exactly. Here I dropped across an old friend, one of the higher officials of the North Eastern, who said he was going up that afternoon to a certain place on business and kindly added that if I liked to accompany him he could show me something that would be of special interest to me. We arrived at our destination as the shadows of a gloomy autumn day were beginning to fall, and to the accompaniment of a fierce north-east gale blowing from the sea, which lifted the spray in clouds over the cliffs of an iron-bound coast. My friend having the company's affairs to attend to, pointed out my direction and left me to my own devices. After proceeding for a short distance, always within sound of the surf beating upon the rocks, I came across a lonely spot, in a half-hidden recess in the hillside, in which there stood a fairly large engine shed containing some thirty engines. They stood inside the shed in tidy rows, silent and deserted, for not a sound could be heard except the roaring of the gale outside. The engines were the "ghosts" of a North Eastern past, mostly old goods engines of the earlier Fletcher era, including many of the old E. B. Wilson and Stephenson engines of 1852 to 1865. A good many were old acquaintances of my early days, when I used to see them regularly at work in the Leeds, York, and Hull district – engines which I had missed from their quondam haunts some years before. Others were old Stockton & Darlington engines, which twenty to thirty years previously might have been seen panting up the heights of Stainmoor. But their day was now completely past; all of them had brought home the last trains they ever were to run, and they were now waiting in this cheerless and lonely spot, many miles away from any locomotive works, until such time as could be conveniently appointed for the executioner's "set" and sledge-hammer to break them up. "Ghost" sheds occasionally exist as outbuildings of the large locomotive works, but rarely will one be found amid such deserted, bleak surroundings as the one "Somewhere on the North-East Coast". It may still be there with a fresh company of "ghosts", but I have not seen it since. ⟨c.1905⟩   E. L. Ahrons, *Locomotive and Train Working in the Latter Part of the Nineteenth Century* (1951–4), i. 93–4

46. THE RAILWAY CARRIAGE AS
A WORK OF ART

The extraordinary steps taken to preserve the coachwork and so give it the superb finish for which the Midland became renowned are set out in an official painting directive of about 1906 for a 54ft carriage. Two coats of priming before filling, then four coats of filling, were described as the ground work. Then followed stopping before rubbing, staining and rubbing. Operation no. 10 was the application of lead colour, then stopping up, facing and a second colour. Colour work began with operation no. 14, which was a coat of lake ground, then lake crimson, followed by lake and varnish. Mouldings were painted black and the first coat of body varnish applied. With that done, it was flatt down, a third coat of body varnish and flatt down. Final operation, no. 25, was a fourth coat of body varnish! ⟨c.1906⟩

George Dow, *Midland Style* (1975), 103

47. MOTIVE-POWER MESS

Four years after establishment on 1 January 1923, the London Midland & Scottish Railway, the largest of the four British Group companies forming the initial stage from private enterprise to nationalisation, had not a single express passenger locomotive worthy of the time. . . .

Paucity of designing skill, and a costive appreciation of the fundamentals of thermodynamics and railway mechanics, were responsible in part for this situation; but more was due to high-level fights for power, in which the dominant contestants up to 1927 were men from the ex-Midland Railway.

As the first chief mechanical engineer, George Hughes, chose to base himself on the homely but extraordinary backwater of Horwich, the "operating" element located at London and Derby soon came to have the upper hand, with increased power after Hughes retired in 1925. John H. Follows, chief general superintendent and John E. Anderson, his superintendent of motive power, were the leading figures. They insisted on the Midland's small-engine policy, with continuance of the Midland standard 4-4-0 compounds for passenger work and 0-6-0s for main-line freight.

Hughes did something to stem this tide with the production of the effective Horwich "Crabs" or 2-6-0 mixed-traffic engines; but he was unable, close on retiring age, to measure up in mechanical design to the needed large and powerful locomotives for long-distance 450-ton express trains. Nor was he able to impose his will on all his widespread staff, let alone on the "operators". He was too much of a gentleman to dive into power politics.

His successor, Henry Fowler, off the Midland, was not particularly interested in locomotive design, being more an administrator with a touch of the metallurgist. His accession to power on the Midland itself in 1909 had been due to his acquiescence in playing second fiddle to the chief general superintendent; his predecessor, R. M. Deeley, went out because he would not suffer any reduction in authority and responsibility as locomotive superintendent.

Anderson thus came to have predominant influence as to what locomotive types should be built. For their size, the Midland compounds were about as good as any existing type on the LMSR; but in overall performance no Midland engine got above mediocrity, mainly because of small bearings, inadequate valve gear, and indifferent piston valves. These defects were common to the larger London & North Western Claughton and Lancashire & Yorkshire four-cylinder and Caledonian two and three-cylinder engines. The much-improved valve motion of the Horwich Crabs was a lecture cut by the Derby motive-power and design authorities.

Anderson's perseverance in Midland policy, carried out by equally narrow and conservative designers, brought the LMSR into a motive-power mess by the summer of 1926. Long-distance express trains on the Western Division were operated by fire-throwing Claughtons, often piloted, and on the northern section by Hughes 4-6-0 locomotives which, having been designed for the short point-to-point runs of the LYR, were unsuited to the 141-mile non-stop or one-stop runs between Crewe and Carlisle.

Both types, and every other main-line class on the LMSR, suffered from excessive steam leakage past the piston valves, to a degree not appreciated. This ruined their coal and steam consumption figures, and also their economic effectiveness between general repairs. . . .

The statistician Sir Josiah Stamp had been appointed as president [of the LMSR] in 1925. Already he had initiated reorganisation; and the early results of his cost-accounting of locomotive operation were making him incredulous as to where all the money could possibly go that was charged to locomotive maintenance, repair, and operation – and with so little to show for it in the way of engine mileage and train speed and punctuality.

Therefore higher management borrowed the brand-new Great Western Railway 4-6-0 No. 5000 *Launceston Castle*, to run for a fortnight between Euston and Crewe and for another fortnight between Crewe and Carlisle in October 1926. Its easy, quiet handling of trains and schedules that were extending the Claughton and Hughes 4-6-0s to their limits sealed the business. The fiat of the board went forth, and in December the North British Locomotive Company Ltd. (NBL) was instructed to build fifty large 4-6-0 engines to a new design, and if possible to have them ready for the next summer's services. None of the LMSR works could have tackled such a design and construction problem; even NBL, with two works and an immense drawing-office staff, could not manage it in the time, though that was largely because when the letter of intent went out little more than an undigested skeleton design existed. The actual order to an agreed price was not signed until February 1927. ⟨1923–7⟩

> Brian Reed, *Locomotives in Profile*, (1971), i. 173–5. The delivery of the whole series of fifty Royal Scot engines between July and December 1927 reflected great credit on NBL, and they came to fulfil the expectations that had been set on them.

48. FROM STEAM TO DIESEL TRACTION

Of the great change in motive power what more is to be said? That it was inevitable is sufficiently clear from objective contemplation of the inherent characteristics of the different forms, and the movement has been world-wide. What is not clear is the reason for the suddenness of the revulsion from steam which has caused many managements the world over, and certainly our own, to embark upon its replacement at so frantic a pace as to discount for a period many of the hoped-for advantages. In the U.S.A., where operating needs brought steam well beyond the possibility of its economic operation, even on so well ordered a line as the Norfolk & Western for example, there was a reason. In Russia, where steam had become associated with the Bolshevik old guard and was chopped off with the lives of some of its adherents in a Stalin purge, there was a reason, if rather a macabre one. In certain countries without coal or water there was also a reason. But for the rest there was no practical reason, only an emotional one, why steam could not have been replaced in an orderly and economical manner, as indeed has been the case in a minority of countries abroad. In its final form it was perfectly capable of continuing to perform its duties with a very acceptable standard of performance and reliability, until it could be replaced, area by area, by more economical successors which had been given time to develop into their natural strides. It was thus capable, subject to one very important proviso, that from top management to shed cleaner its *esprit de corps* be actively maintained for as long as it was expected to give good service. . . . It is a matter of some wonder how fashions race round the world leaping the frontiers of geography and political thought. The bee-hive hair style and the same brand of "pop" music appear as readily in Madrid and Moscow as in Manchester, but one could perhaps expect that such submission to fashion would less affect hard-headed administrators. But the rage to throw away steam which their people understood and to replace it suddenly by the fashionable but untried diesel has suffused the minds of many distant administrators in emergent overseas railways, equally with their brethren in more sophisticated environments. . . .

It was unfortunate in this country that the advent of the change-over coincided with the big change in the status and authority of the Railway Engineer. There is no doubt whatever in my mind that if they had retained as much responsibility for their actions as did the former Chief Mechanical Engineers, the pace of the change would have been more restrained. Being human, they could well have made plenty of mistakes, but were unlikely to have made the mistake of accepting that, because a new form of motive power was working apparently satisfactorily in some other country, it should be applied at once and in bulk over here. This was the mistake the administrators made, unambiguously recorded in numerous reports and memoranda. ⟨1955–65⟩   E. S. Cox, *Locomotive Panorama* (1965), ii. 152–3

49. INDUSTRIAL ARCHAEOLOGY

Railway carriages were the embodiment of certain social distinctions to such an extraordinary degree that to study such rolling stock is to study some of the most telling archaeological remains of Victorian society. ⟨1969⟩   H. J. Dyos and D. H. Aldcroft, *British Transport: an Economic Survey from the Seventeenth Century to the Twentieth* (1974 ed.), 213

50. THE BEAUTY OF THE VICTORIAN LOCOMOTIVE

Like Eric Gill, I have never lost my affection and respect for the work of the great locomotive engineers of the nineteenth century. The sense of balance they achieved by such details as the spacing of springs on the tenders, by the excellence of lettering, by even the pattern of rivet heads – never for one moment forgetting that their aim was efficiency in operation – was something to marvel at. ⟨1969⟩
Sir Gordon Russell in preface to Ernest Gimson exhibition catalogue (Leicestershire Museums, 1969)

4

Opening, Closing, Revival

51. OPENING THE NEWCASTLE & CARLISLE RAILWAY

It was past six o'clock when the last train [from Redheugh, the temporary station outside Newcastle] arrived at the Canal Basin, Carlisle, an hour after it was timed to leave. A disorderly stampede for refreshments took the place of a procession into the town which was to have formed part of the day's proceedings. At half-past six o'clock a number of passengers arrived at the London Road station, where the trains were being marshalled for the return journey. These early comers took possession of the covered carriages, entering by the windows when the doors were locked. Several ladies and portly town councillors, with a temporary loss of dignity, secured comfortable seats in this way. No train, however, according to the arrangements might start until the engineer had gone ahead to see that all was right along the line, and as he was also required to superintend the preparations at Carlisle – the shunting and turning of the engines, the replenishing of the tenders with coke and water, the oiling of the axles of the carriages, etc. – he could not leave until every train was in travelling order. The consequence was that, long after the trains were due at Redheugh, they were still standing at Carlisle. Passengers who had taken their seats at 6.30 did not get away until nearly ten o'clock, having had to remain for over three hours exposed to the drenching showers in a comfortless station. In the open carriages were hundreds of ladies who, in expectation of a sunny day and an early return, had come in light thin dresses without any preparations for unfavourable weather and a night journey. Even after starting from Carlisle, which took place amid the roar of thunder and the flash of lightning, the unfortunate passengers had not got to the end of their troubles. A short distance from Milton station, the *Carlisle* engine came into collision with the hinder part of the preceding train. Some carriages and a tender were thrown off the line and two passengers injured, one having a rib broken and the other a hip dislocated. This accident brought all the trains in the rear of the *Carlisle* to a standstill and there, on the verge of the Cumberland fells, they were obliged to remain until one o'clock in the morning when, the line being cleared, they were able to resume their journey. In Newcastle and Gateshead the greatest anxiety was felt, as hour after hour passed and none of the travellers returned. Thousands of people waited all night at Redheugh for tidings of these trains, the first of which arrived about three o'clock, and as the passengers walked through the streets of Newcastle people threw up their bedroom windows to ask for news of their friends. The last train did not arrive until after six o'clock. ⟨1838⟩

W. W. Tomlinson, *The North Eastern Railway*
(1915), 317–18

52. LAVISH ENTERTAINMENT

At the opening of the branch line to Ashbourne on 31 May 1852 Brassey, the contractor, entertained 250 guests, brought in by special train. They were beguiled by "a party of vocalists" from Manchester, and this is what they had to eat. The quantity was not extravagant, in the scale of these feasts.

Baron of beef, 16 dishes potted trout, 16 ditto pickled salmon, 52 lobsters, 10 pigeon pies, 42 couple roast chickens, 6 turkeys, 10 quarters lamb, 8 haunches mutton, 16 pieces ribs beef, 10 ditto boiled ditto, 24 tongues, 8 hams, 12 joints veal, 6 venison pasties, 6 savoury pies, 12 couple boiled chickens, 2 couple guinea fowls, jellies, custards, blancmanges, lemon cheese cakes, Bakewell puddings, rhubarb tarts, preserve ditto, hunting puddings. – Dessert, grapes, oranges, gingerbread, figs, and sponge-cakes. ⟨1852⟩   *Staffordshire Advertiser*, 5 June 1852

53. THE PAIGNTON PUDDING

It was at length determined to feast the poor and make a monster pudding. It is said that, according to an old charter, the inhabitants of Paignton every fifty years give a large plum pudding to the poor. The previous one was made on the 1st of June 1819, and although the jubilee of fifty years was short by a whole decade, the inhabitants resolved to anticipate it on the ground that so great an event as the opening of a railway could only be adequately commemorated by the eating of a great pudding. . . . It was arranged that the pudding should be baked in sections, eight sections forming one layer, the whole being afterwards built together. The pudding consisted of 573 lbs of flour, 191 lbs of bread, 382 lbs of raisins, 191 lbs of currants, 382 lbs of suet, 320 lemons, 144 nutmegs, 95 lbs of sugar, a quantity of eggs, and 360 quarts of milk; the cost was £45. When completed the weight of it was one ton and a half. Besides this remarkable pudding there were provided 1900 lbs of meat, 1900 lbs of bread, and an unlimited supply of the staple product of the Paignton orchards – cider. The intention of the promoters was to feast the poor of the parishes of Paignton, Marldon, and Stoke Gabriel, as well as the navvies who had worked on the line, and their wives and families. Twelve lines of tables were erected on the Green, where the dinner was to take place. The best arrangements had been made by Mr John Belfield, of Primley, but unfortunately that gentleman had been subpoenaed to attend the assizes at Exeter on the day of the feast, and to his absence may be attributed the untoward contretemps which afterwards occurred. At twelve o'clock the procession moved off from Primley towards the Green; the prominent features in it were the waggon of bread, two waggons of meat, each drawn by three horses, and the great pudding, drawn by eight horses. Arrived at the Paignton Green, the people took their seats and were supplied with the bread, meat, and cider by a number of gentlemen, farmers, and tradesmen, who acted as carvers and waiters. The pudding was to have been cut up and served after the dinner; for that purpose the waggon containing it was brought within the rope fence which surrounded the tables, and placed in the centre. As the pudding was about to be distributed, the outside public clamoured for slices; and, breaking down the fence, attempted to help themselves. Five policemen mounted the waggon to protect the committee as well as the pudding. Seeing the turn affairs were taking, the navvies and others at the tables, imagining that they were likely to be deprived of the toothsome delicacy, left their seats and swelled the tumultuous throng by whom the unfortunate pudding, committee, and policemen were beleaguered. The mob literally swarmed round the waggon, and mounting the wheels, proceeded to demolish the pudding; alarmed at the menacing attitude of the crowd, the committee threw the pudding piecemeal amongst them. A disgraceful scene followed, in which men, women, and boys struggled and fought for the possession of the pieces thrown out from the waggon; and this continued until not a morsel was left. At three o'clock in the afternoon the first train came in with excursionists; but there were neither addresses presented nor speeches made, for the majority of the directors were in London. It was estimated that there were not less than eighteen thousand persons present at Paignton on that day. ⟨1859⟩

J. T. White, *History of Torquay* (1878), 231–3

54.   THE CLOSING OF A RAILWAY

On the morning of Saturday, October 13, 1956, rather more than the usual flow of passengers was to be seen converging on one of the western bay platforms at Newcastle Central station to join the 11.10 a.m. train for Hexham, Riccarton Junction, and Hawick. Some people were taking it as usual back to Blaydon or Prudhoe, but for most of them it was an occasion – a melancholy occasion, indeed; for it was the last day when regular passenger trains would run up the North Tyne valley. There were some visitors from a distance, but most of those who were taking the train – not the very last to run, but the best out-and-back trip in the daylight hours – had known the line and the valley for years; some were bringing their children to show them how things had been. It felt like a family occasion, a little bit like a family funeral; shyness was loosened, so that complete strangers spoke to each other and were gathered into the community for the trip.

Six coaches were provided for the train, and they were fully loaded. The locomotive, K3 class 2-6-0 62022, was adorned (like all the other engines working on the line that day) with a funeral wreath, and the preliminaries made a late start. The run lay over former North Eastern metals as far as Hexham, and there was no question of lament for this busy piece of line. From Newcastle Central, which could with care and attention be one of the best-looking stations in the country, the train passed through some of the most regrettable Newcastle outskirts and then ran across the river at Blaydon, within sight of George Stephenson's birthplace at North Wylam, and into the gentler scenery of the Tyne valley, which – above Prudhoe – has its points. Most of the main lines of the North Eastern have been modernised and to some extent standardised, but on this section the great high signal-boxes at Wylam, and the station buildings like Riding Mill built for the original low platforms, point to an older, more rugged age of railway work. There was just time to notice wagons marked "Not to leave Riding Mill", and wonder what sort of an existence theirs must be; a few more minutes, and the train was at Hexham. A sizeable crowd was on the platform, and two more coaches were added to accommodate the curious and the sentimental. If only, one thought, a few more of these people had come for the trains before this day, they might not be having to come now; but three weekday trains (with Saturday extras) have been much more than enough for the traffic offering ever since the line was opened throughout in 1862. . . .

As the train got under way again, feeling became sharper. Nobody was thinking of closing the Newcastle & Carlisle; but from Border Counties Junction, a mile beyond Hexham, where the Border Counties line left the North Eastern and turned up the North Tyne valley, it was track that passengers would not travel again, except rail fans on their excursions. At Wall – "a fine station it was" (burnt down in the second war) – someone observed that the villages on this stretch were mostly rather far from the station: a remark that might justifiably have been put the other way round, for the villages were there first.

Soon came the house and park of Chesters, where the line of the Wall crossed the North Tyne and the bath-house of the Roman soldiers. This is the only place among the railway crossings of Hadrian's wall where anything of it was to be seen, and the October sun lent colour to the woods and hills. But the more knowing prophesied cloud and perhaps rain higher up. Humshaugh had the remains of a wonderful summer's display in the station garden to show, and an inhabitant saying: "We used to walk into Hexham and take the train back. What'll we do now?" (to which and similar questions the British Transport Commission had obligingly supplied answers on a poster liberally applied). From here the line climbed up through Chollerton and Barrasford, giving views over the river to Haughton Castle and woods and pasture land, with low moors above them; Chipchase Castle was seen for a moment, Countess Park wood was pierced (where the line terminated for a few months in 1859), and Reedsmouth Junction was reached. . . . Here was a passing place – the only one on the line designed for two passenger trains to pass – and a train waiting to cross. A few more minutes, and most of the population of Bellingham, the chief settlement of the valley, seemed to be on the platform for the occasion. There was some interchange of passengers, and we were joined by a lady who could and did tell us the name of every house and farmstead as far as the top of the valley. "A blow to North Tyne, this will be", she said. She was terribly distressed.

The scenery changed; fields gave place to moorland, and the hills came closer. At Tarset was the only relic of the North British, proclaiming its origin, that the passing traveller could descry – a cast-iron drinking fountain with the admonitory words, "Keep Platform Dry". The stations, of course, are much more than relics; they bear a stern and stony aspect, and they will serve as houses for many years yet. Thornleyburn was but a halt, though not in name; at one period it was served by one train each way a week – on Tuesdays. Falstone was more of a place, but by now the late start, the heavy load, and the drawing-up required at most stations had pulled the train behind its timetable; some anxiety began to be felt by those who were counting on a southbound connection at Riccarton. At Plashetts the remains of a siding to two worked-out collieries could be seen, but also the evidences of the valley's most recent source of livelihood. The conifer plantations of the state forest of Kielder lay on both sides and began to obscure the firm outlines of the hills. Lewiefield Halt groaned beneath the load of passangers waiting to join. Kielder Castle was visible for a moment from the bridge over the burn – tricked out with battlements so as not to spoil the view from the castle windows. At Kielder Forest was a 2-6-4 tank with the Saturday train – and a wreath. It was almost 2 o'clock, instead of 1.35, and the stationmaster was begged to send word to Riccarton about the Carlisle connection.

The 2-6-0 set off again with its unaccustomed load, up to Deadwater, the last station in England, where the falling raindrop may roll into the Tyne and the North Sea or into Liddel Water and Solway Firth. Deadwater station was opened in 1880; seeing it and its surroundings, we could not help wondering why. Anxiety about the 2.1 from Riccarton was now so acute – for if it was gone there was no making London that night – that we felt almost disposed to grudge the stop – for handshaking only that day – at Saughtree (two minutes extra allowed on Mondays, Thursdays, and Saturdays).

But all was well; as the Border Counties train rounded Shiel Knowe, Arnton Fell came into sight across the Riccarton Burn and – more important – so did the Carlisle train, with an impatient-looking Pacific, *Sir Visto*, and several heads out of windows inquiring what the delay was and marvelling at the spectacle of an eight-coach train, garlanded at the front and quite full of passengers, coming off the single line.

Riccarton Junction, with its railwaymen's co-operative shop on the island platform, has no connection with the outside world by road. Although the "Junction" part lost its meaning on that day, you can still in 1967 travel to and from it by train – there is no other way but walking. ⟨1956⟩ Michael Robbins, *Points and Signals* (1967), 107–12. The main line running down to Carlisle was itself closed in 1969

55.   THE BRANCH LINE

This poem relates to the closing of the line from Sidmouth Junction to Exmouth in 1967.

One train was the last.
Decorated with a crowd
Of people who like last things,
Not normally travellers,
Mostly children and their fathers,
It left to a theatrical blast
As the guard for once played
At his job, with mixed feelings.

Photographers were there,
For the only time perhaps
Since the railway groped
Down into these shires
First of all, and the squires
Fretted about their deer.
There were flags and a few maps,
And cheers as the signal dropped.

The platform is now old
And empty, but still shows
The act of waiting.
Beyond it the meadows,
Where once the toy shadows
Of funnel and smoke bowled,
Are pure green, and no echoes
Squeeze into the cutting.

The villages that gave
The stations their names
Were always out of sight,
Behind a hill, up a lane,
Dead, except when a train
Fetched somebody forth alive.
But now no one at all comes
Out of them by this route.

The level-crossing gates
Guard passers-by from nothing
Now. The railway's bite
Is dislocated by time,
Too out-of-date to harm
Like a gummy old cat's.
The road is the frightening
Power, the current favourite. . . .

⟨1967⟩   Patricia Beer, *The Estuary*
            (1971), 15–16

56.   THE PRESERVATION OF A RAILWAY

The Talyllyn Railway in Merioneth (now Gwynedd) closed in 1950 after the death of Sir Haydn Jones, who had held the controlling interest in it since 1911. Since it was entirely unprofitable it appeared almost certain that his executors would sell it for scrap. Under the energetic and imaginative leadership of L. T. C. Rolt a society was formed to acquire the railway and to run a passenger service on it similar to the one offered in Sir Haydn's lifetime, on several days a week during the summer. It was the first operation of this kind and may be said to have initiated the railway preservation movement. Here Rolt describes the first day's traffic.

It had always been the custom to open the railway for traffic during the Whitsun holiday. This year Whitsun fell in mid-May whereas we did not feel that regular running would prove economic until early June. Moreover we wanted to give the permanent-way workers "total occupation" of the line east of Rhydyronen until the last possible moment. But because we were anxious to observe local custom as far as possible, it was decided to stage a formal opening of the line on Whit Monday by working a token shuttle service between Towyn and Rhydyronen. On his little press in Towyn, Mr Basil Jones was commissioned to print a special announcement to this effect which was suitably displayed, and activity on the line quickened as the day approached. Whit Saturday saw an influx of volunteer helpers and for the first time that year a passenger train ran the length of the line carrying these volunteers and a van load of new sign-boards which were off-loaded as we went along. Sunday was mainly devoted to tidying and cleaning-up operations. I had previously found time to give the red livery of the coaches a coat of varnish, and when the windows had been cleaned and the brass door handles polished the antiquated four-wheelers put the average modern main-line train to shame in appearance, though not, it must be admitted, in comfort. The "Old Lady", too [the locomotive *Dolgoch*, built in 1866], had been most carefully groomed and made up for the occasion. There had been no opportunity yet to repaint her completely or to add the new finery of brass name plates or transfers. But the judicious use of oily rags had made lustrous her old green coat, and like a dash of lipstick the fresh scarlet enamel on buffer beams which had previously been a sober black gave her a jaunty air of renewed youth which was no less effective for being superficial. The hand rail along the top of her boiler barrel, the balances of her safety valves, and even her cab spectacle frames, which had hitherto been painted over, all had been polished till they shone like gold.

It would have been too bad if such careful preparation had been greeted by a day of rain, but fortunately for once the Welsh weather was kind on this eighty-fifth birthday of the Talyllyn, and all that Monday the sun shone down from a sky of cloudless blue.

In such weather it seemed that summer had arrived overnight. Mountains which had so recently looked sombre and brown under cloud now lay basking in a fresh green coat of newly-unfolded bracken fronds, while every gorse bush was ablaze with a flame which rivalled the glittering brasswork of *Dolgoch* as she slowly propelled her empty train down to the Wharf station. Here a sizeable crowd was awaiting her arrival, grouped about a station building which, with a newly-painted nameboard and a red ensign floating from the mast that over-topped the roof ridge, looked as worthy of the occasion as the glittering train. . . .

There was a good muster of passengers who had come early to the scene to claim the distinction of having travelled on the first train of the season. When they were all aboard, Bill Trinder, as chairman of the Society, made a short speech before ceremonially cutting a tape, which had been stretched across the track, and declaring the line open. His action was answered by a shrill blast of *Dolgoch*'s whistle and, punctually to the minute, the first service to run under the new management drew out to the accompaniment of much excitement and acclamation.

A gang of volunteers was awaiting the arrival of the train at Rhydyronen, for as there is no loop at this station the task of turning round the train involved man-handling the coaches. First the passengers were asked to disembark on to the platform, then the train was run back and held on the brakes until *Dolgoch* was manoeuvred slowly and carefully over the points on to the disused dead-end siding. Once she was safely clear of the running line, everyone breathed a sigh of relief and proceeded to push the train past her and back into the platform. This procedure was repeated successfully throughout the day as trainload after trainload made the short journey up from Towyn. ⟨1951⟩

L. T. C. Rolt, *Railway Adventure* (Pan Books ed., 1971), 63–5, 72

5

Opposition, Fear, Hatred

57. OBJECTIONS TO THE BUILDING OF RAILWAYS

(a)

The line is not 5½ miles in length, and there is not any direct traffic between Sheffield and Rotherham. It enters neither Rotherham nor Sheffield, and parallel therewith is a canal and navigable river and an excellent public road. ⟨1835⟩

> *Sheffield & Rotherham Railroad. Reasons against the Bill. Session 1835*: Darlington Public Library: copy in Pease-Stephenson Papers, vol. ii. The railway was nevertheless authorised in 1836 and opened two years later

(b)

The Trustees of the Dartford & Strood Turnpike Road here petition Parliament against a projected Kent Railway, running parallel with their road, close to the southern shore of the Thames estuary. They had a cogent case, and they set it out quietly. The railway promoters' application was rejected.

[The petition] showeth, that the Trustees of the said road have bestowed great attention on the management of the same, and by a careful and judicious expenditure of a portion of the funds arising from the tolls thereon have brought the said road into the highest state of perfection and that it is now in the best possible condition. That having good reason to consider the debt for which such tolls were pledged sufficiently secure, and being desirous to accommodate the public to the utmost their revenues would admit, the Trustees have since the passing of the last Act in 1832, instead of paying off their debt, obtained further advances on the credit of the tolls and by means thereof and their annual income have lowered the hills in many parts of the said road and otherwise greatly improved it, at a cost of about £8000 over and above the yearly expenditure for repairs. And that all the sums at present charged on the said tolls amount to about £9000. . . .

That your petitioners view with serious alarm the projected scheme of a Kent Railway parallel with the said road inasmuch as if it succeed the revenue of the said road from Dartford to Strood must be materially diminished and the Trustees thereby prevented . . . from fulfilling their engagements with those persons of whom they have borrowed money under the sanction of the legislature. . . .

Your petitioners further respectfully submit that there is at present an excellent turnpike road from London through Dartford, Gravesend, Rochester, and Canterbury to Dover, Ramsgate, and other parts of the coast and a communication by means of steamboats along the River Thames perhaps more frequent as well as cheaper and more commodious than between any other towns in England, there being even during the winter months six and in the summer about twice as many regular passage boats plying between London and Gravesend alone which go and return every day, . . . besides which said regular steam packets to and from London and Gravesend a vast number more ply between the metropolis and the towns of Greenwich, Dartford, Chatham, Herne Bay, Margate, Ramsgate, and Dover between which the competition is so great that the fares are in many instances less than a penny a mile, and the speed of the packets is such as to render the communication along some parts parallel with the great Dover road much more rapid than that by the Royal Mail.

Your petitioners also submit to your Honourable House not only that there is no evidence of railways answering when opposed to conveyance by water and that experience has proved the superiority of communication even by canals for all heavy commodities, and that the transport by means of a great navigable river like the Thames has a still more decided advantage over railway communications.

Your petitioners further humbly but earnestly submit that it would be unjust to favour adventurers, in a speculative scheme undertaken solely for their own profit and advantage, at the expense of those who have advanced money at fixed legal and moderate interest on the credit of turnpike tolls, which have for many years been treated by repeated Acts of Parliament as valid and acknowledged securities. ⟨1837⟩

Kent Archives Office, Maidstone: AG.54

58. THE SENSE OF BEAUTY

In the choice of a line it is disgraceful that not one thought should be bestowed upon the character of the natural scenery which is threatened with destruction. It is highly desirable that there should be a railway to Brighton; scarcely any one which could be constructed would be convenient to such a multitude of persons, or is likely to be so profitable to the subscribers. But of the five rival lines which have been proposed two, if not three, and particularly Stephenson's, would, to a great degree, annihilate the peculiar beauty of a spot unrivalled in the world for the exquisiteness, combined with the accessibility, of its natural scenery: the vale of Norbury, at the foot of Box Hill. Yet into the head of hardly one Member of Parliament does it appear to have come, that this consideration ought to weigh one feather, even on the question of preference among a variety of lines, in other respects probably about equal in their advantages. Yet these men have voted £11,000 of the people's money for two Correggios, and many thousands more for a building to put them in,[1] and will hold forth by the hour about encouraging the fine arts, and refining the minds of the people by the pleasures of imagination. We see, by this contrast, what amount of real taste, real wish to cultivate in the people the capacity of enjoying beauty, or real capacity for enjoying it themselves, is concerned in this profuse expenditure of public money, although two-thirds of these men would shout in chorus against "political economists" and "utilitarians" for having no imagination, and despising that faculty in others. The truth is, that in this country the sense of beauty, as a national characteristic, scarcely exists. ⟨1836⟩

John Stuart Mill, Collected Works, (1982), vi. 327–8

[1] A reference to the foundation of the National Gallery, under an Act of 1834.

59. JUDGMENT IN A FAMOUS CASE

The Eastern Counties Railway entered into an agreement with Lord Petre in 1836 concerning the purchase of land belonging to him in Essex. Its line could take one of two routes through his property. To one of these routes he offered no objection, but he was implacably opposed to the other for the way in which it would cut up his estates. If the company decided to take the route he objected to it agreed to pay him the very large sum of £100,000 as special compensation, over and above £20,000 for the value of the land itself. It chose this route and then dishonourably refused to pay what it had promised. Here is the judgment of the Vice-Chancellor (10 May 1838).

My Lord Petre according to his own affidavit was determined to oppose the Bill unless they [the Eastern Counties company] would, by the Bill, take the Writtle road, or if they would not take the Writtle road then that they should be bound to pay him £100,000 and £20,000; and it really does not appear to' me that there is any general ground whatever for imputing anything like an improper motive to Lord Petre for so doing, because you will recollect it appears in his own affidavit that this was a place, as I understand it, built by his own grandfather, and that great pains were taken to improve the place by plantations and by making it agreeable to all the members of his family; and he represents that he himself was very partial to ... fox-hunting, which afforded great amusement not only to himself but to all the gentlemen of the county, and he naturally would stand forth as their champion against an unnecessary violation of that amusement in which they had all so long participated; therefore he said he did not regard the price so much, but that he wished if the company would not adopt the Writtle line and would come on the south side of the road, that then they should pay these enormous sums, meaning of course to have some sort of security against their doing a thing which was so adverse to their own interest. ... He meant the company should most distinctly understand that if they would interfere with his patrimonial enjoyments and the comforts of the country gentlemen whom he considered himself as protecting, that then they should pay this enormous sum. ⟨1838⟩

> The Vice-Chancellor accordingly ordered that the railway should pay Lord Petre the sum agreed between them, and after a very long delay it did so. Copy of the judgment in Essex Record Office, D/DP.E51/8

60. A JUST DISDAIN

Proud were ye, Mountains, when in times of old,
Your patriot sons, to stem invasive war,
Intrenched your brows; ye gloried in each scar:
Now, for your shame, a Power, the Thirst of Gold,
That rules o'er Britain like a baneful star,
Wills that your peace, your beauty, shall be sold,
And clear way made for her triumphal car
Through the beloved retreats your arms enfold!
Heard YE that Whistle? As her long-linked Train
Swept onwards, did the vision cross your view?
Yes, ye were startled; – and, in balance true,
Weighing the mischief with the promised gain,
Mountains, and Vales, and Floods, I call on you
To share the passion of a just disdain.

⟨1844⟩   William Wordsworth: *Shorter Poems*
                                (Everyman ed.), 664–5

61. A DUCAL OPPONENT OF RAILWAYS

The 5th Duke of Cleveland receives a deputation of persons anxious to bring a railway to Barnard Castle, crossing his Raby estate.

The Duke replied that he could not see the necessity for these branch lines; it was well enough for through lines, they might be desirable for the country, but branch lines were uncalled for. If a place was within twenty miles of a railway it was all that could be wished or desired. His Grace also added that when he came to Raby he looked at the beautiful valley of the Tees and said to himself, surely they will never think of bringing one of those horrid railways through this Paradise of a country. That he did not think a line was wanted for the interests of the country, and would oppose it to the utmost of his power. Mr [Joseph] Pease reminded His Grace that it was all very well for him, he could order out his carriage at any moment and go with ease and comfort any distance, but every one could not do this, and that the facilities and comfort of a railway were of the utmost importance to the great mass of the population.

The Duke was at ease in his possessions and remained firm in his refusal, and the inhabitants had to submit to the disappointment. ⟨1844⟩

History of the Darlington & Barnard Castle Railway
(1877), 27. The branch line was authorised nevertheless ten
years later, and opened in 1856

62. INTRUSIONS OF THE PRESS

From a diary recording the journey made through England in 1846 by the King of Saxony, kept by his physician, Dr Carus.

The latest newspapers were constantly offered at the stations [in Derbyshire]; we bought some, and the rapidity with which news is circulated here may be guessed from the circumstance that the *Times* of this morning, just arrived, gave a full and minute account of His Majesty's visit to Hatfield House yesterday! In this manner all that takes place at the court in London, visits, invitations, excursions, etc., are particularly chronicled and printed in all the newspapers, and now I see that the reporters, even on their journey, report with the same rapidity. At every station a person in one of the nearest carriages kept continually looking towards our carriage, and fixed his eyes upon us as if he were working upon a sketch of the travelling equipage for a woodcut in the *Illustrated News*! I confess that all this spying and universal small talk of the newspapers seems to me to be doubly mischievous: first, to the people who are thus accustomed to trouble themselves about a multitude of trivial circumstances, family affairs, and the most ordinary events; and secondly, for those who are the objects of such incessant prying and observation. Such a people as the English should be far above such littleness! ⟨1846⟩

C. G. Carus, *The King of Saxony's Journey* (1846), 156–7

63. FEAR OF RAILWAYS

(a)

Though I am so *greatly benefiting* by the railway [a projected line to Colne, for which she had sold some property], I should have a horror in travelling by it. ⟨1847⟩   Miss Ellen Wilson to her solicitor, Edward Parker,
12 June 1847: Lancashire Record Office, DDB/75

(b)

My father, being in bad health, travelled to Malvern, and my step-mother, for his sake only, took her place in the train. I see her still, sitting in the carriage, as we children were taking leave of her. She had her handkerchief tightly pressed to her eyes, so that she might see nothing, and begged us not to make her uncover them. A more abject picture of terror and dejection I never saw. ⟨? c.1855⟩   Sir J. H. A. Macdonald, *Life Jottings of an Old Edinburgh Citizen* (1915), 16–17

64. POLLUTION

Sir,

Between Slough and Wycombe the country is poisoned and the passengers asphyxiated by the foulest, and the blackest, and the most sulphurous pest of smoke that ever came from fuel. It is a peril to health to ride along the line or to stand near a train.

As we go up and down we cough and groan and wonder whether the Parliament has repealed the law that provided against this nuisance, and directed that coke only should be burnt. A gentleman on Saturday suggested that Mr Milner Gibson [President of the Board of Trade] gets we don't know how much every year for seeing that the railways obey the law; if so, we should be very much obliged to him to do his duty.

SMOKED BUT NOT CURED

⟨1864⟩   Letter in *The Times*, 25 July 1864

65. SCANDALOUS AND IRRETRIEVABLE UGLINESS

Our train went out of what lately was Hungerford market [i.e. Charing Cross station, which had replaced it], over what was Hungerford Bridge: instead of the graceful curves of that, we have now a horizontal line of huge gratings, between the bars of which the folks on the footway stood to gaze at us. All the rest of the way, our Asmodeus-machine looks over the roofs of poor men's houses which it has made horrible to live in, and passes across the sites of infinite dwellings destroyed: two other unfinished destroyers are seen on the way: then we stare impudently *down* upon the glorious old church of St Saviour [Southwark cathedral], lying in the pit which we have made for it: and finally crawl into the miserable makeshift station at London Bridge. No words are strong enough to condemn the scandalous and irretrievable ugliness which has spoilt the old station and the entrance to the Borough. Leasehold houses are ugly, but they are built to fall down at the end of the lease, so their baseness will at least have a speedy end: but these railways are meant to last; and who are we, that we should decimate the population and defile our children's minds with the sight of these monstrous and horrible forms, for the sake of gaining half an hour on the way to our work or our dinner? Few things of the kind are more distressing than the absolute divorce of strength and skill from beauty, which such buildings speak of. ⟨1865⟩

A. L. Munby: Derek Hudson, *Munby: Man of Two Worlds* (1972), 175

66. "IT'S ALL RIGHT"

The contractor for the Pembroke & Tenby Railway, David Davies, speaks:

When I first came into the district, about 1862, I was told that the best and ablest engineers had failed to find out a way of placing Tenby on a railway. They had said Tenby must be on a spur [i.e. a branch line]. I said, however, that a main line was practicable. I said that I certainly would have no spur, and now here you have Tenby on a main line. I knew we had hills in the way, and that if we could not get over them, we must get under them; but there was still a more formidable difficulty in the way, and which I was told I could not get over. I was informed that a lady – a Miss Richards – was opposed to our railway. I must confess I could not see my way clear through her. I was told Miss Richards represented in herself one-half of Tenby, and carried the other half with her. Our intention, however, was to make a railway, not for one-half but for the whole of Tenby; but you all know, if a lady is against you and thinks otherwise, there is an end of it. . . .

Mr Mathias and I talked the matter over, and I said: "We'll call upon her". We went to her house, and tapped at the door. We were shown into a room, and as I had never seen Miss Richards, I need not say how anxious I was to see what kind of a face she had. As soon as she made her appearance, I saw in a moment from her face what I could not say to Mr Mathias in her presence, but I said to myself: "It's all right". The fact is I twigged a smile on her face. She said: "I cannot say No, but I hope your scheme will tumble to pieces before you want my land". I said: "Well, that is quite as much as we can expect".

I had early seen that Tenby could support a railway, and I knew very well that it was not what a railway would cost, whether £5000 or £50,000 a mile, that mattered, but its value, as estimated by its earnings. The recent money panic [of May 1866] had dismayed me, but happily my partner and I had three good banks to draw upon when it came. I had prophesied the panic and prepared for it. The first and best bank was our own pockets; the second, our personal friends who knew and cared nothing about the railways, but who did know and cared for us, so they came out like bricks; and thirdly, the Tenby people themselves, who responded nobly.

Of course, our own pockets have been our best bank. Mr Roberts and I brought hard cash to the work in addition to our labour, our time, and our energy. If it had not been for that, we should not have got through, but have been compelled to do the same as the others – stop in the middle. All the money in this railway (except £5000) belongs to Mr Roberts and myself. We have also personally attended to the work, and the line has been completed twelve months before the time named in the contract. I asked Captain Rich, the government inspector, on Saturday if he had ever heard of a railway sixteen miles in length being completed as soon as this, and he replied "Never". That could not have been done if we had no money, and if I had not myself stood upon the works day after day, night after night, to see how they were progressing. ⟨1862–6⟩

Ivor Thomas, *Top Sawyer* (1988 ed.), 78–80

67.   DETESTABLE LITTLE RAILWAY

The Isle of Wight is at first disappointing. I wondered why it should be, and then I found the reason in the influence of the detestable little railway. There can be no doubt that a railway in the Isle of Wight is a gross impertinence, is in evident contravention to the natural style of the place. The place is pure picture or is nothing at all. It is ornamental only – it exists for exclamation and the water-colour brush. It is separated by nature from the dense railway-system of the less diminutive island, and is the corner of the world where a good carriage-road is most in keeping. Never was a clearer opportunity for sacrificing to prettiness; never was a better chance for not making a railway. But now there are twenty trains a day, so that the prettiness is twenty times less. The island is so small that the hideous embankments and tunnels are obtrusive; the sight of them is as painful as it would be to see a pedlar's pack on the shoulders of a lovely woman. This is your first impression as you travel (naturally by the objectionable conveyance) from Ryde to Ventnor; and the fact that the train rumbles along very smoothly and stops at half a dozen little stations, where the groups on the platform enable you to perceive that the population consists almost exclusively of gentlemen in costumes suggestive of unlimited leisure for attention to cravats and trousers (an immensely large class in England), of old ladies of the species denominated in France *rentières*, of young ladies of the highly educated and sketching variety, this circumstance fails to reconcile you to the chartered cicatrix which forms your course. ⟨1879⟩

Henry James, *English Hours* (1905), 232

68.   BETTER RAILWAY FACILITIES
NOT DESIRED

'Tis well from far to hear the railway scream
And watch the curling lingering clouds of steam,
But let not Bournemouth – health's approved abode,
Court the near presence of the iron road.

⟨1882⟩   Verses recited at a public meeting there,
discussing proposals for new lines in 1882:
C. H. Mate and C. Riddle, *Bournemouth,*
1810–1910 (1910), 135

69.   CARRIAGES OF DAMNED SOULS

Railroads ... are to me the loathsomest form of devilry now extant, animated and deliberate earthquakes, destructions of all wise social habit or possible natural beauty, carriages of damned souls on the ridges of their own graves. ⟨1887⟩   John Ruskin, Letter to *The Times*, 3 March 1887: *Works*, ed. E. T. Cook and A. Wedderburn (1903–12), xxxiv. 604

70.   ADVERTISING IN FIELDS

Loud protests arose in the 1890s against the erection of large hoardings to display advertisements – especially of patent medicines – in open fields close to railway lines.

URBS IN RURE

There are who love, while woodlands shy
    And pastures green they haunt,
To meet – in letters four feet high –
    The legend SOZODONT;
Who deem that it adornment lends
    To vernal meads and hills,
When Mr Carter recommends
    His LITTLE LIVER PILLS!

They say it gives attraction new
    To Nature's simple charm
And adds considerably to
    The value of a farm;
Though agricultural distress
    Affects my feeling heart,
I still prefer a somewhat less
    Obtrusive style of art. . . .
  ⟨c.1900⟩   A. D. Godley, *Reliquiae*
                  (1926), i. 355

71. THE WHISTLING OF ENGINES

(a)

For a generation past the stupid English public have tamely submitted to the enormous evil inflicted upon them by railway companies in every large town in the kingdom – the evil of peace disturbed day and night by the shrieks of railway whistles. With their dull, bovine unintelligence they have let it be tacitly assumed that railway companies, and even private manufacturers, have a right to make noises of any degree of loudness, with any degree of frequency, at whatever time they please. . . . These daily aggressions on hundreds of thousands of people . . . ought to be peremptorily forbidden, even had railway companies to suffer in consequence considerable inconvenience and cost. But they need suffer no inconvenience and no cost. This immense nuisance is wholly superfluous – nay more than that, it is continued at the same time that there might be a signalling system far more efficient, while entailing relatively little annoyance. ⟨1892⟩　　Herbert Spencer to the Earl of Wemyss, 1 June 1892: D. Duncan, *Life and Letters of Herbert Spencer* (1908), 314

(b)

Sir,
　If you will instruct your drivers to blow their blasted whistles every twenty yards instead of every fifty there will be a fine chance of reducing their wages sheet – for I know a number of passengers who have been driven insane by that devilish screech and only wait an opportunity to shoot either the driver or the engine. ⟨1903⟩
　　　　Anonymous letter to general manager of the North London Railway, 22 September 1903: Public Record Office, RAIL 529/113

72. A WATCHFUL CRITIC

Death has removed the Rev. W. J. Jenkins, at the age of seventy-eight. We had a slight personal acquaintance with him. So long as his particular rights were not in danger of curtailment, he was of a pleasant disposition, and an interesting companion. His persistent attempts at prosecuting railway, tramway, and omnibus companies had a good effect.
　It cannot be supposed that large concerns like railways can be efficiently

managed without stringent rules. These rules very often nearly overstep the border of legality, and minor officials, having or using no discretion, at times enforce such rules in such a manner that their actions become illegal, and the companies have to put up with the consequences when a man of Mr Jenkins's force of character insists on his rights.

These rules and regulations had been unconditionally accepted as legal for so many years before the rev. gentleman began to question them that the railway companies had regarded them as a law unto themselves, and in consequence were rather surprised when the rector of Fillingham was successful in his suits. . . .

He wrote many subtly-worded pamphlets, which he stated "exposed the iniquity of railways" and kindred concerns. These productions were remarkable for the venom displayed, but the literary style was good. Of the latter he was very proud.

It has been stated that the Rev. W. J. Jenkins had only two pleasures in life. One consisted in obtaining a summons against somebody, and the other in having one served upon himself for something. When ticket-collectors refused to oblige him in either capacity, he kept himself acquainted with legal procedure by quarrelling with his housekeepers and coal-merchants. *Railway Magazine*, 1 (1897), 187

6

Danger and Disaster

73. HUSKISSON'S DEATH

My dear Professor,

I have come to Liverpool only to see a tragedy. Poor Huskisson is either dead, or must die before tomorrow. He has been killed by a steam carriage. The folly of 700 people going fifteen miles an hour, in six carriages on a narrow road, exceeds belief. But they have paid a dear price. ⟨1830⟩

> Henry Brougham to Macvey Napier, 16 September 1830:
> *Selections from the Correspondence of the late Macvey*
> *Napier* (1879), 88

74. FRACAS IN LANCASHIRE

In March 1849 the Lancashire & Yorkshire and East Lancashire Railways, in dispute about a payment of tolls over a five-mile section of the Lancashire & Yorkshire east of Manchester, came into physical collision at Clifton Junction, each company attempting to blockade the other. Eight trains were stuck fast until the sensible Lancashire & Yorkshire superintendent withdrew those of his company. Verbal argument then ensued, which kept the companies' officials and lawyers busy for nearly four years.

The extraordinary scene which occurred last week at the Clifton railway station . . . ought not to be allowed to drop from memory without the indignant reprobation of the public. Our police regulations will not tolerate that two rival omnibus drivers should block up a street to impede traffic and endanger life by their quarrels, neither should the infinitely more dangerous blockade of a line of railway be allowed to pass unpunished. By all Acts authorising the formation of railways, the directors are empowered to punish any person who may wilfully place obstruction on the railways, and that too whether damage to property or loss of life have or have not occurred. A wilful obstruction on the part of railway officials themselves is an offence still more flagrant and dangerous. . . . These railway gentry, who seem inclined to carry things with so high a hand, both in their relations with other companies and with the public, should remember, too, in their own interest that railway dividends are not entirely composed of fares received from persons who travel on business, but that large numbers of their best customers travel for pleasure and recreation. This class are very sensitive to danger and will transfer their favours to other lines, where civil war is not raging, and where there is no more than the ordinary risk to life and limb. The everyday casualties of railway travelling are quite sufficient of themselves to deter the timid from all unnecessary travelling. It is a suicidal policy, as well as a public offence, to increase these risks by such reckless conduct as was exhibited at Clifton. ⟨1849⟩   *Illustrated London News*, 24 March 1849

75. MODERN TRIUMPHS?

I see long trains of strange machines on wheels,
With one in front of each, puffing white smoke
From a black hollow column. Fast and far
They speed, like yellow leaves before the gale,
When autumn winds are strongest. Through their windows
I judge them thronged with people; but distinctly

Their speed forbids my seeing. . . .
But while I look, two of them meet and clash,
And pile their way with ruin. One is rolled
Down a steep bank; one through a broken bridge
Is dashed into a flood. Dead, dying, wounded,
Are there as in a battlefield. Are these
Your modern triumphs? Jove preserve me from them.

⟨1860⟩   T. L. Peacock, *Gryll Grange*, chap. 28:
Novels, ed. D. Garnett (1948), 933

76. THE ABERGELE ACCIDENT

A collision between the Irish Mail, making for Holyhead, and some wagons, running back towards it down an incline.

The most terrible railway accident that ever happened in this country . . . took place on Thursday week [20 August 1868]. A passenger train ran into some wagons laden with barrels of petroleum; the inflammable oil took fire from the engine; thirty-three persons, unable to get out of the carriages, were burnt alive; their bodies were reduced to heaps of cinders. . . .

One of the passengers, the Marquess of Hamilton (eldest son of the Duke of Abercorn, Lord-Lieutenant of Ireland), gives the following account: "We were startled by a collision and a shock which, though not very severe, were sufficient to throw everyone against his opposite neighbour. I immediately jumped out of the carriage, when a fearful sight met my view. Already the whole of the three passenger carriages in front of ours, the vans, and the engine were enveloped in dense sheets of flame and smoke, rising fully 20ft high, and spreading out in every direction; it was the work of an instant. No words can convey the instantaneous nature of the explosion and conflagration. I had actually got out almost before the shock of the collision was over, and this was the spectacle which already presented itself. Not a sound, not a scream, not a struggle to escape, or a movement of any sort was apparent in the doomed carriages. It was as though an electric flash had at once paralysed and stricken every one of their occupants. So complete was the absence of any presence of living or struggling life in them that, as soon as the passengers from the other parts of the train were in some degree recovered from their first shock and consternation, it was imagined that the burning carriages were destitute of passengers; a hope soon changed into feelings of horror when their contents of charred and mutilated remains were discovered about an hour afterwards. From the extent, however, of the flames, the suddenness of the conflagration, and the absence of any power to extricate themselves, no human aid would have been of any assistance to the sufferers, who, in all probability, were instantaneously suffocated by the black and fetid smoke peculiar to paraffin, which rose in volumes around the spreading flames". . . .

Probably this is the only very disastrous railway accident in which there have been no wounded, with the exception of one individual. It has been death in a most dreadful form or an entire escape. ⟨1868⟩

Illustrated London News, 29 August 1868

77.   SUICIDE AT WILLESDEN

It is quite unnecessary to describe the Tenway Junction [Willesden], as everybody knows it. From this spot, some six or seven miles distant from London, lines diverge east, west, and north, north-east and north-west, round the metropolis in every direction, and with direct communication with every other line in and out of London. It is a marvellous place, quite unintelligible to the uninitiated, and yet daily used by thousands who only know that when they get there, they are to do what someone tells them. The space occupied by the convergent rails seems to be sufficient for a large farm. And these rails always run one into another with sloping points, and cross passages, and mysterious meandering sidings, till it seems to the thoughtful stranger to be impossible that the best trained engine should know its own line. Here and there and around there is ever a wilderness of wagons, some loaded, some empty, some smoking with close-packed oxen, and others furlongs in length black with coals, which look as though they had been stranded there by chance, and were never destined to get again into the right path of traffic. Not a minute passes without a train going here or there, some rushing by without noticing Tenway in the least, crashing through like flashes of substantial lightning, and others stopping, disgorging and taking up passengers by the hundreds. Men and women – especially the men, for the women knowing their ignorance are generally willing to trust to the pundits of the place – look doubtful, uneasy, and bewildered. But they all do get properly placed and unplaced, so that the spectator at last acknowledges that over all this apparent chaos there is presiding a great genius of order. . . .

At Tenway Junction there are half-a-dozen long platforms, on which men and women and luggage are crowded. On one of these for a while Ferdinand Lopez walked backwards and forwards as though waiting for the coming of some especial train. The crowd is ever so great that a man might be supposed to walk there from morning to night without exciting special notice. But the pundits are very clever, and have much experience in men and women. A well-taught pundit, who has exercised authority for a year or two at such a station as that of Tenway, will know within a minute of the appearance of each stranger what is his purpose there – whether he be going or has just come, whether he is himself on the way or waiting for others, whether he should be treated with civility or with some curt command – so that if his purport be honest all necessary assistance may be rendered him. As Lopez was walking up and down, with smiling face and leisurely pace, now reading an advertisement and now watching the contortions of some amazed passenger, a certain pundit asked him his business. He was waiting, he said, for a train from Liverpool, intending, when his friend arrived, to go with him to Dulwich by a train which went round the west of London. It was all feasible, and the pundit told him that the stopping train from Liverpool was due there in six minutes, but that the express from the north would pass first. Lopez thanked the pundit and gave him sixpence – which made the pundit suspicious. A pundit hopes to be paid when he handles luggage, but has no such expectation when he merely gives information.

The pundit still had his eye on our friend when the shriek and the whirr of the express from the north was heard. Lopez walked quickly up to the edge of the platform, when the pundit followed him, telling him that this was not his train. Lopez then ran a few yards along the platform, not noticing the man, reaching a spot that was unoccupied – and there he stood fixed. As he stood the express flashed by. "I am fond of seeing them pass like that", said Lopez to the man who had followed him.

"But you shouldn't do it, sir," said the suspicious pundit. "No one isn't allowed to stand near like that. The very hair of it might take you off your legs when you're not used to it."

"All right, old fellow", said Lopez, retreating. The next train was the Liverpool train; and it seemed that our friend's friend had not come, for when the Liverpool passengers had cleared themselves off, he was still walking up and down the platform.

"There ain't another from Liverpool stopping here till the 2.20", said the pundit. "You had better come again if you mean to meet him by that."

"He has come on part of the way, and will reach this by some other train", said Lopez.

"There ain't nothing he can come by", said the pundit. "Gentlemen can't wait here all day, sir. The horders is against waiting on the platform."

"All right", said Lopez, moving away as though to make his exit through the station.

Now Tenway Junction is so big a place, and so scattered, that it is impossible that all the pundits should by any combined activity maintain to the letter that order of which our special pundit had spoken. Lopez, departing from the platform which he had hitherto occupied, was soon to be seen on another, walking up and down, and again waiting. But the old pundit had had his eye upon him, and had followed him round. At that moment there came a shriek louder than all the other shrieks, and the morning express down from Euston to Inverness was seen coming round the curve at a thousand miles an hour. Lopez turned round and looked at it, and again walked towards the edge of the platform. But now it was not exactly the edge that he neared, but a descent to a pathway – an inclined plane leading down to the level of the rails, and made there for certain purposes of traffic. As he did so the pundit called to him, and then made a rush at him – for our friend's back was turned to the coming train. But Lopez heeded not the call, and the rush was too late. With quick, but still with gentle and apparently unhurried steps, he walked down before the flying engine – and in a moment had been knocked into bloody atoms. ⟨1876⟩ Anthony Trollope, *The Prime Minister* (old World's Classics ed.), ii. 231–5. Tolstoy read and admired *The Prime Minister* while he was writing *Anna Karenina*, published in 1877. His account of her suicide under a train seems to have been influenced by this one

78. THE ABBOT'S RIPTON ACCIDENT

It was a frightful catastrophe, and the horrors of the scene were much enhanced by the state of the weather. In that part of the country it had been snowing all day . . . and where the collision took place, in a deep cutting, the snow lay deep – it was still falling in heavy showers and a strong wind was blowing.

Although the first collision, between the Scotch express and the coal-train, was a frightful one, I do not think that any great loss of life or damage had taken place. But when the engine of the "down-train" dashed in, sweeping before it the debris of the first accident, that was the climax of horrors and a sight that I shall never forget.

I had *two* miraculous escapes. I was in the third carriage from the front. The compartment was full. I was in the far seat with my back to the engine. Opposite to me was an officer of artillery, whom I subsequently saw, a good deal shaken.

The centre seats were occupied by two very nice-looking lads, apparently travelling together, and in the remaining seats, by the door, were two gentlemen.

There was no warning – but, in a moment, there was an awful shock, and utter darkness. The end of my carriage seemed to sink down on the rails. I doubled myself up – and put my arms over my head to protect my surviving eye. The cushion from the opposite seat fell on my head and, I believe, protected me much. When, at last, we stopped I was still in my seat, but I *stepped off my cushion into the snow* – NOT THROUGH THE DOOR, *the whole side of the compartment was gone.*

A few minutes after this, being uninjured and in full possession of my senses – I, with another gentleman, assisted a Scotchwoman and "her lassie" as she called her – out of a portion of a shattered carriage laying across the down line – we had JUST got them into an uninjured carriage in the Scotch Express when the engine of the down-train, having leaped over the tender of the Scotch Express engine which was laying across the down-line, dashed past us, and turned over on the top of the very carriage from which, *two minutes* before, we had rescued the Scotchwoman and her "lassie"!!

I remained at the scene for upward of four hours after the catastrophe – and as I never saw either of the lads who were in the carriage with me I felt certain that something had happened to them. I mentioned this to Mr Cockshott, a Great Northern official who had arrived on the spot, and I described their dress, etc., etc. He told me yesterday that their bodies had been found – *the lowest down of eight*, under the wrecked carriage the engine had fallen upon – so disfigured he could only recognise them by my description of their dress. How *they* got there and *I* did not, God only can tell, *I* shall never know. I had my feet on the same foot-warmer with one of them when the collision took place! ⟨1876⟩

Lord Colville of Culross to Henry Ponsonby, 23 January
1876: A. Ponsonby, *Henry Ponsonby* (1942), 312–13

79. RACING BETWEEN TRAINS

Mr Francis Jones, clerk of the peace and under sheriff for the city of Gloucester, . . . said that . . . about 12 months ago he was in the habit of passing between Gloucester and Oxford both ways about six times a week; he therefore had ample opportunity of observing the running of the trains between Standish junction and Gloucester. Almost every morning he came from Oxford by the 6.0 a.m. train from London. This train used very frequently to meet a slow train from Bristol, and he has many times noticed that they have come neck and neck at about Haresfield, or between that and Standish Junction. From his observation he considers that there is a decided tendency on the part of both companies to race one another, and he has on many occasions heard remarks from servants of both companies as to which engine was for the time being the better of the two. He has also very frequently, when looking out of the window of the Great Western train, seen the Midland driver turn the circular reversing gear to its full extent for forward motion, and as he thought for gaining the utmost speed possible, and he recollects on one occasion seeing the Midland train, on this being done, run completely away from the Great Western train, and as it was running away he saw not only the guards of the Midland train but many of the passengers put their heads out of the windows, as much as to say "we have done you today". He has noticed great interest being evinced by the fair sex as to the success of the trains in the race. . . .

Mr William Nicks, of Greville House, Gloucester, a magistrate, then said that about 10 years ago he was travelling a great deal. . . . There was constant racing between the trains at that point, and in fact it was impossible to travel over it without having a race; he had seen racing scores of times. . . . There was a common rumour that the engine drivers used to have bets on, and that they used to have a supper every Saturday night. He said everyone in Gloucester knew that this racing went on continuously. One night, a little before the alteration of the gauge (in May 1872), he was in a train from London, and when at Stonehouse he heard the driver of his train and the driver of the Midland train whistling like two call-birds. When the trains got to Standish junction they were alongside, and they had the most fearful race he ever saw in his life. His train was the 4.50 p.m. from Paddington. He could produce three gentlemen who saw it as well as himself. He believed the racing was chiefly due to a belief among the men that the broad gauge could beat the narrow. Since the alteration of the gauge he had not seen any racing. ⟨1877⟩

> From evidence given at an inquiry into the death of a plate-layer on the Great Western Railway on 27 January 1877: *Parliamentary Papers*, 1877, lxxvii. 393–4

80.   A "WILD RUN"

"Wild runs" were frequently made on the Brecon & Merthyr Railway, descending the Seven Mile Bank between Torpantau and Talybont, nearly all of it on a gradient of 1 in 38. The brakes often proved quite inadequate to control the trains, even when as in this case three engines were employed, handling thirty-six freight vehicles.

We came into the tunnel, and kept on steam until half the train was in the tunnel. I remember coming to the (north) side of the tunnel, but did not stop, because we could not. I had my brake on tight, but could not stop the train. We opened the whistle for the others to stop, but they did not. Joseph Thomas was my driver. Joseph Thomas said to me, "Joe, do you see anybody your side giving signals?" I said "No". "Well", he said, "there is something not right." We kept on; the train had overpowered us. I never spoke to him or he to me afterwards. I remember going down the bank all the way. I looked back, and saw we were all together. The engine was rolling; we were coming very fast, and the fire was flying out of the chimney. We came near the bridge. I felt a crash, and felt as if the engine jumped up in the air. I found myself on my head, and the scalding water coming over me. I began struggling. I did not know where I was. I struggled

and got free. I felt the air reviving me, and I jumped, but did not know where. I got against some railings, and went down on my knees, and thanked God that I was safe. I am sure we could not stop when we got out of the tunnel. My driver tried to stop. I heard no whistle from the other engines. My driver gave two short whistles on coming out of the tunnel as a signal for the drivers behind to stop. . . . We began work at 3 o'clock in the morning, and we ought to have finished at 5 o'clock that night, but we had extra work to do, because of some coals being wanted immediately at Birkenhead. ⟨1878⟩　Account given by the fireman of the leading engine, Joseph
Davies, taken down at the inquiry by the Board of Trade
inspector, Col. F. H. Rich, into the accident at
Talybont on 2 December 1878: *Parliamentary Papers,*
1878–9, lxii. 219

81. THE TAY BRIDGE
28 December 1879

When shall we three meet again?
Macbeth

"When shall we three meet again?"
　　"At the seventh hour, on the viaduct."
　　　"At the central pier."
　　　　　　　　"I'll quench the flame."
"I'll be there too."
　　　　　　"I'll be arriving from the north."
"And I from the south."
　　　　　　　"And I from the sea."

"Hurrah! What a ring-a-ring-o'-roses there'll be,
And the bridge will have to tumble to the sea-bed."

"And the train which advances on to the bridge
At the seventh hour?"

　　　　　　"Why, it will have to go with the bridge."

"It will, indeed."

　　　　"Nick-nacks and playthings
Are the creations of man."

*

On the north side the bridgemaster's house —
All its windows look to the south,
And the bridgemaster's men restless and agitated
Anxiously keep watch to the south,
Keep watch and wait to see whether a light
From across the water announces, "I am coming,
I am coming despite the night and raging gale,
I, the Edinburgh train."

And then the bridgemaster speaks, "I can see a glimmer of light
On the opposite shore. It must be her.
Now, Mother, forget your fearful apprehensions,
Our Johnny is coming and wants his Christmas tree,
And whatever candles are now left on the tree,
Light them all as though it were Christmas Eve,
This year he intends to be with us twice, —
And in eleven minutes time he'll be at home with us.

*

And it was the train. Past the southern tower
It chugs now against the storm,
And Johnny speaks, "Only the bridge to go now!
But so what. We'll manage it, of course.
A sturdy boiler, full steam-up,
In such a conflict, they'll be the winners.
And no matter how much the storm roars and rages and raves,
We'll succeed in defeating the elements.

And our bridge is our pride and joy;
I cannot but laugh when I think of how things were,
Of all the misery and of all the dangers
With that wretched old ferry-boat.
How many a blessed Christmas night
I've spent in the ferryhouse,
Watching the bright gleam of our windows,
Counting them and yet not being able to be across there."

On the north side, the bridgemaster's house —
All its windows look to the south,
And the bridgemaster's men, restless and agitated,
Anxiously keep watch to the south;
For the wind began to sport more violently,
And then, it was as though fire fell from the heavens,
And plummeted in glowing splendour
Above the waters below . . . and then again all was darkness.

*

"When shall we three meet again?"
  "At midnight, on the mountain ridge."
    "On the high moor, at the trunk of the alder."

"I'll come."
    "I, too."
        "I'll give you the numbers."
"And I'll give you the names."
  "And I'll tell of the suffering."
    "Hey! The timberwork broke apart like splinters."

"Nick-nacks and playthings
Are the works of mankind."
⟨1879⟩

Theodore Fontane translated by David Jeffreys. First published in *Die Gegenwart*, 10 January 1880. German text in *Die Eisenbahn*, ed. W. Minaty (1984), 95–6

82. SNOW IN GALLOWAY

The evening of 7 December 1882 was a bad one. Snow came on shortly after midday, by 3 o'clock it was blowing a blizzard, and the Mail, which left St Enoch [Glasgow] for Carlisle at 5 p.m., walked right out into the thick of it. John Emmerson of Carlisle was driving, with a Stirling 4-4-0, no. 36, and the pilot was of the same type, no other than no. 6, the famous pioneer of that famous class. Wee Jimmy O'Brien of Hurlford was driving her, and Andrew Gilchrist firing. Well, approaching Sanquhar they got the distant off, but the home and the starter were red, and with the scanty warning and brakes impeded by frost and snow they were well past the station before they managed to pull up. John Emmerson ran back through the storm and met an unknown man who shouted "Go on. The signals are out of order". They took his word for it and went on.

But there had been grievous blundering at Sanquhar that night. The way was not clear. At Mennock box, 2¼ miles south of Sanquhar, the Glasgow-Carlisle goods was lying on the up line. It had been buffeting the drifts, and Maxwell McIntosh, the driver, had to stop at Mennock to get his ashpan cleared of snow. He had 249, a Stirling 0-4-2, and a big train of 40 wagons, with a hundred head of cattle in it bound from Dublin to Newcastle. By the time they got the pan cleared the signalman was shouting that he'd have to shunt them for the Mail. But now the points were clogged with snow. Surfacemen were digging them out; the first guard went back to assist, and presently the fireman came along to see what was holding them.

In a lull of the storm they heard the Mail bearing down upon them. The fireman ran shouting to the van, for in it were Gavin Morrison, the second guard, and the two Irish owners of the cattle. Gavin and the first cattleman got clear, the second man hesitated, went back for his boots, and was caught. The Mail men got hardly any warning, for all signals at Mennock were hanging "off" with the snow. Jimmy O'Brien had only time to shut his regulator when they struck and he was sent flying past the cab head-over-heels into a five-foot snowdrift. Emerging unhurt, he floundered around in snow and darkness looking for his fireman, and to his joy discovered him, also unhurt. "Gie me yer haun', man Andra!" cried the little driver. "I thought we would never chow cheese mair!" The Carlisle men on the second engine were not so fortunate. They were pinned in by coal and rather badly burnt. I think a glass burst.

A strange mystery hung over the Mennock business. Who was the unknown man who came out of the storm that night and told them to go? It was eventually discovered to have been the young booking clerk, John Stitt, conveying that fatal order from the stationmaster, George Little. Little was dismissed from the service, although at the High Court trial at Dumfries he and the drivers of the Mail were all acquitted.

The later careers of some of the men involved in this accident were strangely interesting and in some cases tragic. Maxwell McIntosh became a famous driver of main-line expresses, but when oiling 384, a 4-6-0, at St Enoch one morning, 327, a Manson 0-4-4 tank, cut his leg off, though he survived many years after that. Gavin Morrison, escaping unscathed from several other accidents, became a passenger guard at Ayr, and his trim figure graced the train conveying the Prince of Wales to Maybole in 1926 on his first visit to his Earldom of Carrick. George Little, discharged for his blunder, made good as inspector of poor for Thornhill, and was a respected townsman there for many years.

Poor wee Jimmy O'Brien had a sadder end. The shock of the accident and the gruelling inquiry weighed heavily upon him. He took on himself blame where there was none, his health suffered, and some years later he committed suicide. But the fate of John Stitt the boy booking-clerk was perhaps the strangest and most tragic of all. After some years in railway service he became a commercial traveller in London. He was known to have intended travelling to Scotland for the Christmas of 1910, but he never reached his destination and is presumed to have perished in the Hawes Junction disaster, though no trace of him, I believe, was ever found. ⟨1882⟩ David L. Smith, *Tales of the Glasgow & South Western Railway* (1970 ed.), 70–1

83. DEATH IN DORSET

Walter Williams, of Cattistock Mill, gives evidence.

About 9.45 a.m. on Tuesday October 24th I was on the line about ten yards from the bridge. I saw the down train approaching very slowly. There was a few inches of water over the rails when the train came on to the bridge. The engine passed over and then the bridge gave way. The engine then dropped back. I looked round and saw the driver fall near where the steam and water were coming from the engine. I ran back a little, fearing the engine might burst. I sent a man off directly to stop any up train, and to report to the stationmaster at Maiden Newton what had occurred. Henry Allen, the man I sent, went off immediately. Ledbury, Mr Wilkin's coachman, was with me. He went to the driver's assistance. [Severely scalded, the driver died next day.] I went round to assist the fireman. He had swam to a tree in my orchard. I got a rope and swam out to him, and got him out and took him up to my house. Shortly afterwards a doctor arrived. When I was on the line I saw nothing whatever the matter with the bridge. I had walked over it about five minutes before. I was out with Ledbury, shooting rats at the time. ⟨1882⟩

> Accident report, 24 November 1882: *Parliamentary Papers*, 1883, ix. 170

84. AT BALLYHAUNIS

After the Famine in the 1840s there was a substantial migration of Irishmen to find work in England during the harvest. Some 8000 men were being conveyed for this purpose every year by the Midland Great Western Railway from Connaught alone, in 1885–9. Though the company made serious efforts to convey all the traffic satisfactorily, stampedes to enter the trains often occurred at the stations. The horrible death inquired into here was a consequence of one of them.

On Friday 14th June an unusually large number of harvestmen presented themselves at various stations on the Mayo line to be taken by special train as passengers for the North Wall [Dublin] and thence to various parts of England. . . . The official charged with the arrangements for the conveyance of harvestmen had considered that he was finding sufficient accommodation on the 14th June by arranging for the dispatch of four special trains, two from Ballina, one from Westport, and one from Claremorris, containing in all 43 carriages and four brake vans, capable of holding about 3000 persons; owing, however, to the unexpectedly early hay harvest in England unusually large numbers of harvestmen presented themselves at the various stations, and no less than 898 had been booked at Ballyhaunis in the course of the morning. When the first special train from Ballina arrived at Ballyhaunis (where it and the following one had to cross the down limited mail) at about 11.30 a.m. it was quite full, as the stationmaster had been informed by telegraph, and as he had endeavoured to explain to the crowds of harvestmen on the platform. There was, however, a rush made upon the carriages as the train drew up at the platform, and a number of harvestmen managed to find room for themselves. The deceased, his brother, and another man had made their way into the front compartment of the eighth carriage from the engine – his brother says by opening the door. The carriage appears to have been overcrowded (there having been from 32 to 40 harvestmen in the compartment intended to hold 28), when the three men made their way into it, and in the commotion that ensued the deceased was thrown on to the floor, his ulcerated leg trampled on, and haemorrhage ensued, from the effects of which he died shortly after being extricated from the carriage. ⟨1889⟩

From the report of the inspector, Major-General
C. S. Hutchinson, to the Board of Trade:
Parliamentary Papers, 1890, lxv. 191–2

85.   THE FORCE OF WATER

In 1898 the Highland Railway opened a new line from Aviemore to Inverness, which reduced the length of its main route up from the south by 26 miles.

Climbing to a height of 1500ft at Slochd Summit and crossing the Findhorn and the Nairn by towering viaducts, it was a heroic feat of engineering, especially when we remember that, by English standards, the Highland was a small and impoverished concern. All the works on this new line were massively constructed, for its engineers were under no illusions about the weather in the Highlands.

Yet on 15 June 1914 circumstances conspired to defeat them. At about noon on this sultry summer day a terrific storm broke over the Grampians and the Monadhliaths which culminated at 2 o'clock in a cloudburst on the high moors above Carr Bridge. All the burns came roaring down their glens in sudden tremendous spate. The railway bridges withstood this onslaught, but the Baddengorm, the stream most affected by the storm, completely carried away the old stone road bridge which stood on the upstream side of the railway. The debris formed an effective dam across the narrow glen so that the floodwaters formed a sizeable lake. As the torrent continued to pour down from the moors above, it was obviously only a question of time before this dam must fail. Meanwhile, all unaware of this fearful trap which had been set for it a little way up the line, the

10 a.m. train from Glasgow to Inverness ran into Carr Bridge station. Fate could not have dealt more hardly with the Highland Railway that day, for just as the train pulled away from the station and approached the Baddengorm bridge the trap was sprung. Those who saw the results of the appalling flood disaster at Lynmouth in 1952 will not need to be reminded of the terrifying power which water can at such times assume. When the dam broke a wall of water, tearing down trees and tossing up two-ton boulders like pebbles, fell upon the bridge as the train of six coaches passed on to it. The engine had just cleared the bridge when it began to subside at the northern end, with the result that the tender and the two leading coaches became derailed. Speed was slow on this long pull up to Slochd Mhuic and the train was quickly brought to a standstill. The two derailed coaches were now clear of the bridge, and the next three stood wholly or partially upon it, while the rearmost was still on the approach embankment. It is small blame to the driver that he did not immediately grasp the peril of the situation. Even had he done so it is highly improbable that he could, in the last few seconds that remained, have dragged his crippled train to safety. As it was he climbed down from the footplate and walked back across the bridge to notify his guard of the derailment. He had an extraordinarily lucky escape from almost certain death, for no sooner had he reached the other side than the bridge collapsed and was swept away. Fortunately the power of the brakes and the parting of couplings prevented the whole train from following it, but the third and fifth coaches reared up on end while the unlucky fourth fell fairly into the torrent and disappeared in a maelstrom of flying boulders and debris. No coach in railway history has ever disintegrated more rapidly and completely. Its bodywork was reduced to matchwood and tatters of upholstery, which were swept far down the burn into the Dulnan and thence into the Spey. When the spate subsided as quickly as it had risen, few traces of it remained. The passengers in the upended coaches luckily escaped with minor injuries; the question was how many people had been travelling in the one ill-fated vehicle. . . . Mercifully the train was unusually empty that day and only five bodies were subsequently recovered from the bed of the burn. The bridge was completely demolished but by a remarkable feat of engineering on the part of the Highland contractor, Sir Robert McAlpine, a new bridge was completed and opened for traffic three weeks after the accident. ⟨1914⟩   L. T. C. Rolt, *Red for Danger* (4th ed., 1982), 107–9

86.   SNOW IN FIFE

My worst experience with "nature in the raw" occurred during the big snow blizzards of 1947. We had been ploughing through it for over a week on the East Coast night trains to and from London, but it was left to the comparatively short forty-eight-mile trip between Edinburgh and Perth to "put us on the spot".

It should be understood that our long night trips on the "Londons" were worked on alternate weeks, and, to give us a glimpse of the daylight and ease the strain of long-road work, the top-link men at my depot ran short trips between Edinburgh and Perth, Edinburgh and Dundee, and Edinburgh and Glasgow.

So it was that we set off on the 7.40 a.m. from Waverley to Perth that Monday morning in the middle of a snowstorm which had been raging almost continuously for the best part of three days. We knew that everyone had been fighting it during the week-end and were warned before we set out that things were pretty tough on the exposed parts of the road.

We weren't unduly concerned. We had our own engine *Spearmint* and quite a wee train which would be reduced from seven coaches to four at Dunfermline, about 16½ miles from Edinburgh, and the worst snow blocks we were told lay beyond that. At least six powerful engines were working with snow ploughs trying to keep the line clear.

I had run the Perth road for years and knew all its moods: its pleasant, smiling Glenfarg in the spring and summer, the snarling winds of autumn and the bleak icy snow-laden blasts and eddies of winter. All the same this was something a bit different in its continued ferocity, and so it proved to be.

We left Dunfermline after being told the road was not too good beyond Kelty, just about half-way between Edinburgh and Perth, and sure enough all the signals were against us as we drew into Kelty platform, with right ahead of us about fifty men with shovels clearing a mountainous drift.

"We are going to clear the loop and you will shove back into it – the road ahead is completely blocked", said the stationmaster. "There's another couple of Austerities coming along with snow-ploughs; we've got to clear the main line to let them through." So we shoved our four carriages into the loop and passed insulting remarks to the Austerities as their huge bulk lumbered past behind a gigantic snowplough.

This was somewhere about 10 a.m., and we stood at Kelty till 10.30 p.m. waiting for the road ahead to be cleared. To keep the passengers comfortable we gave them all the heat we could until the water in our tank was nearly finished. This meant that we had to be dug out of the loop to allow us to move the few hundred yards to the water column on the main line, after which the road had to be cleared behind our train to allow us to shove back. . . .

At midday we determined to cut a path to the Kelty Colliery canteen, a few hundred yards away, so that our passengers could get something warm inside them, and had to clear the path again to return to the train. The same performance was gone through at tea-time.

At 10 p.m. we got word that one line was cleared. "Would we try it?" Off we went into the "white darkness" ahead with a pilot-man on the footplate to keep us company. I had run through snow many times before, but that twenty-four miles to Perth gave me a few new angles.

The usual technique is almost to close the damper through the drifts to prevent the ashpan being choked, then open the damper on the clear stretches to let air into the fire. But it seemed to be all drift for the first ten miles – drifts which we couldn't see, but very often felt!

Green lights guided us through a narrow lane of snow fifteen or twenty feet high in one of the dips before reaching Loch Leven, and we crawled past no less than six engines buried on the other line to plough through our own particular drifts which we hit with a feeling of sinking our nose into a cushion.

This was the sign to give old *Spearmint* "all the works", and as we smashed into and out of each succeeding drift it cascaded into the cab like a gigantic and solid waterfall. It was solid all right – the cab windows knew that, when the cascade hit them and they caved in.

We got through the worst at last and down Glenfarg we went, the Glen a beautiful sight even to the three of us on *Spearmint* who were anything but beautiful to look at.

We were black as crows, strips of sacking tied round our legs, our waterproofs belted round us with odds and ends of string, in a perfectly useless attempt to keep dry; but our train got through, and as far as I know it was the only one which did so that day.

It took us sixteen hours to do that forty-eight miles, which normally we ran in 1½ hours with a whole lot of stops. That trip at its conclusion gave us a good laugh as well as a grand example of kindness.

We, of course, couldn't return to Edinburgh that night, and were recommended to one of the more modest hotels, but on our ring at the bell being answered by the proprietor, it wasn't surprising that he slammed the door in our faces when he saw the three awful-looking figures confronting him. We stood helplessly laughing on the pavement when we saw his horrified look.

So we decided, if we could not enter the modest portals, we would go to the other extreme, and make straight for one of the biggest hotels which the Fair City boasted. There we were received with calm acceptance as if we weren't the filthy tramps we looked. Lashings of hot water, hot towels, and literally bathfuls of soapsuds made new men of us all, ready to eat the huge meal the manageress of the Queen's Hotel had ready for us when we came downstairs. A warm bed and a dreamless long sleep and we travelled home to Edinburgh "on the cushions" next morning, glad to see a bright sun – the end of that memorable 1947 blizzard. ⟨1947⟩

Norman McKillop, How I became an Engine Driver
(1953), 113–16

7

Travelling

87. LONDON – BIRMINGHAM – LIVERPOOL

1 Sept. 1838. Started, in company with Hume, for Birmingham and Liverpool by the railroad. . . . On our arrival at Vauxhall (near Birmingham), where the train stopped, the whole scene but too strikingly bore out the notion of those who see a tendency to *Americanise* in the whole course of the world at present. The way in which we were trundled out of the carriages, like goods, and all huddled together in the same room – the rush upstairs to secure beds – the common supper-room for the whole party – and the small double-bedded room in which Hume and I were (to my no small uncomfort) forced to pig together – all struck me as approaching very fast the sublime of Yankeeism.

2 Sept. Took the railroad to Liverpool, and was quite enchanted with the swiftness and ease of the course. There I sat, all the way, lolling in a most comfortable arm-chair and writing memorandums in my pocket-book as easily and legibly as I should at my own study-table, while flying through the air at the rate of thirty miles an hour. Did the journey in about four hours and twenty minutes, and had but little time to look about us when we found ourselves on board the Liverpool packet. ⟨1838⟩

Memoirs, Journal, and Correspondence of Thomas Moore,
(1856), vii. 231

88. NO. 1 TICKET

I happened to be on the spot [at Derby, on 12 August 1839], the day on which the line to London was first opened. As a matter of study and curiosity, I determined on taking my departure by it for the capital. . . .

All Derby was in a bustle on that eventful morning. . . . I was the first on the spot, and had ticket No. 1. Every director was present. Preliminary experiments had been made daily for a week and upwards; yet everything seemed in a state of confusion, everybody spoke or commanded, and when the carriages were to be brought up to the temporary platform it was found that something had to be done to the iron stop of one of those circular moving machines in the ground which serve to turn the vehicles. The operation was performed with bad and inefficient tools, and took some time to be completed. This was not very encouraging to me, who was silently watching every movement, and saw all the hesitation and whispering and going to and fro around us.

When all was ready, it was found that there were but few persons who would proceed, and the train ended by being composed of three or four first-class carriages only, certainly very splendid and comfortable. With these we started for Stonebridge, a few miles north-west of Coventry, where we expected to be taken in tow by a train from Birmingham. But we were not quite ready when the train came in sight, and it whisked along, giving us the go-by and leaving us in the lurch.

However, a locomotive with suitable fuel and water was soon procured and tacked to our three or four solitary vehicles, which started on their venture at the risk of finding every impediment and none of the ordinary aids on the road, inasmuch as we were interlopers on the line, appearing for the first time upon it, and not in our right and pre-concerted time.

The consciousness of this made my travelling companions in the same carriage and myself somewhat nervous; yet we could hardly help smiling, in the midst of our apprehensions, at the vacant and stupefied stare of the workmen we found on the road and our own line, who had just time to scamper off; and at the astonishment of some of the policemen who were seen running to take up their flags which they had not expected to be so soon called upon to wave again after the passing of the last Birmingham train; and above all at the gaze of wonder and curiosity of all the people employed at the different stations, upon beholding the arrival of a total stranger on their premises.

We made our journey good, nevertheless, and I inwardly thanked my stars to find myself again upon my legs, passing under Hardwick's splendid arch at Euston Grove, where we arrived in seven hours from Derby: no great performance truly, nowadays, for a distance of 135 miles! ⟨1839⟩

A. B. Granville, *The Spas of England: Midland Spas* (1841), 125–7

89.   AMENITIES OF TRAVELLING PROPHESIED

If a reasonable time for refreshments cannot be allowed, and if the necessary viands for breakfast and luncheon are not provided at the stations, a refreshment carriage should be fitted up for those who choose to take any, which might very simply be done with a stage on sliding parts to lead to it, or the carriages might be made high enough to walk in, and have a communication from one end to the other of the train, as is done on some of the American railways, the passengers sitting along the sides. This would enable every accommodation to be afforded, including portable water-closets. . . . A smoking carriage might also be fitted up, as this habit has become almost a necessary of life with many people. ⟨1839⟩

Peter Lecount, *Practical Treatise on Railways* (1839), 194. British railway companies were required to provide smoking accommodation in their trains in 1868. The dining car first appeared in regular service in Britain in 1879. Lavatory accommodation began to be provided in 1880, the corridor train was introduced in 1892

90.   MR WELLER ON RAILWAYS

"It wos on the rail," said Mr Weller, with strong emphasis; "I wos a goin' down to Birmingham by the rail, and I wos locked up in a close carriage with a living widder. Alone ve wos; the widder and me wos alone; and I believe it wos only because ve *wos* alone and there wos no clergyman in the conwayance, that that 'ere widder didn't marry me afore ve reached the half-way station. Ven I think how she began a screaming as ve wos a goin' under them tunnels in the dark, – how she kept on a faintin' and ketchin' hold o' me, – and how I tried to bust open the door as was tight-locked and perwented all escape – Ah! It was a awful thing, most awful!"

Mr Weller was so very much overcome by this retrospect that he was unable, until he had wiped his brow several times, to return any reply to the question whether he approved of railway communication, notwithstanding that it would appear from the answer which he ultimately gave, that he entertained strong opinions on the subject.

"I con-sider," said Mr Weller, "that the rail is unconstitootional and an inwaser o' priwileges, and I should wery much like to know what that 'ere old Carter[1] as once stood up for our liberties and wun 'em too, – I should like to know wot he vould say, if he wos alive now, to Englishmen being locked up with widders, or vith anybody again their wills. Wot a old Carter vould have said, a old Coachman may say, and I as-sert that in that pint o'view alone, the rail is an inwaser. As to the comfort, vere's the comfort o' sittin' in a harm-cheer lookin' at brick walls or heaps o' mud, never comin' to a public-house, never seein' a glass o' ale, never goin' through a pike, never meetin' a change o' no kind (horses or othervise), but alvays comin' to a place, ven you come to one at all, the wery picter o' the last, vith the same p'leesemen standin' about, the same blessed old bell a ringin', the same unfort'nate people standin' behind the bars, a waitin' to be let in; and everythin' the same except the name, vich is wrote up in the same sized letters as the last name, and vith the same colours. As to the *honour* and dignity o' travellin', vere can that be vithout a coachman; and wot's the rail to sich coachmen and guards as is sometimes forced to go by it, but a outrage and a insult? As to the pace, wot sort o' pace do you think I, Tony Veller, could have kept a coach goin' at, for five hundred thousand pound a mile, paid in adwance afore the coach was on the road? And as to the ingein, – a nasty, wheezin', creakin', gaspin', puffin', bustin' monster, alvays out o' breath, vith a shiny green-and-gold back, like a unpleasant beetle in that 'ere gas magnifier, – as to the ingein as is alvays a pourin' out red-hot coals at night, and black smoke in the day, the sensiblest thing it does, in my opinion, is, ven there's somethin' in the vay, and it sets up that 'ere frightful scream vich seems to say, 'Now here's two hundred and forty passengers in the wery greatest extremity o' danger, and here's their two hundred and forty screams in vun!'" ⟨1840⟩

Charles Dickens, *Master Humphrey's Clock*
(Oxford Illustrated ed.), 79–80

91.   A CHILDREN'S EXCURSION

It is gratifying to think how inexpensive are some of the purest pleasures of life. There can be no doubt, for instance, that a little tea-party, or railway trip, is among the most interesting events of the year to the children in our

[1] Magna Carta

Sunday schools. Yet quite a luxurious treat of tea and its accompaniments can now be supplied at less than sixpence per head. To give an idea of the cheapness of travelling, I need only mention that our scholars and teachers were taken, last Whitsuntide, above 70 miles, including both going and returning, for ninepence each, or at the rate of half a farthing per mile. For this they paid but sixpence each, the remaining expenses, together with their usual entertainments of tea, buns, and buttermilk, being provided for by their friends of the Cross Street and Brook Street Congregations. ⟨1850⟩

John Layhe, Minister to the Poor in Manchester: *Sixteenth Report to the Ministry of the Poor* (1850), 47

92.   EXCURSION TRAIN TO THE GREAT EXHIBITION

The request for her to come to him was a less one to make than it would have been when he first left Stickleford, or even a few months ago; for the new railway into South Wessex was now open, and there had just begun to be run wonderfully-contrived special trains called excursion-trains, on account of the Great Exhibition; so that she could come up easily alone.

She said in her reply how good it was of him to treat her so generously, after her hot and cold treatment of him; that though she felt frightened at the magnitude of the journey, and was never as yet in a railway-train, having only seen one pass at a distance, she embraced his offer with all her heart; and would, indeed, own to him how sorry she was, and beg his pardon, and try to be a good wife always, and make up for lost time.

The remaining details of when and where were soon settled, Car'line informing him, for her ready identification in the crowd, that she would be wearing "my new sprigged-laylock cotton gown", and Ned gaily responding that, having married her the morning after her arrival, he would make a day of it by taking her to the Exhibition. One early summer afternoon, accordingly, he came from his place of work, and hastened towards Waterloo Station to meet her. It was as wet and chilly as an English June day can occasionally be, but as he waited on the platform in the drizzle he glowed inwardly, and seemed to have something to live for again.

The "excursion-train" – an absolutely new departure in the history of travel – was still a novelty on the Wessex line, and probably everywhere. Crowds of people had flocked to all the stations on the way up to witness the unwonted sight of so long a train's passage, even where they did not take advantage of the opportunity it offered. The seats for the humbler class of travellers in these early experiments in steam-locomotion, were open trucks, without any protection whatever from the wind and rain; and damp weather having set in with the afternoon, the unfortunate occupants of these vehicles were, on the train drawing up at the London terminus, found to be in a pitiable condition from their long journey; blue-faced, stiff-necked, sneezing, rain-beaten, chilled to the marrow, many of the men being hatless; in fact, they resembled people who had been out all night in an open boat on a rough sea, rather than inland excursionists for pleasure. The women had in some degree protected themselves by turning up the skirts of their gowns over their heads, but as by this arrangement they were additionally exposed about the hips, they were all more or less in a sorry plight.

In the bustle and crush of alighting forms of both sexes which followed the entry of the huge concatenation into the station, Ned Hipcroft soon discerned the slim little figure his eye was in search of, in the sprigged lilac, as described. She came up to him with a frightened smile – still pretty, though so damp, weather-beaten, and shivering from long exposure to the wind.

"O Ned!" she sputtered, "I – I – " He clasped her in his arms and kissed her, whereupon she burst into a flood of tears. ⟨1851⟩

From Thomas Hardy, "The Fiddler of the Reels": *Collected Short Stories* (1988 ed.), 500–1. Written in 1893

93. LUGGAGE

(a)

One would wonder how people contrived in former days to get themselves and their wants into a stage-coach or a carriage and pair, so greatly have our wants expanded with railway times. It is not now the carrying but the paying for it that forms the difficulty; and twenty shillings is soon run away with for extra luggage by express train. In going to London it may be well to remember that as it is the real place for choice and fashion, it is no use taking antiquated garments that are sure to be laid aside as soon as you get there. The better plan is to have such things as can be ordered without inspection, to be ready against you arrive – as, for instance, papa's hat, coats, boots, shoes, stockings, etc.

If, notwithstanding this precaution, the luggage is still likely to be onerous, pack all the heavy articles into one box and, a day or two before you go yourselves, send them by goods train, directed to the care of any friend or tradesman; or, if a total stranger, to be left till called for at the station luggage-office. . . .

After money, luggage-labels are the greatest conducers to comfort in travelling. Leather or parchment directions are the best for carpet bags.

95

Cards are apt to come off. Direct with a large initial as

"T"

for Tomkinson, which will save trouble at the end of the journey, as the porters will catch the "T" in half the time they will take to spell the "Tomkinson". Besides, it gives you the chance of being taken for ex-Lord Chancellor Truro, or lord anybody else whose name begins with a "T". If your packages are numerous, which if a family man they are pretty sure to be, number them thus:

1 to 40 inclusive

2 to 40 inclusive

3 to 40 inclusive

and make a list of the general contents of each; by which means you will be able to tell at a glance whether it contains Lady Truro's trinkets or Tommy's toys.

Have such things as you require on the night of your arrival in separate bags, so that you need not disturb the bulk of the luggage until you have settled in your lodgings. ⟨1851⟩

R. S. Surtees, *Town and Country Papers*, ed. E. D. Cuming (1929), 231–3

(b)

Perhaps some restraints came to be accepted in this matter. The advice given in a guidebook of 1859 was more stringent.

The traveller is advised to take as little luggage as possible; and ladies are earnestly entreated not to indulge in *more* than seven boxes and five small parcels for the longest journey. ⟨1859⟩

G. Measom, *Official Illustrated Guide to the North Western Railway* (1859), 13

(c)

Some railway companies came to insist very strictly on the payment of what was due to them, like the London Brighton & South Coast, which

scrupulously weighed very particle of luggage . . . [with a care that] would have done credit to the troy methods of a dispensing chemist in the poison business. ⟨? c.1885⟩   E. L. Ahrons, *Locomotive and Train Working in the Latter Part of the Nineteenth Century* (1951–4), v. 67

94. THIRD CLASS

The mode in which our third-class travellers are treated is a scandal to an age which legislates for the comfort of a cab-horse and places water-troughs along the Strand for the benefit of any lost sheep or idle dog that may feel disposed to take to drinking in that crowded locality. . . . It is, certainly, as cruel to expose a number of thinly-clad women and children to rain and wind for several hours on a railway train, as it is to exact from an unhappy donkey more than a fair day's work for a fair day's thistles. ⟨1854⟩   *Punch*, 26 (1854), 133

95. THE SOLEMNITY OF FIRST-CLASS TRAVEL

It is foolish ever to travel in the first-class carriages except with ladies in charge. Nothing is to be seen or learnt there; nobody to be seen except civil and silent gentlemen, sitting on their cushioned dignities. In the second class, it is very different. ⟨1855⟩

> Nathaniel Hawthorne, *English Notebooks*, ed. R. Stewart (1941), 119

96. WRITING IN THE TRAIN

It was while I was engaged on *Barchester Towers* that I adopted a system of writing which, for some years afterwards, I found to be very serviceable to me. My time was greatly occupied in travelling, and the nature of my travelling was now changed. I could not any longer do it on horseback. Railways afforded me my means of conveyance, and I found that I passed in railway carriages many hours of my existence. Like others, I used to read. . . . But if I intended to make a profitable business out of my writing, and, at the same time, to do my best for the Post Office, I must turn these hours to more account than I could do even by reading. I made for myself therefore a little tablet, and found after a few days' exercise that I could write as quickly in a railway carriage as I could at my desk. I worked with a pencil, and what I wrote my wife copied afterwards. In this way was composed the greater part of *Barchester Towers* and of the novel which succeeded it [*The Three Clerks*], and much also of others subsequent to them. My only objection to the practice came from the appearance of literary ostentation, to which I felt myself to be subject when going to work before four or five fellow-passengers. But I soon got used to it. ⟨1855⟩

> Anthony Trollope, *Autobiography* (new World's Classics ed.), 102–3

97.   A RELIGIOUS EXCURSION IN SCOTLAND

Between Keith and Aberdeen I came across a cheap excursion train, its carriages crammed with people. They were all on their way to a religious meeting, a "revival" at which a number of famous preachers would be speaking. The crowd of people wishing to attend was so great that the railway company had to telegraph for extra carriages, and even so girls had to sit on the young men's knees in many of the compartments. My neighbour told me there would be twenty thousand people at the meeting, some of them coming great distances, fifty or sixty miles. While the train was waiting, the women sang hymns with an air of great conviction and serious purpose. Religious music here is always grave and sweet and never fails to give me pleasure. The carriages were all third-class, and the people shopkeepers, working people, and small farmers all dressed like our lower-middle classes: clean suits of grey or brown cloth, often new; the faces were lively and intelligent. They were all of the common people but they were obviously better educated than our own villagers in France. ⟨1862⟩   Hippolyte Taine, *Notes on England*,
trans. E. Hyams (1957), 281–2

98.   AN OLD LADY ON HER WAY

An elderly lady presents herself at the ticket-counter, and expresses a wish to go to some place at a short distance, say Putney. She first of all inquires what is the fare first, second, and third class; upon being told that, she hesitates a few seconds, and then thinks she will travel first-class. Being asked whether she requires a single or return-ticket, she appears to be astounded at the proposition, ejaculates "Eh! oh! ah!" at wide intervals, and finally decides upon a single ticket, giving at the same time her reasons for doing so. Having been informed that the fare is ninepence, she dives for her purse into some apparently unfathomable chasm connected with her dress, and after considerable rummaging, accompanied by a jingling of keys and the production in succession of a pocket-handkerchief, a smelling-bottle, a pair of mittens, spectacle-case, a fan, and an Abernethy biscuit, she at length succeeds in drawing forth an article which resembles an attenuated eel. Thrusting her long bony fingers into this receptacle, she draws out what she conceives to be a shilling, but on nearer inspection she discovers it to be a sovereign. She makes another dive and produces a half-crown, as she supposes, but this proves to be only a penny-piece: finally, she manages to fish out sixpence, and connecting this with the penny-piece, and vaguely wondering whether she can find twopence more to make up the required amount, but without arriving at any satisfactory conclusion, she is at length constrained to give over further search, and to lay down the sovereign. Upon receiving her change, she examines each piece leisurely to ascertain if it be genuine; satisfied on this point, she counts her change over, repeating the process some four or five times, and on each occasion arriving at a different result. At length she makes out the matter to her satisfaction, then having carefully stowed away her change in such a manner that the first pickpocket may abstract it, she looks about to see that she has left nothing behind, and after remarking how wonderfully the clerk resembles her nephew who has gone to the Indies, she somewhat reluctantly makes way for the next person. ⟨1862⟩

The Railway Traveller's Handy Book (1971 ed.), 58

99. FROM WINDSOR TO BALMORAL

As Superintendent of the Line on the London & North Western Railway from 1862 to 1895, the writer made 112 journeys with the Queen's trains between England and Scotland.

The routine of the clerical arrangements at Euston for a Queen's journey became a thoroughly settled formula. The dates of each coming journey were in the first place given by the Private Secretary as approximate, but probably correct, and any desired modification in time of departure or of arrival as compared with the previous journey indicated. Then correspondence commences with all the companies interested.[1] A draft timetable is sent with the letter showing the suggested times at every station on the route. By the time these letters are acknowledged, and the draft timetable returned with any needed corrections, in all probability the list of the suite to be accommodated will have been received, and this requires the selection of saloons and vehicles suited to the respective groups of the household and official guests included in the list. The carriages must be fitted alike for the night journey and for daylight travelling. A diagram showing the proposed allocation of carriages is exchanged with the authorities at Wolverton, and the desired carriages, in accordance with their distinctive numbers as shown on it, have to be withdrawn from traffic and thoroughly overhauled. The Queen's own saloon is always kept in special care at an equable temperature. The electricians are apprised, so as to have all electric couplings and appliances in perfect order. The Locomotive Department and the District Superintendents are advised, the latter having to ensure the clear road required not only for the train but for the pilot engine running fifteen minutes in advance. . . .

The Engineering Department also receive notice, so that the whole

[1] After 1866 there were normally four: the Great Western, London and North Western, Caledonian, and Great North of Scotland.

length of the line may be watched and patrolled on the occasion; and since the days of Fenian threats, additional precautions are taken of placing men at each overbridge and underbridge to prevent any trespass on the line. . . .

Any danger from trains passing in the opposite direction, from goods loading shifting, or doors being open, was originally intended to be guarded against by ordering all such goods trains to come to a stand when the royal train was approaching, and for passenger trains to slacken, but these restrictions were ultimately strengthened, and goods trains are kept back entirely, between the pilot and the royal train running; and the brakesmen being under orders to walk along the shunted trains to ensure there being no overhanging load; the only trains in motion that might meet the royal train are the mail trains.

The requirement for privacy, during Her Majesty's journeys, was frequently pressed on us, and certainly almost a funereal silence was observed; perhaps this was more the case in England than north of the Border; the journey generally taking place during the night may be largely responsible for this; occasionally, request was made that the people at Perth might be allowed to come nearer to the train. Ferry Hill, outside Aberdeen, was almost always an exception to the restrictive orders, and Her Majesty was always greeted there with a bright gathering of her lieges. ⟨1862–1895⟩   G. P. Neele, *Railway Reminiscences* (1904), 465–6

100. DTs IN THE TRAIN

9 August 1864. In one of the third-class compartments of the express train leaving King's Cross station at 9.15 p.m. a tall and strongly-built man, dressed as a sailor and having a wild and haggard look, took his seat about three minutes before the train started. . . . It had scarcely done so when, on putting his hand to his pocket, he called out that he had been robbed of his purse, containing £17, and at once began to shout and gesticulate in a manner which greatly alarmed his fellow-travellers, four in number, in the same compartment. He continued to roar and swear with increasing violence for some time, and then made an attempt to throw himself out of the window. He . . . had just succeeded in placing one of his legs out when the other occupants of the carriage, who had been endeavouring to keep him back, succeeded in dragging him from the window. Being foiled in this attempt, he turned round upon those who had been instrumental in keeping him back. After a long and severe struggle, which, notwithstanding the speed the train was running at, was heard in the adjoining compartments, the sailor was overcome by the united exertions of the party and was held down in a prostrate position by two of their number. Though thus secured he still continued to struggle and shout vehemently, and it was not till some time afterwards, when they managed to bind his hands and strap him to the seat, that the passengers in the compartment felt themselves secure. This train, it may be explained, makes the journey from London to Peterborough, a distance little short of eighty miles, without a single stoppage. . . . Almost frantic attempts were made to get the train stopped. The attention of those in the adjoining compartment was readily gained by waving handkerchiefs out of the window, and by and by a full explanation of the circumstances was communicated through the aperture in which the lamp that lights both compartments is placed. A request to communicate with the guard was made from one carriage to another for a short distance, but it was found impossible to continue it. . . . All the way along to Peterborough a succession of shouts of "Stop the train", mixed with the frantic screams of female passengers, was kept up. On the arrival of the train at Peterborough the man was released by his captors and placed on the platform. No sooner was he there, however, than he rushed with a renewed outburst of fury on those who had taken the chief part in restraining his violence, and as he kept vociferating that they had robbed him of his money it was some time before the railway officials could be got to interfere – indeed it seemed likely for some time that he would be allowed to go on in the train. As remonstrances were made from all quarters to the stationmaster to take the fellow into custody, he at length agreed, after being furnished with the names and addresses of the other occupants of the carriage, to hand him over to the police. The general impression on those who witnessed the sailor's fury seemed to be that he was labouring under a violent attack of *delirium tremens*, and he had every appearance of having been drinking hard for some days. ⟨1864⟩

Annual Register, 1864 (Chronicle), 117–18

101. A BEASTLY FUNK

I was put in a beastly funk the other day by a woman. I had travelled towards town as far as Wandsworth in a compartment to myself when a female got in; she had her hair in short curls and wore no gloves. She first of all sat in the opposite seat, then she moved to the opposite corner, then to the middle, three seats in as many minutes! I began to speculate as to where she would sit next – perhaps on my knee, and then would charge me with an indecent assault. Happily she got out at the next station, Clapham Junction, but my mind was not at ease, for she stood outside the carriage door and just as the train started, got into the next compartment. Perhaps she was relating to her new companion how she had been grossly insulted by a lewd gent in the place she had just left. I assure you I was "much exercised" (as the Methodists have it) by this little adventure. These unfounded charges of indecent assault have been very common of late, and I have determined to object in future to the entry of any unprotected female into a carriage where I may be alone. ⟨1866⟩

Sir William Hardman: The Hardman Papers, ed. S. M. Ellis (1930), 153–4

102.   EDWARD LEAR PROVES HIS IDENTITY

A few days ago in a railway as I went to my sister's a gentleman explained to two ladies (whose children had my "Book of Nonsense") that thousands of families were grateful to the author (which in silence I agreed to) who was not generally known – but was really Lord Derby: and now came a showing forth, which cleared up at once to my mind why that statement has already appeared in several papers. Edward Earl of Derby (said the Gentleman) did not choose to publish the book openly, but dedicated it as you see to his relations, and now if you will transpose the letters LEAR you will read simply EDWARD EARL. Says I, joining spontanious in the conversation – "That is quite a mistake: I have reason to know that Edward Lear the painter and author wrote and illustrated the whole book". "And I", says the Gentleman, says he – "have good reason to know Sir, that you are wholly mistaken. There is no such a person as Edward Lear". "But", says I, "there is – and I am the man – and I wrote the book!" Whereupon all the party burst out laughing and evidently thought me mad or telling fibs. So I took off my hat and showed it all round, with Edward Lear and the address in large letters – also one of my cards, and a marked handkerchief: on which amazement devoured those benighted individuals and I left them to gnash their teeth in trouble and tumult. ⟨1866⟩

Edward Lear to Lady Waldegrave, 17 October 1866: Later Letters of Edward Lear, ed. Lady Strachey (1911), 78–9

103.   HAVERFORDWEST TO BRECON

18 October 1871. We left Haverfordwest by train for Neath at 11.30. A boy travelled with us who seemed to have just left home. He was weeping bitterly. At Neath the lower station was full of Breconshire people who had been at Neath Market and were waiting for the train to take them home towards Brecon. They were a nice set of people, pleasant, courteous, and obliging, and all seemed quiet and sober. A number of them got into the carriage next to ours, and soon they began to sing. It was a rich treat. They sang in perfect time and tune, altogether, the trebles of the women

blending exquisitely with the tenors and basses of the men. Then a man sang a solo to the company and then they all chimed in together again. At every station some of the simple kindly folk got out with their large baskets.

A strange wild-looking woman was sitting opposite to me with light blue eyes almost starting out of her head. She had conceived a mortal dislike to a man who sat in another corner of the carriage and she kept on glancing round over her shoulder at him, poking me violently in the ribs when she thought he was not looking, to make me look at him, and turning away from him with a shudder and horrible grimaces. "Do you know him?" she whispered looking stealthily round at her enemy, at the same time pushing me and poking my leg till I was bruised and sore. "Do you know him?" she repeated. "No", I said extremely amused. "Who is he?" "He's a wicked man" she said making a horrible face as if she had taken a draught of nauseous salts, and giving me another tremendous push and agonising poke in the leg and ribs.

Soon after we left Neath we crossed and recrossed the beautiful Dulas winding through a lovely valley among gorgeous woods. Then we came into a wild bare region of mountain and deep desolate valleys, with waterfalls leaping down the steep hill sides. The mountains loomed in gloomy grandeur, dark grey, indigo and purple under a heavy cloudy sky. As we drew near Brecon again we got into a beautiful rich woodland country highly cultivated, with lovely dingles and deep green meadows, and a fine gleam of sunshine at sunset lit the dingles and hill slopes and set the gorgeous woods aflame. The country about Aberbran, Abercamlais and Penpont seemed to me unusually beautiful. ⟨1871⟩

Francis Kilvert, *Diary*, (1939), ii. 70–1

104. TRAVELLING UNDERGROUND

I met with a gentleman from the New York *Tribune*, with whom I fraternised, and learnt from him that there existed an underground railway, with its terminus near the Houses of Parliament. . . . The trains run every few minutes, and are lighted up with coal gas, which is carried in a gasometer on the top of the car and which has an instrument for indicating when it is full and when it is approaching emptiness. This is an improvement which might be advantageously imitated by us. The English railway carriage is, however, a disgrace to the age. There is nothing comfortable or elegant about it, and it is broken up into boxes into which it would be well enough to cram pigs. The employees are, however, most attentive and civil men. Indeed the underground railway carriages are quite an improvement upon the overground carriages. For the sake of the gas lights, the compartments only extend half way up towards the roof, and they are better cushioned and finished. The fine station houses underground caused me a considerable surprise. At the stations there is light from heaven and the usual blaring advertisements in every imaginable coloured ink. Descending to this station, you present your ticket, which you have obtained above ground, to an official whom you meet upon the stairs, and who permits you to pass as soon as he has nipped it with his punchers, and you give it up on reaching your destination to another official similarly placed. ⟨1873⟩

C. Roger, *Glimpses of London and Atlantic Experiences* (1873), 20–1. The writer had come from Canada

105. THE CATTLE TRAIN

PENMAENMAWR

All light or transient gloom – no hint of storm –
White wreaths of foam, born in blue waters, broke
Among the mountain shadows; all bespoke
A summer's day on Mona and the Orme.
My open window overlook'd the rails,
When, suddenly, a cattle-train went by;
Rapt, in a moment, from my pitying eye,
As from their lowing mates in Irish vales,
Close-pack'd and mute they stood, as close as bees,
Bewilder'd with their fright and narrow room;
'Twas sad to see that meek-eyed hecatomb,
So fiercely hurried past our summer seas,
Our happy bathers, and our fresh sea-breeze,
And hills of blooming heather, to their doom.

⟨1873⟩   Charles Tennyson Turner, *Sonnets, Lyrics, and Translations* (1873), 27

106. NOTHING LIKE BEING WELL KNOWN

29 June 1882. Meeting of Sunday-School teachers at Hingham. I missed the train at Dereham. Another train was starting in half an hour, but alas! did not stop at Hardingham, which is the station for Hingham. There is nothing like being well known in a place and on good terms with its people, to which I attribute an order from our stationmaster to the driver to stop at

Hardingham to let me get out. Getting a lift into Hingham in a butcher's cart, I arrived in the middle of the service to the great surprise of my friends. ⟨1882⟩   B. J. Armstrong, *A Norfolk Diary* (1949), 249

107.   EXCURSION TRAIN TO BRIGHTON

Chorus of Directors

With out slap dash, crack, crash
And here and there a glorious smash,
     And a hundred killed and wounded! –
It's little we jolly Directors care
For a passenger's limbs if he pays his fare,
So away you go at a florin the pair,
     The signal whistle has sounded!
⟨1884⟩   H. Cholmondeley Pennell,
                    From Grave to Gay (1884), 119

108.   LANCASHIRE & YORKSHIRE EXPRESS

Taking a Lancashire express leaving Bradford, a stroll up to the engine before the start probably introduced the traveller to one of the 2-4-0 outside-cylinder engines, . . . the driver of which was engaged in effecting temporary light repairs by trying to fasten a recalcitrant coupling-rod cotter with a piece of millband or other handy material. The train having started, a dense cloud of escaping steam conveyed the information that one of the piston-rod glands was sadly in need of new packing, and also incidentally helped to thicken the atmosphere of the "bottle-neck" tunnel. The engine clanked laboriously up the 1 in 50 bank at an average rate of 8 to 10 miles an hour with a load of some 50 tons, "exclusive of passengers and luggage", as the usual formula has it. At Bowling Junction, just as things seemed about to move, a dead stop for signals occurred. After a six or seven minute wait, and the passengers were becoming restive, it was gathered from information conveyed by the signalman to the driver that the cause "wor that theer owd injun o' Ephraim Sutcliffe's as 'ad 'appen brokken dahn agen, same as it wor allus doin'".

At this point the ringing of a bell in the signal box announced that driver Ephraim had succeeded in getting the steed in question to emerge at the other end of Wibsey Tunnel, and leave the road clear to Low Moor station, where our train pulled up in 22 minutes odd seconds from the dead start (distance 3 miles). At Low Moor a wait of seven or eight minutes would occur. Late as the Bradford train was, the Leeds train, which had encountered troubles of its own, was worse, but eventually put in an appearance with four six-wheeled coaches and a Hirst "straight-back" 2-4-0 engine in charge, and backed on to the Bradford portion. The load from Low Moor would now be about 90 to 100 tons, and a start was proposed – "Halifax next stop", as the officials announced. This information was quite superfluous and moreover absolutely untrue, for the train just went five yards when the discovery was made that a party of women destined for Cleckheaton and the Spen Valley had stowed themselves into the Manchester train. Result: another minute gone in getting them and their bundles and baskets out on to the platform. A real start was finally made, and the train was running well – say 25 miles an hour – when one of those unfortunate signal stops, that are such a source of annoyance to the speed observer, occurred. This time it was on the Halifax side of Hipperholme; somebody had got a train into Beacon Hill Tunnel and did not seem to know how to get it out again. After a five-minute stop at Halifax the mournful procession began to wend its way in the direction of Dryclough Junction. It was proposed D.V. that the next stop should be Sowerby Bridge, but it proved to be Copley Junction to allow a train from Manchester to Wakefield to cross the lines in front. After one such journey to Sowerby Bridge . . . I returned on my tracks and made for Halifax by the quickest and most direct route, *viz*.: by walking over King Cross Hill. ⟨?1880s⟩   E. L. Ahrons, *Locomotive and Train Working in the Latter Part of the Nineteenth Century* (1951–4), ii. 53–4

109.   CATCHING THE TRAIN

One of the important duties which ladies had to perform was going to London for the day to shop. They had to catch the 8.30 Great Northern train [from Cambridge] to King's Cross. In those days no one ever went to St Pancras by the Great Eastern Railway if they could help it; and Liverpool Street was unknown to the genteel. The early start put a great strain on the whole household. Sometimes the Bull bus came to fetch my mother; it went round the town picking up such people as had bespoken its services. It cost sixpence, luggage and all. But sometimes the bus was booked up, and then a fly from the Bull yard was ordered to come at 8 o'clock. But when red-faced Ellis drew up to the door, my mother was nowhere near being ready. Once, when she was leaving to catch the boat-train for New York, she was still in her nightdress when Ellis came; and she caught the train, too. If not actually in her nightdress when he came, she was always still in her bedroom; perfectly calm, though all the three maids, and Nana, and I, were running about to fetch things and to help her to dress; while my father stood at the foot of the stairs, watch in hand, looking worried, and calling up in his patient voice: "Maud, you'll miss the train". Of course she had not attempted breakfast, and I used to put slices of buttered toast on the seat of the cab for her. This was important, as her day's work was so absorbing that she never had time for lunch, and used to come home in the evening quite famished and worn out. When she was in the fly I used to hand in through the window her boots and a button-hook, so that she could put them on as she went; while she gave me in exchange her slippers to take back.

Then, just as Ellis was gathering up the reins and chucking to the horse, she would call suddenly: "Oh, wait a minute – there's that little dressing-table I was going to take for a wedding present to Mrs X's daughter – it's in the attic, Isabel, just run and fetch it; and the silver teapot needs mending, will you get that, Alice, please; and Gwen, just run up on my washstand and get that empty bottle of cough-mixture" and so on. But at last, the dressing-table on the roof of the fly, and buttoning her boots and eating her toast, off they drove. We then went back and ate an enormous, leisurely holiday breakfast, and a feeling of delicious peace descended on the house. But she never, never missed the train. ⟨?1880s⟩

Gwen Raverat, *Period Piece* (1960 ed.), 93–5

110. TIPPING

Goldfinch. – "I hope you've had a comfortable journey [from Sheffield to London]."
Gregory. – "Yes, I'd a third-class compartment all to myself."
Mrs Goldfinch. – "The train was not full?"
Gregory. – "Crammed. But I had the door locked."
Dick. – "What, you tipped the guard?"
Gregory. – "He hung about, but I referred him to the by-laws."
⟨1890⟩   Sydney Grundy, *A Pair of Spectacles* (1890):
                                Nineteenth-Century Plays (old World's
                                Classics ed.), 517–18

111. AN INCIDENT ON ONE OF QUEEN VICTORIA'S JOURNEYS

The only special incident on our journey took place on nearing Forfar. One of the two engines of the Caledonian had a very hot axle. For some little time prior to our stoppage we had detected the pungent smell of hot oil, but observation along the train as it was running failed to elucidate the cause; at Forfar the train pulled up. "The Queen wants to know 'What gars this stink?'" is John Brown's remark as we pass along the platform by the side of the Queen's saloon. . . . The locomotive was detached and we travelled with one engine the rest of our way. ⟨1892⟩

G. P. Neele, *Railway Reminiscences* (1904), 521

112. MIDNIGHT ON THE GREAT WESTERN

In the third-class seat sat the journeying boy,
        And the roof-lamp's oily flame
Played down on his listless form and face,
Bewrapt past knowing to what he was going,
        Or whence he came.

In the bend of his hat the journeying boy
        Had a ticket stuck; and a string
Around his neck bore the key of his box,
That twinkled gleams of the lamp's sad beams
        Like a living thing.

What past can be yours, O journeying boy
        Towards a world unknown,
Who calmly, as if incurious quite
On all at stake, can undertake
        This plunge alone?

Knows your soul a sphere, O journeying boy,
        Our rude realms far above,
Whence with spacious vision you mark and mete
This region of sin that you find you in,
        But are not of?

Thomas Hardy, *Complete Poems*, ed. J. Gibson (1978 ed.), 514. It is impossible to give a date for the composition of any of the train poems by Hardy included in this book. This was published in 1917, nos. 113 and 142 in 1922; but all were certainly written much earlier in his life

113. FAINTHEART IN A RAILWAY TRAIN

At nine in the morning there passed a church,
At ten there passed me by the sea,
At twelve a town of smoke and smirch,
At two a forest of oak and birch,
      And then, on a platform, she:

A radiant stranger who saw not me.
I said, "Get out to her do I dare?"
But I kept my seat in my search for a plea,
And the wheels moved on. O could it but be
      That I had alighted there!

Thomas Hardy, *Complete Poems*, ed. J. Gibson (1976), 576. For dating, see note to
no. 112

114. THE PILLORY AT CLAPHAM JUNCTION

On November 13th 1895 I was brought down here [to Reading] from
London. From two o'clock till half-past two on that day I had to stand on
the centre platform of Clapham Junction in convict dress and handcuffed,
for the world to look at. I had been taken out of the Hospital Ward without
a moment's notice being given to me. Of all possible objects I was the most
grotesque. When people saw me they laughed. That was of course before
they knew who I was. As soon as they had been informed, they laughed still
more. Nothing could exceed their amusement. For half an hour I stood
there in the grey November rain surrounded by a jeering mob. . . .

    Well, now I am beginning to feel more regret for the people who laughed
than for myself. Of course when they saw me I was not on my pedestal. I
was in the pillory. A pedestal may be a very unreal thing. A pillory is a
terrific reality. ⟨1895⟩

Oscar Wilde to Lord Alfred Douglas, 1897: *The Letters of
Oscar Wilde*, ed. R. Hart-Davis (1962), 490–1

115. THE SEAL

Henry Moat's brother, Bill, was a fisherman, and used to bring over to see
us from Whitby a tame seal. . . . The reader may wonder how such a
slippery customer was conveyed to us. Unlikely as it sounds, by train, and
then by cab. Bill was a well-known character in Whitby, and was allowed

to take his seal with him in a third-class carriage. He would have charge of its head, a porter would help him by pushing from below, and the sleek creature would ride beside him, giving a delicious breath of the ocean – and of fish – to the whole of the compartment. Once arrived at Scarborough, they would take a cab, sent by my mother, the seal again sitting beside him, and looking around with interest at place and people. ⟨c.1900⟩

> Sir Osbert Sitwell, *Left Hand! Right Hand!* (Reprint Society ed., 1946), 126

116. FROM RAVENGLASS TO IRTON ROAD

North of Barrow-in-Furness is a junction called Ravenglass. "Change here for the Eskdale line" calls the porter. As your ticket is for Irton Road on that line you dismount and look around for your train. The porter collects your goods and, stepping across the rails past a goods shed, leads you to a tiny siding whereby is a tar-coated wooden shed, covering some extremely crookedly-laid rails, three feet in gauge. On the rails are an engine of primitive design, a van ditto, and one coach still more so. The coach is a "composite" one, containing a guard's box, one third "smoker" and an ordinary third. These carriages hold at a pinch four slim adults-a-side, and are innocent alike of racks, cushions, or communication cords. As, however, the pace never exceeds five miles per hour, nervous passengers need not be deterred from journeying on the line on this account, for it is quite within the bounds of safety to alight while the train is going at full speed. Behind these vehicles, but not coupled to them, is another passenger coach, containing a first-class carriage – the royal saloon, so to speak. Tonight this is left behind to ease the engine's burden.

There are no porters visible, but presently a guard arrives, and the engine, which has been employing its leisure in giving rides to two small boys, is coupled on ahead, and the guard, a composite official, unlocks a cupboard in the dim recesses of the shed and doles out four third-class tickets to the three others and yourself who comprise his load. He then locks up his ticket office and, packing you in, starts his tiny train on its perilous career up the valley. It lurches, and groans, and rolls along in a manner that makes you wonder why you did not invest your spare coppers in insurance tickets. You also speculate whether the bottom will fall out of the carriage, the train pull up the rails, or the whole affair topple over into the river.

Thick bracken brushes the footboards at either side, from out of which the head of an ancient Herdwick ram gazes up at the snorting, labouring engine. It is evidently an old acquaintance, and he pays but little heed to it. The stoker, whistling cheerfully, sits on the cab, swinging one leg over the side with an airy grace all his own. Presently, with a dislocating jerk, the train pauses dead with an abruptness that lands your portmanteau on your toes, and the stoker descends leisurely to drive a misguided ewe and lamb off the track into the clustering bracken. This act of mercy being accomplished, and a pedestrian who suddenly appears over a wall having climbed on board for a "lift", this weird express grunts its toilsome way at last into "Irton Road Station", a wooden hut with a siding whereon reposes a decaying truck filled with bricks. Here you dismount, and the guard, who has unlocked the hut and doled out more tickets, starts his comic-opera collection of relics off again on its uncertain way round a bend, up into the beautiful cleft among the hills where, several stations away, lies the terminus, which is known as Boot. ⟨1903⟩

Mary C. Fair: *Wide World*, 19 December 1903

117. THE PERSONAL ELEMENT

The atmosphere of the waiting-room set at naught at a single glance the theory that there can be no smoke without fire. The stationmaster, when remonstrated with, stated, as an incontrovertible fact, that any chimney in the world would smoke in a south-westerly wind, and further, said there wasn't a poker, and that if you poked the fire the grate would fall out. He was, however, sympathetic, and went on his knees before the smouldering mound of slack, endeavouring to charm it to a smile by proddings with the handle of the ticket-punch. Finally, he took me to his own kitchen fire and talked politics and salmon-fishing, the former with judicious attention to my presumed point of view, the latter with no less tactful regard for my admission that for three days I had not caught a fish, while the steam rose from my wet boots, in witness of the ten miles of rain through which an outside car had carried me.

Before the train was signalled I realised for the hundredth time the magnificent superiority of the Irish mind to the trammels of officialdom, and the inveterate supremacy in Ireland of the Personal Element.

"You might get a foot-warmer at Carrig Junction", said a species of lay porter in a knitted jersey, ramming my suit-case upside down under the seat. "Sometimes they're in it, and more times they're not."

The train dragged itself rheumatically from the station, and a cold spring rain – the time was the middle of a most inclement April – smote it in flank as it came into the open. I pulled up both windows and began to smoke; there is, at least, a semblance of warmth in a thoroughly vitiated atmosphere.

It is my wife's habit to assert that I do not read her letters, and being now on my way to join her and my family in Gloucestershire, it seemed a sound thing to study again her latest letter of instructions.

"I am starting today, as Alice wrote to say we must be there two days before the wedding, so as to have a rehearsal for the pages. Their dresses have come, and they look too delicious in them –"

(I here omit profuse particulars not pertinent to this tale) –

"It is sickening for you to have had such bad sport. If the worst comes to the worst couldn't you buy one? –"

I smote my hand upon my knee. I had forgotten the infernal salmon! What a score for Philippa! If these contretemps would only teach her that I was not to be relied upon, they would have their uses, but experience is wasted upon her; I have no objection to being called an idiot, but, that being so, I ought to be allowed the privileges and exemptions proper to idiots. Philippa had, no doubt, written to Alice Hervey, and assured her that Sinclair would be only too delighted to bring her a salmon, and Alice Hervey, who was rich enough to find much enjoyment in saving money, would reckon upon it, to its final fin in mayonnaise.

Plunged in morose meditations, I progressed through a country parcelled out by shaky and crooked walls into a patchwood of hazel scrub and rocky fields, veiled by rain. About every six miles there was a station, wet and windswept; at one the sole occurrence was the presentation of a newspaper to the guard by the stationmaster; at the next the guard read aloud some choice excerpts from the same to the porter. The Personal Element was potent on this branch of the Munster & Connaught Railway. Routine, abhorrent to all artistic minds, was sheathed in conversation; even the engine-driver, a functionary ordinarily as aloof as the Mikado, alleviated his enforced isolation by sociable shrieks to every level crossing, while the long row of public-houses that formed, as far as I could judge, the town of Carrig, received a special and, as it seemed humorous salutation.

The Timetable decreed that we were to spend ten minutes at Carrig Junction; it was fifteen before the crowd of market people on the platform had been assimilated; finally, the window of a neighbouring carriage was flung open, and a wrathful English voice asked how much longer the train was going to wait. The stationmaster, who was at the moment engrossed in conversation with the guard and a man who was carrying a long parcel wrapped in a newspaper, looked round, and said gravely –

"Well now, that's a mystery!"

The man with the parcel turned away, and convulsively studied a poster. The guard put his hand over his mouth.

The voice, still more wrathfully, demanded the earliest hour at which its owner could get to Belfast.

"Ye'll be asking me next when I take me breakfast", replied the stationmaster, without haste or palpable annoyance.

The window went up again with a bang, the man with the parcel dug the guard in the ribs with his elbow, and the parcel slipped from under his arm and fell on the platform.

"Oh my! oh my! Me fish!" exclaimed the man, solicitously picking up a remarkably good-looking salmon that had slipped from its wrapping of newspaper.

Inspiration came to me, and I, in my turn, opened my window and summoned the stationmaster.

Would his friend sell me the salmon? The stationmaster entered upon the mission with ardour, but without success.

No; the gentleman was only just after running down to the town for it in the delay, but why wouldn't I run down and get one for myself? There was half a dozen more of them below at Coffey's, selling cheap; there would be time enough, the mail wasn't signalled yet.

I jumped from the carriage and doubled out of the station at top speed, followed by an assurance from the guard that he would not forget me.

Congratulating myself on the ascendancy of the Personal Element, I sped through the soapy limestone mud towards the public-houses. *En route* I met a heated man carrying yet another salmon, who, without preamble, informed me that there were three or four more good fish in it, and that he was after running down from the train himself.

"Ye have whips of time!" he called after me. "It's the first house that's not a public house. Ye'll see boots in the window – she'll give them for tenpence a pound if you're stiff with her!"

I ran past the public-houses.

"Tenpence a pound!" I exclaimed inwardly, "at this time of year! That's good enough."

Here I perceived the house with boots in the window, and dived into its dark doorway.

A cobbler was at work behind a low counter. He mumbled something about Herself, through lengths of waxed thread that hung across his mouth, a fat woman appeared at an inner door, and at that moment I heard, appallingly near, the whistle of the incoming mail. The fat woman grasped the situation in an instant, and with what appeared but one movement, snatched a large fish from the floor of the room behind her and flung a newspaper round it.

"Eight pound weight!" she said swiftly. "Ten shillings!"

A convulsive effort of mental arithmetic assured me that this was more than tenpence a pound, but it was not the moment for stiffness. I shoved a half-sovereign into her fishy hand, clasped my salmon in my arms, and ran.

Needless to say it was uphill, and at the steepest gradient another whistle stabbed me like a spur; above the station roof successive and advancing puffs of steam warned me that the worst had probably happened, but still I ran. When I gained the platform my train was already clear of it, but the Personal Element held good. Every soul in the station, or so it seemed to me, lifted up his voice and yelled. The stationmaster put his fingers in his mouth and sent after the departing train an unearthly whistle, with a high trajectory and a serrated edge. It took effect; the train slackened, I plunged from the platform and followed it up the rails, and every window in both trains blossomed with the heads of deeply-interested spectators. The guard met me on the line, very apologetic and primed with an explanation that the gentleman going for the boat-train wouldn't let him wait any longer, while from our rear came an exultant cry from the stationmaster.

"Ye *told* him ye wouldn't forget him!"

"There's a few countrywomen in your carriage, sir", said the guard, ignoring the taunt, as he shoved me and my salmon up the side of the train, "but they'll be getting out in a couple of stations. There wasn't another seat in the train for them!"

My sensational return to my carriage was viewed with the utmost sympathy by no less than seven shawled and cloaked countrywomen. In order to make room for me, one of them seated herself on the floor with her basket in her lap, another, on the seat opposite me, squeezed herself under the central elbow flap that had been turned up to make room. The aromas of wet cloaks, turf smoke, and salt fish formed a potent blend. I was excessively hot, and the eyes of the seven women were fastened upon me with intense and unwearying interest.

"Move west a small piece, Mary Jack, if you please", said a voluminous matron in the corner, "I declare we're as throng as three in a bed this minute!"

"Why then Julia Casey, there's little throubling yourself", grumbled the woman under the flap. "Look at the way meself is! I wonder is it to be putting humps on themselves the gentry has them things down on top o' them! I'd sooner be carrying a basket of turnips on me back than to be scrooged this way!"

The woman on the floor at my feet rolled up at me a glance of compassionate amusement at this rustic ignorance, and tactfully changed the conversation by supposing that it was at Coffey's I got the salmon.

I said it was.

There was a silence, during which it was obvious that one question burnt in every heart.

"I'll go bail she axed him tinpence!" said the woman under the flap, as one who touches the limits of absurdity.

"It's a beautiful fish!" I said defiantly. "Eight pounds weight. I gave her ten shillings for it."

What is described in newspapers as "sensation in court" greeted this confession.

"Look!" said the woman under the flap, darting her head out of the hood of her cloak, like a tortoise, "'t' is what it is, ye haven't as much roguery in your heart as'd make ye a match for her!"

"Divil blow the ha'penny Eliza Coffey paid for that fish!" burst out the fat woman in the corner. "Thim lads o'her's had a creel full o' thim snatched this morning before it was making day!"

"How would the gentleman be a match for her!" shouted the woman on the floor through a long-drawn whistle that told of a coming station. "Sure a Turk itself wouldn't be a match for her! That one has a tongue that'd clip a hedge!"

At the station they clambered out laboriously, and with groaning. I handed down to them their monster baskets, laden, apparently, with ingots of lead; they told me in return that I was a fine *grauver* man, and it was a pity there weren't more like me; they wished, finally, that my journey might well thrive with me, and passed from my ken, bequeathing to me, after the agreeable manner of their kind, a certain comfortable mental sleekness that reason cannot immediately dispel. They also left me in possession of the fact that I was about to present the irreproachable Alice Hervey with a contraband salmon.

The afternoon passed cheerlessly into evening, and my journey did not conspicuously thrive with me. Somewhere in the dripping twilight I changed trains, and again later on, and at each change the salmon moulted some more of its damp raiment of newspaper, and I debated seriously the idea of interring it, regardless of consequences, in my portmanteau. A lamp was banged into the roof of my carriage, half an inch of orange flame, poised in a large glass globe, like a gold-fish, and of about as much use as an illuminant. Here also was handed in the dinner basket that I had wired for, and its contents, arid though they were, enabled me to achieve at least some measure of mechanical distension, followed by a dreary lethargy that was not far from drowsiness. . . .

I awoke in total darkness; the train was motionless, and complete and profound silence reigned. We were at a station, that much I discerned by the light of the dim lamp at the far end of a platform glistening with wet. I struck a match and ascertained that it was eleven o'clock, precisely the hour at which I was to board the mail train. I jumped out and ran down the platform; there was no one in the train; there was no one even on the engine, which was forlornly hissing to itself in the silence. There was not a human being anywhere. Every door was closed, and all was dark. The name-board of the station was faintly visible; with a lighted match I went along it letter by letter. It seemed as if the whole alphabet were in it, and by the time I had got to the end I had forgotten the beginning. One fact I had, however, mastered, that it was not the junction at which I was to catch the mail.

I was undoubtedly awake, but for a moment I was inclined to entertain the idea that there had been an accident, and that I had entered upon existence in another world. Once more I assailed the station house and the appurtenances thereof, the ticket-office, the waiting room, finally, and at some distance, the goods store, outside which the single lamp of the station commented feebly on the drizzle and the darkness. As I approached it a crack of light under the door became perceptible, and a voice was suddenly uplifted within.

"Your best now agin that! Throw down your Jack!"

I opened the door with pardonable violence, and found the guard, the stationmaster, the driver, and the stoker, seated on barrels round a packing case, on which they were playing a game of cards.

To have too egregiously the best of a situation is not, to a generous mind, a source of strength. In the perfection of their overthrow I permitted the driver and stoker to wither from their places, and to fade away into the outer darkness without any suitable send-off; with the guard and the stationmaster I dealt more faithfully, but the pleasure of throwing water on drowned rats is not a lasting one. I accepted the statements that they thought there wasn't a Christian in the train, that a few minutes here or there wouldn't signify, that they would have me at the junction in twenty minutes, and it was often the mail was late.

Fired by this hope I hurried back to my carriage, preceded at an emulous gallop by the officials. The guard thrust in with me the lantern from the card table, and fled to his van.

"Mind the goods, Tim!" shouted the stationmaster, as he slammed my door, "she might be coming any time now!"

The answer travelled magnificently back from the engine.

"Let her come! She'll meet her match!" A war-whoop upon the steam whistle fittingly closed the speech, and the train sprang into action.

We had about fifteen miles to go, and we banged and bucketed over it in what was, I should imagine, record time. The carriage felt as if it were galloping on four wooden legs, my teeth chattered in my head, and the salmon slowly churned its way forth from its newspaper, and moved along the netting with dreadful stealth.

All was of no avail.

'Well", said the guard, as I stepped forth on to the deserted platform of Loughranny, "that owld Limited Mail's the unpunctualest thrain in Ireland! If you're a minute late she's gone from you, and may be if you were early you might be half-an-hour waiting for her!".... ⟨1908⟩

At this point narrative turns away from railways. But the fate of the salmon will reward anyone who looks for it in the original tale.

From "Poisson d'Avril": Edith Œnone Somerville and Martin Ross, *Further Experiences of an Irish R.M.* (1908), 57–69

118.   USING BRADSHAW

(a)

"I wonder whether I can get on to Brighton tonight if I take the six train?" Hilda asked. . . .

At the station the head porter received their inquiry for a Bradshaw with a dull stare and a shake of the head. No such thing had ever been asked for at Bursley station before, and the man's imagination could not go beyond the soiled timetables loosely pinned and pasted up on the walls of the booking-office. Hilda suggested that the ticket-clerk should be interrogated, but the aperture of communication with him was shut. She saw Edwin Clayhanger brace himself and rap on the wood; and instead of deploring his diffidence she liked it and found it full of charm. The partition clicked aside, and the ticket clerk's peering suspicious head showed in its place mutely demanding a reason for this extraordinary disturbance of the dream in which the station slumbered between two half-hourly trains. With a characteristic peculiar slanting motion Edwin nodded.

"Oh, how-d'ye-do, Mr Brooks?" said Edwin hastily, as if startled by the sudden inexplicable apparition of the head.

But the ticket-clerk had no Bradshaw either. He considered it probable, however, that the stationmaster would have a Bradshaw. Edwin had to brace himself again, for an assault upon the fastness of the stationmaster.

And in the incredibly small and incredibly dirty fastness of the stationmaster, they indeed found a Bradshaw. Hilda precipitately took it and opened it on the stationmaster's table. She looked for Brighton in it as she might have looked for a particular individual in a city. . . .

"Here", said Edwin brusquely, and with a certain superiority, "you might just let me have a look at it myself."

She yielded, tacitly admitting that a woman was no match for Bradshaw.

After a few moments' frowning Edwin said:

"Yes, there's a train to Brighton at eleven-thirty tonight!"

"May I look?"

"Certainly", said he, subtly condescending.

She examined the page, with a serious deliberation.

"But what does this '*f*' mean?" she asked. "Did you notice this '*f*'?"

"Yes. It means Thursdays and Saturdays only", said Edwin, his eyes twinkling. It was as if he had said: "You think yourself very clever, but do you suppose that I can't read the notes in a timetable?"

"Well – " she hesitated.

"Today's Thursday, you see", he remarked curtly. . . .

"I'm all right then", she said aloud, and smiled. ⟨1911⟩

Arnold Bennett, *Hilda Lessways* (1911), 385–90

(b)

She wheeled round and swiftly glided to that little table on which stood her two books. She snatched Bradshaw.

We always intervene between Bradshaw and anyone whom we see

consulting him. "Mademoiselle will permit me to find that which she seeks?" asked Melisande.

"Be quiet", said Zuleika. We always repulse, at first, anyone who intervenes between us and Bradshaw.

We always end by accepting the intervention. "See if it is possible to go direct from here to Cambridge", said Zuleika, handing the book on. "If it isn't, then – well, see how one *does* get there."

We never have any confidence in the intervener. Nor is the intervener, when it comes to the point, sanguine. With mistrust mounting to exasperation Zuleika sat watching the faint and frantic researches of her maid.

"Stop!" she said suddenly. "I have a much better idea. Go down very early to the station. See the stationmaster. Order me a special train. For ten o'clock, say."

Rising, she stretched her arms above her head. Her lips parted in a yawn, met in a smile. With both hands she pushed back her hair from her shoulders, and twisted it into a loose knot. Very lightly she slipped up into bed, and very soon she was asleep. ⟨1911⟩

Max Beerbohm, *Zuleika Dobson* (1947 ed.), 251–2

119. MORNING EXPRESS

Along the wind-swept platform, pinched and white,
The travellers stand in pools of wintry light,
Offering themselves to morn's long, slanting arrows.
The train's due; porters trundle laden barrows.
The train steams in, volleying resplendent clouds
Of sun-blown vapour. Hither and about,
Scared people hurry, storming the doors in crowds.
The officials seem to waken with a shout,
Resolved to hoist and plunder; some to the vans
Leap; others rumble the milk in gleaming cans.
Boys, indolent-eyed, from baskets leaning back,
Question each face; a man with a hammer steals
Stooping from coach to coach; with clang and clack
Touches and tests, and listens to the wheels.
Guard sounds a warning whistle, points to the clock
With brandished flag, and on his folded flock
Claps the last door: the monster grunts: "Enough!"
Tightening his load of links with pant and puff.
Under the arch, then forth into blue day,
Glide the processional windows on their way,
And glimpse the stately folk who sit at ease
To view the world like kings taking the seas

In prosperous weather: drifting banners tell
Their progress to the counties; with them goes
The clamour of their journeying; while those
Who sped them stand to wave a last farewell.
⟨1917⟩   Siegfried Sassoon, *Collected Poems*
(1961), 44–5

120. JOURNEY TO A COUNTRY HOUSE

Next day, at Victoria, I saw strolling on the platform many people, male
and female, who looked as if they were going to Keeb – tall, cool, ornate
people who hadn't packed their own things and had reached Victoria in
broughams. I was ornate, but not tall nor cool. My porter was rather
off-hand in his manner as he wheeled my things along to the 3.30. I asked
severely if there were any compartments reserved for people going to stay
with the Duke of Hertfordshire. This worked an instant change in him.
Having set me in one of those shrines, he seemed almost loth to accept a tip.
A snob, I am afraid.

A selection of the tall, the cool, the ornate, the intimately acquainted
with one another, soon filled the compartment. There I was, and I think
they felt they ought to try to bring me into the conversation. As they were
all talking about a cotillion of the previous night, I shouldn't have been
able to shine. I gazed out of the window, with middle-class aloofness.
Presently the talk drifted on to the topic of bicycles. But by this time it was
too late for me to come in.

I gazed at the squalid outskirts of London as they flew by. I doubted, as I
listened to my fellow-passengers, whether I should be able to shine at Keeb.
I rather wished I were going to spend the week-end at one of those little
houses with back gardens beneath the railway line. I was filled with fears.

For shame! thought I. Was I nobody? Was the author of "Ariel in
Mayfair" nobody?

I reminded myself how glad Braxton would be if he knew of my
faint-heartedness. I thought of Braxton sitting, at this moment, in his room
in Clifford's Inn and glowering with envy of his hated rival in the 3.30, and
after all how enviable I was!

My spirits rose. I would acquit myself well. . . .

I much admired the scene at the little railway station where we alighted.
It was like a *fête* by Lancret. I knew from the talk of my fellow-passengers
that some people had been going down by an earlier train, and that others
were coming by a later. But the 3.30 had brought a full score of us. That
was the final touch of beauty. ⟨c.1917⟩

Max Beerbohm, from "Maltby and Braxton": *Seven Men
and Two Others* (old World's Classics ed.), 72–4

121. THE MISERY

From February 1917 to April 1919 a through service was run, for naval men only, over the 717 miles from Euston to Thurso, the railhead for the Grand Fleet's base at Scapa Flow.

The Naval Special maintained a good reputation for punctuality. Only once was its running interrupted, and that was due to the weather. It happened on 12 January 1918, during a snowstorm in Caithness. A snowplough sent ahead to clear the line got stuck near Scotscalder, as did the Special itself close behind, together with three engines and another snowplough sent up as reliefs, with bread for the sailors carried in hampers on the engines' tenders. There the whole lot remained for a week before they could be dug out. The sailors meanwhile had left the train and made their way on foot along the eight miles of snowbound road to Thurso, except for some who fell by the way in the pubs at Halkirk. While the line was out of action the Special stopped short at Invergordon and the sailors went on by sea.

The Special was known to the Navy as "The Misery", and it is easy to see why. After a long night in the train – or almost a day and a night in some cases – came the final interminable crawl through the northern wilderness, the delights of leave receding, the rigours of duty ahead. If anything were needed to add to the depression, it was the scenery over the last stage of the journey. I affirm that nowhere in Britain is there a stretch of country so utterly desolate, empty and bleak as the twenty-odd miles between Forsinard and Georgemas Junction. ⟨1918⟩

J. A. B. Hamilton, *Britain's Railways in World War I*
(1967), 178

122. ALL LONDON THEIRS

Great was my joy with London at my feet –
All London mine, five shillings in my hand
And not expected back till after tea!
Great was our joy, Ronald Hughes Wright's and mine,
To travel by the Underground all day
Between the rush hours, so that very soon
There was no station, north to Finsbury Park,
To Barking eastwards, Clapham Common south,
No temporary platform in the west
Among the Actons and the Ealings, where
We had not once alighted. Metroland

Beckoned us out to lanes in beechy Bucks —
Goldschmidt and Howland (in a wooden hut
Beside the station): "most attractive sites
Ripe for development"; Charrington's for coal;
And not far off the neo-Tudor shops.
We knew the different railways by their smells.
The City and South reeked like a changing-room;
Its orange engines and old rolling-stock,
Its narrow platforms, undulating tracks,
Seemed even then historic. Next in age,
The Central London, with its cut-glass shades
On draughty stations, had an ozone smell —
Not seaweed-scented ozone from the sea
But something chemical from Birmingham.
When, in a pause between the stations, quiet
Descended on the carriage we would talk
Loud gibberish in angry argument,
Pretending to be foreign.
⟨c.1920⟩   John Betjeman, *Summoned By Bells*
                           (1960), 56–7

123. THE FOREIGN SECRETARY DEPARTS
FOR LAUSANNE

The train was waiting at Victoria Station and there remained but three minutes to the time when it was scheduled to leave. In front of the Pullman reserved for Lord Curzon clustered the photographers, holding their hooded cameras ungainlily. The station-master gazed towards the barrier. Already the two typists were ensconced in the saloon: Sir William Tyrell in the next compartment had disappeared behind a newspaper: the red despatch boxes were piled upon the rack, and on the linoleum of the gangway Lord Curzon's armorial dressing-case lay cheek by jowl with the fibre of Miss Petticue's portmanteau. I waited with Allen Leeper on the platform. We were joined by Mr Emmott of Reuter's. "Is the Marquess often as late as this?" he inquired. "Lord Curzon", I answered, "is never late", and as I said the words a slight stir was observable at the barrier. Majestically, and as if he were carrying his own howdah, Lord Curzon proceeded up the platform accompanied by the police, paused for a moment while the cameras clicked, smiled graciously upon the station-master, and entered the Pullman. A whistle shrieked, a flag fluttered, the crowd stood back from the train and began to wave expectantly. It was then that I first saw Arketall. He was running with haste but dignity along the platform: in his left hand he held his bowler, and in his right a green baize foot-rest. He jumped on to the step as the train was already moving. "Crakey", said Arketall, as he entered the saloon. ⟨1922⟩

Harold Nicolson, *Some People* (2nd ed., 1927), 187–8

124.   THE ANCIENT MARINER OF RAILWAY TRAVELLERS

There is one more type of traveller that must be mentioned here, if only for the guidance of the young and simple. He is usually an elderly man, neatly dressed, but a little tobacco-stained, always seated in a corner, and he opens the conversation by pulling out a gold hunter and remarking that the train is at least three minutes behind time. Then, with the slightest encouragement, he will begin to talk, and his talk will be all of trains. As some men discuss their acquaintances, or others speak of violins or roses, so he talks of trains, their history, their quality, their destiny. All his days and nights seem to have been passed in railway carriages, all his reading seems to have been in timetables. He will tell you of the 12.35 from this place and the 3.49 from the other place, and how the 10.18 ran from So-and-so to So-and-so in such a time, and how the 8.26 was taken off and the 5.10 was put on; and the greatness of his subject moves him to eloquence, and there is passion and mastery in his voice, now wailing over a missed connection or a departed hero of trains, now exultantly proclaiming the glories of a non-stop express or a wonderful run to time. However dead you were to the passion, the splendour, the pathos, in this matter of trains, before he has done with you you will be ready to weep over the 7.37 and cry out in ecstasy at the sight of the 2.52.

Beware of the elderly man who sits in the corner of the carriage and says that the train is two minutes behind time, for he is the Ancient Mariner of railway travellers, and will hold you with his glittering eye. ⟨1922⟩

J. B. Priestley, *Papers from Lilliput* (1922), 163–4

125.   JOURNEY TO LONDON

It was always a solemn thing for a Boot to go to London; solemn as a funeral for William on this afternoon. Once or twice on the way to the station, once or twice as the train stopped on the route to Paddington, William was tempted to give up the expedition in despair. . . .

He went to the dining-car and ordered some whiskey. The steward said "We're serving teas. Whiskey after Reading". After Reading he tried again. "We're serving dinners. I'll bring you one to your carriage". When it came, William spilled it down his tie. He gave the steward one of Nannie Bloggs's sovereigns in mistake for a shilling. It was contemptuously refused and everyone in the carriage stared at him. A man in a bowler hat said, "May I look? Don't often see one of them nowadays. Tell you what I'll do, I'll toss you for it. Call".

William said "Heads".

"Tails it is", said the man in the bowler hat, putting it in his waistcoat pocket. He then went on reading his paper and everyone stared harder at William. His spirits began to sink; the mood of defiance passed. It was always the way; the moment he left the confines of Boot Magna he found himself in a foreign and hostile world. There was a train back at ten o'clock that night. Wild horses would not keep him from it. . . . The man opposite him looked over the top of his paper. "Got any more quids?"

"No", said William.

"Pity."

At seven he reached Paddington and the atrocious city was all around him. ⟨1938⟩   Evelyn Waugh, *Scoop* (1938), 27–9

126.   RESTAURANT CAR

Fondling only to throttle the nuzzling moment
Smuggled under the table, hungry or not
We roughride over the sleepers, finger the menu,
Avoid our neighbours' eyes and wonder what

Mad country moves beyond the steamed-up window
So fast into the past we could not keep
Our feet on it one instant. Soup or grapefruit?
We had better eat to pass the time, then sleep

To pass the time. The water in the carafe
Shakes its hips, both glass and soup-plate spill,
The tomtom beats in the skull, the waiters totter
Along their invisible tightrope. For good or ill,

For fish or meat, with single tickets only
Our journey still in the nature of a surprise,
Could we, before we stop where all must change,
Take one first look and catch our neighbours' eyes?
⟨1960⟩   Louis MacNeice, *Collected Poems*,
                                ed. E. R. Dodds (1966), 504

127.   INTER-CITY TRAINS

A small comfort. Oxford, although a city, for some unsearchable reason does not qualify for the latest Inter-City trains. These have small tinted windows which cannot be opened; artificial temperature which cannot be adjusted; spring-loaded doors, Symplegades which shut automatically with a loud thump; and painful strip lighting which always stays on and whines like a distant dentist's drill. They make it impossible either to hear station announcers or to bid friends farewell. They resemble modern crematoria, even, in some cases, having piped musak to sing you to your rest. They have been appropriately named. They do indeed inter their passengers. A recent poster reads: "Inter-City – the easy way to go". ⟨1984⟩   Tiresias [Roger Green], *Notes from Overground* (1984), 21

8

Stations

128. CONFUSION AT YORK

Arrived at the bridge, Captain Wragge stopped, and looked idly over the parapet at the barges in the river. It was plainly evident that he had no particular destination to reach, and nothing whatever to do. While he was still loitering, the clock of York Minster chimed the half-hour past five. Cabs rattled by him over the bridge on their way to meet the train from London, at twenty minutes to six. After a moment's hesitation, the captain sauntered after the cabs. When it is one of a man's regular habits to live upon his fellow-creatures, that man is always more or less fond of haunting large railway stations. Captain Wragge gleaned the human field; and on that unoccupied afternoon the York terminus was as likely a corner to look about in as any other.

He reached the platform a few minutes after the train had arrived. That

entire incapability of devising administrative measures for the management of large crowds, which is one of the national characteristics of
Englishmen in authority, is nowhere more strikingly exemplified than at
York. Three different lines of railway assemble three passenger mobs,
from morning to night, under one roof; and leave them to raise a travellers'
riot, with all the assistance which the bewildered servants of the company
can render to increase the confusion. The customary disturbance was
rising to its climax as Captain Wragge approached the platform. Dozens of
different people were trying to attain dozens of different objects, in dozens
of different directions, all starting from the same common point, and all
equally deprived of the means of information. A sudden parting of the
crowd, near the second-class carriages, attracted the captain's curiosity.
He pushed his way in; and found a decently-dressed man – assisted by a
porter and a policeman – attempting to pick up some printed bills scattered
from a paper parcel, which his frenzied fellow-passengers had knocked out
of his hand. . . .

The unfortunate traveller wrapped up his parcel as he best might, and
made his way off the platform; after addressing an inquiry to the first
official victim of the day's passenger traffic who was sufficiently in
possession of his senses to listen to it. ⟨1846⟩

> Wilkie Collins, *No Name* (1967 ed.), 142–3. *No Name* was
> published in 1862; but the story is assigned to 1846, and
> the description of the station is appropriate to that year

129.   BLACKBURN STATION

*The original station at Blackburn (it was rebuilt in 1888) was notable on
two counts. (a) It was, so far as I know, the only station in Great Britain at
which the Continental practice of keeping passengers off the platforms
until the arrival of the trains was followed. See nos. 137, 138, below. (b) It
was a handsome classical building, which aroused strong local pride – even
in Lancashire, where such buildings abounded.*

(a)

The apartments etc. in the station are so planned that all the passengers can
be kept off the platform till the proper time to enter the carriages; an
arrangement the convenience and safety of which is immediately
apparent. ⟨1846⟩   *Blackburn Standard*, 3 June 1846, quoted in G. C. Miller,
Blackburn: the Evolution of a Cotton Town (1951), 316

(b)

The station is a noble building of polished stone, perfectly Grecian in its style of architecture; possessing a fine portico supported by six double square pillars, and otherwise adorned. There are fifteen windows to the front, cased and bracketed cornices beautify the apex of each window. The cornice and frieze running the whole length and sides of the edifice is extremely rich and elegant, and the design is far too superb for a station in that part of the town; and, under the circumstances, years will have to pass over before suitable buildings will be erected to correspond with it. ⟨1852⟩

P. A. Whittle, *Blackburn As It Is* (1852), 361

130. EUSTON ILLUMINATED

In a clear winter's night the arrival of an up-train at the platform before us forms a very interesting picture.

No sound is heard in the cold air but the hissing of a pilot engine, which, like a restless spirit advancing and retrograding, is stealing along the intermediate rails, waiting to carry off the next down train; its course being marked by white steam meandering above it and by red-hot coals of different sizes which are continually falling from beneath it. In this obscure scene the company's interminable lines of gaslights (there are 232 at the Euston station), economically screwed down to the minimum of existence, are feebly illuminating the damp varnished panels of the line of carriages in waiting, the brass door-handles of the cabs, the shining haims,[1] brass brow-bands and other ornaments on the drooping heads and motionless backs of the cab-horses; and while the blood-red signal lamp is glaring near the tunnel to deter unauthorised intrusion, the stars of heaven cast a faint silvery light through the long strips of plate-glass in the roof above the platform. On a sudden is heard – the stranger hardly knows whence – the mysterious moan of compressed air, followed by the violent ringing of a bell. That instant every gaslight on and above a curve of 900 feet suddenly bursts into full power. The carriages, cabs, etc., appear, comparatively speaking, in broad daylight, and the beautiful iron reticulation which sustains the glazed roof appears like fairy work. ⟨1849⟩

Sir Francis Head, *Stokers and Pokers* (2nd ed., 1849), 47

[1] Later more usually spelt "hames": strips of metal attached to the collar of a draught-horse.

131. TEMPLES OF DISCOMFORT

Another of the strange and evil tendencies of the present day is to the decoration of the railroad station. Now, if there be any place in the world in which people are deprived of that portion of temper which is necessary to the contemplation of beauty, it is there. It is the very temple of discomfort, and the only charity that the builder can extend to us is to show us, plainly as may be, how soonest to escape from it. . . . The railroad is in all its relations a matter of earnest business, to be got through as soon as possible. It transmutes a man from a traveller into a living parcel. For the time he has parted with the nobler characteristics of humanity for the sake of a planetary power of locomotion. Do not ask him to admire anything. You might as well ask the wind. Carry him safely, dismiss him soon: he will thank you for nothing else. . . . There never was more flagrant nor impertinent folly than the smallest portion of ornament in anything concerned with railroads or near them. Keep them out of the way, take them through the ugliest country you can find, confess them but the miserable things they are, and spend nothing upon them but for safety and speed. Give large salaries to efficient servants, large prices to good manufacturers, large wages to able workmen; let the iron be tough, and the brickwork solid, and the carriages strong. The time is perhaps not distant when these first necessities may not be easily met: and to increase expense in any other direction is madness. Better bury gold in the embankments than put it in ornaments on the stations. . . . Railroad architecture has, or would have, a dignity of its own if it were only left to its work. You would not put rings on the fingers of a smith at his anvil. ⟨1849⟩

John Ruskin, *The Seven Lamps of Architecture: Works*, ed. E. T. Cook and A. Wedderburn (1903–12), viii. 159–60

132. STATION REFRESHMENT ROOMS

(a)

I travel by railroad. I start from home at seven or eight in the morning, after breakfasting hurriedly. What with skimming over the open landscape, what with mining in the damp bowels of the earth, what with banging booming and shrieking the scores of miles away, I am hungry when I arrive at the refreshment station where I am expected. Please to observe, expected. I have said, I am hungry; perhaps I might say, with greater point and force, that I am to some extent exhausted, and that I need – in the expressive French sense of the word – to be restored. What is provided for my restoration? The apartment that is to restore me is a wind-trap, cunningly set to inveigle all the draughts in that country-side and to communicate a special intensity and velocity to them as they rotate in two hurricanes: one, about my wretched head; one, about my wretched legs. The training of the young ladies behind the counter who are to restore me has been from their infancy directed to the assumption of a defiant dramatic show that I am *not* expected. . . . I turn my disconsolate eyes on the refreshments that are to restore me. I find that I must either scald my throat by insanely ladling into it, against time and for no wager, brown hot water stiffened with flour; . . . or I must extort from an iron-bound quarry, with a fork, as if I were farming an inhospitable soil, some glutinous lumps of gristle and grease, called pork pie. While thus forlornly occupied, I find that the depressing banquet on the table is, in every phase of its profoundly unsatisfactory character, so like the banquet at the meanest and shabbiest of evening parties that I begin to think I must have "brought down" to supper the old lady unknown, blue with cold, who is setting her teeth on edge with a cool orange at my elbow – that the pastrycook who has compounded for the company on the lowest terms per head is a fraudulent bankrupt, redeeming his contract with the stale stock from his window – that, for some unexplained reason, the family giving the party have become my mortal foes, and have given it on purpose to affront me. ⟨1860⟩   Charles Dickens, "Refreshments for Travellers": *The Uncommercial Traveller*

(b)

Here and there soup may be had – scalding hot water which removes the skin from the palate, and destroys all power of taste for hours – but with this exception there is little relief from the weary round of ham and beef sandwiches, pork pies, sausage rolls, stale buns, and fossil cakes. None of those appetizing dainties which greet one at Amiens, Dijon, or Macon, the fresh roll neatly bisected and filled with a cold cutlet or a slice of galantine. No fruit but sour oranges, no drink but deleterious spirits or British beer. . . . No wary traveller will nowadays risk present discomfort and future indigestion by trusting to railway bars for refreshment. He will rather take with him all that he requires from home. ⟨1883⟩

    T. H. S. Escott, *England: its People, Polity, and Pursuits* (1885 ed.), 264

133. A SEASIDE STATION

Bray station . . . is a long building with dormer windows projecting from its slanting roof, the sea on the eastern face, the mountains on the western.

The roof is supported by a number of iron pillars and projects to a considerable distance from the offices of the station, thus covering a broad extensive platform, sometimes turned into a fashionable promenade when stress of weather drives the band from the gardens of Briskin's Marine Hotel. In wet weather, or during the dead heat of summer, it forms a lively and pleasant resort. The station has well arranged waiting rooms, and first and second class places of refreshment. The stationmaster, Mr Tozier, is always in his room, should any assistance be required by strangers. As the tourist alights on the platform, the first sight of the fine bold Head beetling over the sea is grand and imposing in the extreme; as we look up, its silent brow rising majestically from the waves, we can hardly believe that an hour since we stepped out of the crush and throng of men. ⟨1860⟩

G. R. Powell, *Official Railway Handbook to Bray, Kingstown, and the Coast of Wicklow* (1860), 12–13

134.   PUZZLE JUNCTION

AN ACCOUNT OF DIDCOT

I will first describe the station itself. It was a junction, and passengers changed there, I might say, for everywhere on the Great Smash Railway [the Great Western]. The trains from the west came there to meet trains from the north, and *vice versa*. Stopping trains shunted there for express trains to pass them; the cheap trains up and down both shunted for an hour and a half, as it was the practice in those days to run one cheap or third-class train only in each direction, and to make that train shunt and stop as often as possible, in order to make people pay second-class and express fares.

No one who travelled third class in those days was apparently entitled to a particle of respect, and the third-class carriages were little better than cattle trucks. What with the stopping, changing, and starting, Puzzle Junction was a very busy place. The station itself was like a dirty old barn, with both ends knocked out to allow the trains to run through; the roofing was blackened with smoke, and the paint all blistered. There were four roads for trains to stand under the roofing, or strictly speaking in the station, and five very narrow platforms.

The only communication between the platforms was by means of an underground passage, so that supposing you alighted on platform 1 and wanted to go to platform 4, you had to go down a little trap-way passage entrance, pass under nos. 2 and 3, and come up again at no. 4.

The passage itself was simply filthy, as the leakage from the engines above, as they stood waiting, caused a continual trickling of water, which corroded on the walls in a slimy coating, sufficiently to spoil any clothes that came in contact with them. There were some directions painted on the walls below, which no one appeared to understand; besides half the passengers did not know if they were going north, south, or west, and as no one was below to direct the passengers they invariably came up at the wrong entrance, and had to go back and up again until they came to the right platform, often missing their train. ⟨c.1862⟩

H. A. Simmons, *Ernest Struggles* (1879), 43–4

135. THE FIRST UNDERGROUND STATIONS

The stations, though not architecturally striking – their style would probably be described now as "debased Italianate" on the original Metropolitan and "engineers' utilitarian" on the Metropolitan District which followed it – were well designed for their purpose, and many of them were spanned by imposing wrought-iron and glass roofs. . . . They were well lit, and the gas lamps encased in large glass globes are a prominent feature of all the early illustrations of underground stations. They soon had bookstalls and poster advertising, too. James Willing . . . was soon doing well as an advertising contractor. In March 1863 he put in a successful tender for the sale of books and for the posting of advertisements at the Metropolitan's stations, for which privileges he was to pay the company £1150 for the year. Later, he started to advertise on its tickets, on the walls between certain stations, and inside carriages. In 1866 he agreed to pay £34,000 for the whole advertising and bookstall contract over the following seven years. The company also gained an income from allowing refreshments to be sold at its stations. It accepted a tender from Spiers and Pond, who, having previously made money in Australia by supplying refreshments to railway travellers between Melbourne and the gold-mining town of Ballarat in the booming 1850s – and organised the first All-England cricket tour of Australia in 1861–2 – shifted their catering activities to London soon afterwards. In 1864 they agreed to pay 10% of their gross takings (and a minimum of £4000 per year) for the refreshment rights at stations between Kings Cross and the City for the following fourteen years, and in 1865 opened a refreshment room at Edgware Road on a percentage basis. ⟨1860s⟩

T. C. Barker and M. Robbins, *A History of London Transport* (2nd ed., 1975), i. 120–1

136. WAITING ROOMS

(a)

That hour at the Taunton station was terrible to her. I know of no hours more terrible than those so passed. The minutes will not go away, and utterly fail in making good their claim to be called winged. A man walks up and down the platform, and in that way obtains something of the advantage of exercise; but a woman finds herself bound to sit still within the dreary dullness of the waiting room. There are, perhaps, people who under such circumstances can read, but they are few in number. The mind altogether declines to be active, whereas the body is seized by a spirit of restlessness to which delay and tranquillity are loathsome. The advertisements on the walls are examined, the map of some new Eden is studied – some Eden in which an irregular pond and a church are surrounded by a multiplicity of regular villas and shrubs – till the student feels that no consideration of health or economy would induce him to live there. Then the porters come in and out, till each porter has made himself odious to the sight. Everything is hideous, dirty, and disagreeable; and the mind wanders away, to consider why stationmasters do not more frequently commit suicide. Clara Amedroz had already got beyond this stage, and was beginning to think of herself rather than of the stationmaster when at last there sounded, close to her ears, the bell of promise, and she knew that the train was at hand. ⟨1866⟩   Anthony Trollope, *The Belton Estate*
(old World's Classics ed.), 81

(b)

It was half-past ten in the morning when Gwendolen Harleth, after her gloomy journey from Leubronn, arrived at the station from which she must drive to Offendene. . . . In her impatience of lingering at a London station she had set off without picturing what it would be to arrive unannounced at half an hour's drive from home – at one of those stations which have been fixed on not as near anywhere but as equidistant from everywhere. Deposited as a *femme sole* with her large trunks, and having to wait while a vehicle was being got from the large-sized lantern called the Railway Inn, Gwendolen felt that the dirty paint in the waiting room, the dusty decanter of flat water, and the texts in large letters calling on her to repent and be converted, were part of the dreary prospect opened by her family troubles; and she hurried away to the outer door looking towards the lane and fields. ⟨1876⟩

George Eliot, *Daniel Deronda* (Everyman ed.), i. 168–9

137. THE FREEDOM OF ACCESS
TO BRITISH TRAINS

How would the British public like to be obliged to come to the station ten minutes before the train started; to have to go to a separate bureau and wait in a long file to have their luggage booked; then to be penned with all their travelling rugs and bags in a crowded room with every one jostling for a front place; at last the doors are opened, and a rush takes place, in which the strong secure the best seats, and the weak and women get separated and shift for themselves. ⟨1873⟩

Samuel Laing, Chairman of the London Brighton & South
Coast Railway: *Parliamentary Papers*, 1874, lviii. 78

138. PRAISE OF ENGLISH STATIONS
FROM A FRENCHMAN

What perhaps strikes foreigners most strongly, and what is certainly most appreciated by travellers, is the freedom of English stations.

They serve a thousand purposes as well as, incidentally, the departure and arrival of trains. The vast, monumental *façades* of the chief terminal stations in London are occupied by large hotels that are a precious convenience for the traveller. You can pass under cover from the arrival platform to a comfortable dwelling, and go away again after you have finished your business, without having had to remove your luggage from the station. These hotels, which usually belong to the railway companies themselves, are heavily used and afford a valuable convenience. The same arrangement is found in most of the large cities. . . .

On the ground floor are the booking offices, with a numerous series of windows and hardly even a microscopic waiting-room, which is always empty. The rest of the buildings and the platforms give the appearance of an immense bazaar. You find everything there, and then something more: buffets and bars, bookstalls, hairdressers and perfumers, shops selling tea and other goods, weighing-scales, instruments for measuring the strength of the breath or the circulation of the blood, Turks' heads for trying the force of your punch – and so on: nothing whatever is lacking.

The walls are covered with numerous advertisements. Not a corner is wasted, and the manager of one second-class line told me that the advertising, at its London station alone, brought his company a revenue of 101,000 francs [£4200] a year.

The public moves about as it likes on the platforms; no locked doors;

travellers arrive with their luggage up to the last minute; relatives and friends can shake hands with the departing traveller up to the very moment when his train begins to move.

Everything is simple, easy, convenient, practical; none of the weighing and registration of luggage, no time lost, no noise; the engine does not whistle on departure, the staff do not shout, everything is done quickly and calmly.

Business is handled like that in some stations that have 600 trains in and out during the fifteen hours of the day.

It is the same on arrival. Tickets are collected at the last station where the train stops, which avoids the tiresome standing about and loss of time that occurs under the French system. . . .

The platforms are always at the level of the carriages, so that ladies and old people, invalids and children have not, as in France, to climb, disagreeably and sometimes dangerously, up and down steps that are often slippery and always inconvenient.

I admit – here is my sole criticism – that the English railways' arrangements are not always easy for foreigners. The names of the stations are not as a rule announced, and it is often impossible to find the one essential indication of the place one has arrived at.

Why have we clung to our old system, and why is there such a great difference between the manner of treating passengers in our stations and in those in England? ⟨1875⟩   Charles Franquet de Franqueville, *Du Régime des travaux publics en Angleterre* (1875), 427–30

139.   LONDON STATIONS

Is it . . . because I like to think how great we all are together in the light of heaven and the face of the rest of the world, with the bond of our glorious tongue, in which we labour to write articles and books for each other's candid perusal, how great we all are and how great is the great city which we may unite fraternally to regard as the capital of our race – is it for this that I have a singular kindness for the London railway-stations, that I like them aesthetically, that they interest and fascinate me, and that I view them with complacency even when I wish neither to depart nor to arrive? They remind me of all our reciprocities and activities, our energies and curiosities, and our being all distinguished together from other people by our great common stamp of perpetual motion, our passion for seas and deserts and the other side of the globe, the secret of the impression of strength – I don't say of social roundness and finish – that we produce in any collection of Anglo-Saxon types. If in the beloved foggy season I delight in the spectacle of Paddington, Euston or Waterloo – I confess I prefer the grave northern stations – I am prepared to defend myself against the charge of puerility; for what I seek and what I find in these vulgar scenes is at bottom simply so much evidence of our larger way of looking at life. The exhibition of variety of type is in general one of the bribes by which London induces you to condone her abominations, and the railway-platform is a kind of compendium of that variety. I think that nowhere so much as in London do people wear – to the eye of observation – definite signs of the sort of people they may be. If you like above all things to know the sort, you hail this fact with joy; you recognise that if the English are immensely distinct from other people they are also socially – and that brings with it, in England, a train of moral and intellectual consequences – extremely distinct from each other. You may see them all together, with the rich colouring of their differences, in the fine flare of one of Mr W. H. Smith's bookstalls – a feature not to be omitted in any enumeration of the charms of Paddington and Euston. It is a focus of warmth and light in the vast smoky cavern; it gives the idea that literature is a thing of splendour, of a dazzling essence, of infinite gas-lit red and gold. A glamour hangs over the glittering booth, and a tantalising air of clever new things. How brilliant must the books all be, how veracious and courteous the fresh, pure journals! Of a Saturday afternoon, as you wait in your corner of the compartment for the starting of the train, the window makes a frame for the glowing picture. I say of a Saturday afternoon because that is the most characteristic time – it speaks most of the constant circulation and in particular of the quick jump, by express, just before dinner, for the Sunday, into the hall of the country-house and the forms of closer friendliness, the prolonged talks, the familiarising walks which London excludes. ⟨1888⟩

Henry James, *English Hours* (1905), 346

140. WATERLOO STATION IN 1889

(a)

We got to Waterloo at eleven, and asked where the eleven-five started from. Of course nobody knew; nobody at Waterloo ever does know where a train is going to start from, or where a train when it does start is going to, or anything about it. The porter who took our things thought it would go from number two platform, while another porter, with whom he discussed the question, had heard a rumour that it would go from platform one. The stationmaster, on the other hand, was convinced it would start from the local.

To put an end to the matter we went upstairs and asked the traffic superintendent, and he told us that he had just met a man who said he had seen it at number three platform, but the authorities there said that they rather thought that train was the Southampton express, or else the Windsor loop. But they were sure it wasn't the Kingston train, though why they were sure they couldn't say.

Then our porter said he thought that it must be on the high-level platform; said he thought he knew the train. So we went to the high-level platform and saw the engine-driver, and asked him if he was going to Kingston. He said he couldn't say for certain of course, but that he rather thought that he was. Anyhow, if he wasn't the 11.5 for Kingston, he said he was pretty confident he was the 9.32 for Virginia Water, or the 10 a.m. express for the Isle of Wight, or somewhere in that direction, and we should all know when we got there. We slipped half-a-crown into his hand, and begged him to be the 11.5 for Kingston.

"Nobody will ever know on this line", we said, "what you are, or where you're going. You know the way, you slip off quietly and go to Kingston."

"Well, I don't know, gents", replied the noble fellow, "but I suppose some train's got to go to Kingston; and I'll do it. Gimme the half-crown."

Thus we got to Kingston by the London & South Western Railway.

Jerome K. Jerome, Three Men in a Boat (Penguin ed.), 47–8

(b)

About twenty minutes after two, on this eventful day [a Sunday], the vast and gloomy shed of Waterloo lay, like the temple of a dead religion, silent and deserted. Here and there, at one of the platforms, a train lay becalmed; here and there a wandering footfall echoed; the cab-horses outside stamped with startling reverberations on the stones: or from the neighbouring wilderness of railway an engine snorted forth a whistle. The main-line departure platform slumbered like the rest; the booking-hutches closed; the backs of Mr Haggard's novels, with which upon a weekday the bookstall shines emblazoned, discreetly hidden behind dingy shutters; and the customary loiterers, even to the middle-aged woman with the ulster and the handbag, fled to more congenial scenes. As in the utmost dells of some small tropic island the throbbing of the ocean lingers, so here a faint pervading hum and trepidation told in every corner of surrounding London.   Robert Louis Stevenson and Lloyd Osbourne, *The Wrong Box* (old World's Classics ed.), 183–4

141.   A STEAM FEELER

They crept along towards a point in the expanse of shade just at hand in which a feeble light was beginning to assert its presence, a spot where, by day, a fitful white streak of steam at intervals upon the dark green

background denoted intermittent moments of contact between their se-
cluded world and modern life. Modern life stretched out its steam feeler to
this point three or four times a day, touched the native existences,
and quietly withdrew its feeler again, as if what it touched had been
uncongenial.

They reached the feeble light, which came from the smoky lamp of a
little railway station. . . . The cans of new milk were unladen in the rain,
Tess getting a little shelter from a neighbouring holly tree.

Then there was the hissing of a train, which drew up almost silently
upon the wet rails, and the milk was rapidly swung can by can into the
truck. The light of the engine flashed for a second upon Tess Durbeyfield's
figure, motionless under the great holly tree. No object could have looked
more foreign to the gleaming cranks and wheels than this unsophisticated
girl, with the round bare arms, the rainy face and hair, the suspended
attitude of a friendly leopard at pause, the print gown of no date or
fashion, and the cotton bonnet drooping on her brow. ⟨1892⟩

Thomas Hardy, *Tess of the Durbervilles*, chap. 30
(New Wessex ed.), 188–9

142. AT THE RAILWAY STATION, UPWAY

"There is not much that I can do,
    For I've no money that's quite my own!"
    Spoke up the pitying child –
A little boy with a violin
At the station before the train came in, –
"But I can play my fiddle to you,
And a nice one 'tis, and good in tone!"

    The man in the handcuffs smiled;
The constable looked, and he smiled, too,
    As the fiddle began to twang;
And the man in the handcuffs suddenly sang
      With grimful glee:
      "This life so free
      Is the thing for me!"
And the constable smiled, and said no word,
As if unconscious of what he heard;
And so they went on till the train came in –
The convict, and boy with the violin.

Thomas Hardy, *Complete Poems*, ed. J. Gibson
(1978 ed.), 607. For dating see note to no. 112

143. STOKE-ON-TRENT STATION

My knowledge of industrial districts amounted to nothing. Born in Devonshire, educated at Cambridge, and fulfilling my destiny as curator of a certain department of antiquities at the British Museum, I had never been brought into contact with the vast constructive material activities of Lancashire, Yorkshire, and Staffordshire. I had but passed through them occasionally on my way to Scotland, scorning their necessary grime with the perhaps too facile disdain of the clean-faced southerner, who is apt to forget that coal cannot walk up unaided out of the mine, and that the basin in which he washes his beautiful purity can only be manufactured amid conditions highly repellent. Well; my impressions of the platform of Knype [Stoke] station were unfavourable. There was dirt in the air; I could feel it at once on my skin. And the scene was shabby, undignified, and rude. I use the word "rude" in all its senses. What I saw was a pushing, exclamatory, ill-dressed, determined crowd, each member of which was bent on the realisation of his own desires by the least ceremonious means. If an item of this throng wished to get past me, he made me instantly aware of his wish by abruptly changing my position in infinite space; it was not possible to misconstrue his meaning. So much crude force and naked will-to-live I had not before set eyes on. In truth, I felt myself to be a very brittle, delicate bit of intellectual machinery in the midst of all these physical manifestations. Yet I am a tallish man, and these potters appeared to be undersized, and somewhat thin too! But what elbows! What glaring egoistic eyes! What terrible decisiveness in action!

"Now then, get in if ye're going!" said a red-headed porter to me curtly.

"I'm not going. I've just got out", I replied.

"Well, then, why dunna ye stand out o' th' wee and let them get in as wants to?"

Unable to offer a coherent answer to this crushing demand, I stood out of the way. In the light of further knowledge I now surmise that that porter was a friendly and sociable porter. But at the moment I really believed that, taking me for the least admirable and necessary of God's creatures, he meant to convey his opinion to me for my own good. I glanced up at the lighted windows of the train, and saw the composed, careless faces of haughty persons who were going direct from London to Manchester, and to whom the Five Towns was nothing but a delay. I envied them. I wanted to return to the shelter of the train. When it left, I fancied that my last link with civilisation was broken. Then another train puffed in, and it was simply taken by assault in a fraction of time, to an incomprehensible bawling of friendly sociable porters. Season-ticket holders at Finsbury Park think they know how to possess themselves of a train; they are deceived. So this is where Simon Fuge came from (I reflected)! The devil it is (I reflected)! I tried to conceive what the invaders of the train would exclaim if confronted by one of Simon Fuge's pictures. . . . Upon my soul, as I stood on that dirty platform, in a *milieu* of advertisements of soap, boots, and aperients, I began to believe that Simon Fuge never had lived, that he was a mere illusion of his friends and his small public. ⟨c.1905⟩

From Arnold Bennett, "The Death of Simon Fuge": *The Grim Smile of the Five Towns* (Phoenix ed., 1928), 211–13

144.   LONDON BRIDGE STATION

. . . Inside the station, everything's so old,
So inconvenient, of such manifold
Perplexity, and, as a mole might see,
So strictly what a station shouldn't be,
That no idea minifies its crude
And yet elaborate ineptitude,
But some such fancied cataclysmal birth: –
Out of the nombles[1] of the martyred earth
This old, unhappy terminus was hurled
Back from a day of small things when the world
At twenty miles an hour still stood aghast,
And thought the penny post mutation vast
As change itself. Before the Atlantic race
Developed turbined speed; before life's pace
Was set by automobilism; before
The furthest stars came thundering at the door
To claim close kindred with the sons of men;
Before the lettered keys outsped the pen;
Ere poverty was deemed the only crime
Or wireless news annihilated time,
Divulged now by an earthquake in the night,
This ancient terminus first saw the light. . . .

⟨c.1909⟩   John Davidson, *Fleet Street and Other Poems* (1909), 39–40

145.   LAST ENCHANTMENTS

That old bell, presage of a train, had just sounded through Oxford station; and the undergraduates who were waiting there, gay figures in tweed or flannel, moved to the margin of the platform and gazed idly up the line.

---

[1] Entrails.

Young and careless, in the glow of the afternoon sunshine, they struck a sharp note of incongruity with the worn boards they stood on, with the fading signals and grey eternal walls of that antique station, which, familiar to them and insignificant, does yet whisper to the tourist the last enchantments of the Middle Age.

At the door of the first-class waiting-room, aloof and venerable, stood the Warden of Judas. An ebon pillar of tradition seemed he, in his garb of old-fashioned cleric. Aloft, between the wide brim of his silk hat and the white extent of his shirt-front, appeared those eyes which hawks, that nose which eagles, had often envied. He supported his years on an ebon stick. He alone was worthy of the background.

Came a whistle from the distance. The breast of an engine was descried, and a long train curving after it, under a flight of smoke. It grew and grew. Louder and louder, its noise foreran it. It became a furious, enormous monster, and, with an instinct for safety, all men receded from the platform's margin. (Yet came there with it, unknown to them, a danger far more terrible than itself.) Ere it had yet stopped, the door of one carriage flew open, and from it, in a white travelling-dress, in a toque a-twinkle with fine diamonds, a lithe and radiant creature slipped nimbly down to the platform. ⟨1911⟩   Max Beerbohm, *Zuleika Dobson* (1947 ed.), 1–2

146.   OUR BIG RAILWAY STATIONS

One reads in the daily papers that one of our biggest railways has commissioned a set of posters from most of the painter-members of the Royal Academy. Whether the R.A.s are equal to this effort in design remains to be seen, but one may take the action of the London Midland & Scottish Railway as a sign of grace – if not exactly a death-bed repentance. After the spirited and successful deeds of the London Underground in this respect, the bigger railways had to do something. Being big, they naturally thought of the Academy; from a great combine one cannot expect any very tiring effort in clear thinking.

But what has all this to do with the big railway stations? I think it lies very near their heart. It gives at any rate a clue to the strange mystery of their shapelessness. The big railway termini in America have no posters, but are in themselves fine architectural schemes. The big termini in this country, especially the recent ones, like Victoria, have no architectural scheme, but plenty of posters. One can imagine the English director saying, "It does not matter about the shape of our stations if we plaster them with these", and then, more touchingly, "If we go to the Royal Academy for the posters, all will indeed be well".

This state of mind, of course, exhibits a fundamental error of the most primitive kind. Our railway companies today seem to have as little faith in their own enterprises as do our banks. If railway transport is the great and important thing a great many people, not even excluding all railway directors, think it to be, the thing in itself is worthy of fine expression.

The terminal station is the gateway of the town, but a gateway through which people are brought from the uttermost parts or through which they set out on illimitable journeys. What structure in the whole of our civilisation should make a finer appeal to the imagination? Yet if we think of our London termini, only King's Cross and Euston express in any sense this gateway idea, and in the latter an hotel belonging to the railway has been allowed to impinge upon and spoil the great gateway symbol – the Doric Propylea – which Hardwick, the architect, invented for this very purpose.

For the rest, our main railway stations are big railway sheds, leaning up against hotels or blocks of railway offices, the details of which are necessarily entirely out of scale with the spans of the train-shed roof. Sometimes this roof, as at St Pancras, is in itself a fine thing; sometimes, as at Waterloo, it is, in the words of Mr Roger Fry, a series of hen-roosts. In no case in England in recent years has the real dignity and importance of the railway as a railway been allowed or given anything like full expression.

In New York the problem has been approached quite differently. There the town has seen in the first place that the railway tracks are below the ground level, and that no steam engine enters the town to befoul it with its smoke. At the Great Central Station there are two tiers of tracks, one for main line and one for suburban traffic, one above the other and both below the surface. With us, especially in the southern lines, the reverse seems to be the general rule. Our railway companies, regardless of all enmity, carry their tracks high in the air, thereby cutting off large districts by embankments and generally deforming the town.

With the sunk railway tracks in New York the structure above ground is left free, and the station problem resolves itself, on the practical side, into gathering together the passengers in the most comfortable way and sending them down to or up from the right railway track at the right time. On the architectural side, the American method has meant that an architect has been called in to express above ground the majesty of the particular railway, while using, of course, the plan forms most convenient to passengers. When he has done that and has thereby made the finest possible advertisement of that particular railway, no other kind of advertisement, either of the railway itself or of anything else, is permitted within the station.

I remember well a New Yorker's view of one of our own termini. He turned to me and said "Say, man, it's a vaudeville show". And he was right. Compared with the great halls of the American stations, our Waterloos and Victorias are comic opera inside and out. Theirs are monumental structures, through which pour with ease vastly greater crowds than we deal with, for New York, with practically the same population as London, has only two great terminal stations.

The fact is our stations take any shape left over by the engineers. No architect of the first rank has been employed since Hardwick at Euston, on any great terminal station, whereas Charles Follen McKim – the Christopher Wren of America – conceived and designed the Pennsylvania Station, and two slightly lesser men had almost more success with the Central Station. Our railway companies are generally content to give the engineer an architectural assistant or to keep in their employ a tame architect, who works for no one else, which is in itself but another confession that they consider the shape and form of their stations a question of very secondary importance.

Such a view is, of course, vastly unpatriotic, an insult to the intelligence of the community, but also a mistake, one would think, on purely commercial grounds. No American walks through the immense concourse hall, lined with Roman travertine, of the Great Central Station in New York or penetrates the series of halls, like some vaster Baths of Caracalla, of the Pennsylvania Station, without a sense of pride in the two great railway companies who have given the country such noble monuments. The average New Yorker feels to these two stations as the average English schoolboy does to express engines. He takes you to see them. Who takes any one to see Waterloo or Victoria? Who is impressed by their combined red brick and stone cinema-architecture? But no one fails to be impressed by the vast simple Roman architecture of the New York stations or the great triple-arched *façade* of the Union Station at Washington.

The Americans believe in architecture; they know its value at its best as both the most abstract and at the same time the most powerful form of human expression, and their railway magnates have the sense to make use of it. Instead, ours go to the Royal Academy for pretty pictures with which to cover up their disgrace. ⟨1924⟩

Charles Reilly, *Some Architectural Problems of Today*
(1924), 31–6

147. BRITISH AND GERMAN STATIONS COMPARED

Whereas the German architect has authority behind him, traditional intelligence to support him, and a widespread sense of what is decent in urban behaviour to secure for his work a fair and independent survival, his English colleague has nothing. Nothing at all. His designs must be submitted to the wholly untrained opinion of so-called business men who "know what they like", are set to save every possible penny, and have never conceived of a railway station as a piece of public responsibility. Further, even suppose it to have been adopted, our architect's design is liable to be plastered with advertisements, obscured with hideous and miscellaneous lettering, and very inadequately cleaned. ⟨1930⟩

Michael Sadleir in *The Nineteenth Century and After*, 108 (1930), 660–1

148. REFINED CALM AT PADDINGTON

The two-forty-five express – Paddington to Market Blandings, first stop Oxford – stood at its platform with that air of well-bred reserve which is characteristic of Paddington trains, and Pongo Twistleton and Lord Ickenham stood beside it, waiting for Polly Pott. The clock over the bookstall pointed to thirty-eight minutes after the hour.

Anyone ignorant of the difference between a pessimist and an optimist would have been able to pick up a useful pointer or two by scanning the faces of this nephew and this uncle. The passage of time had done nothing to relieve Pongo's apprehensions regarding the expedition on which he was about to embark, and his mobile features indicated clearly the concern with which he was viewing the future. As always when fate had linked his movements with those of the head of the family, he was feeling like a man floating over Niagara Falls in a barrel.

Lord Ickenham, on the other hand, was all that was jovial and debonair. Tilting his hat at a jaunty angle, he gazed about him with approval at the decorous station which has for so many years echoed to the tread of county families.

"To one like myself", he said, "who, living in Hampshire, gets out of the metropolis, when he is fortunate enough to get into it, *via* Waterloo, there is something very soothing in the note of refined calm which Paddington strikes. At Waterloo, all is hustle and bustle, and the society tends to be mixed. Here a leisured peace prevails and you get only the best people – cultured men accustomed to mingling with basset hounds and women in tailored suits who look like horses. Note the chap next door. No doubt some son of the ruling classes, returning after a quiet jaunt in London to his huntin', shootin', and fishin'."

The individual to whom he alluded was a swarthy young man who was leaning out of the window of the adjoining compartment, surveying the Paddington scene through a pair of steel-rimmed spectacles. Pongo, who thought he looked a bit of a blister, said so, and the rancour of his tone caused Lord Ickenham to shoot a quick, reproachful glance at him. Feeling himself like a schoolboy going home for Christmas, he wanted happy, smiling faces about him.

"I don't believe you're enjoying this, Pongo. I wish you would try to get the holiday spirit. That day down at Valley Fields you were the life and soul of the party. Don't you like spreading sweetness and light?"

"If by spreading sweetness and light, you mean gate-crashing a strange house and –"

"Not so loud", said Lord Ickenham warningly, "stations have ears". ⟨1939⟩
P. G. Wodehouse, *Uncle Fred in the Springtime* (Penguin ed.), 78–9

149. PADDINGTON IN 1944

In November 1944 I received a letter from Queen Mary asking me to spend from December 22nd to 28th at Badminton. I wrote to Her Majesty at once to accept. . . . Claud Hamilton, the Comptroller of Queen Mary's Household, and a former brother-officer of mine in the Grenadiers, telephoned to me a few days before I left Renishaw to tell me (for war always makes inroads on royal privilege) that, after five years of war, it was not possible to guarantee a reserved seat for me, but that if I reported to the stationmaster's office at one o'clock on Friday the 22nd – the train started at two – that important person had promised to do all he could to find me a place. Accordingly, as I was anxious not to have to stand in the corridor the entire way – since though the whole journey should only occupy two hours, it was plain that, in their war-Christmas state of overcrowding, the trains would run very late – I arrived at the station at twelve-thirty, only to find a howling pack of distracted people rushing about in every direction. There were no porters, and I had been obliged to take a good deal of luggage with me. Eventually I discovered a dazed adolescent who seemed not unwilling to help, and, making him mount guard over my suitcases, I left him with strict instructions not to move, even for an instant, until I returned. Next, I fought my way to the stationmaster's office, and back again to the entrance with a porter. My luggage was still where I had left it, but without the boy in charge of it; he had absolutely disappeared. I then accompanied the luggage to the office, where I was given a chair and sat in a corner, hearing the trampling of the mob outside.

The stationmaster's real office had been bombed, so the staff were using temporarily the royal waiting-room, a pretty octagonal room, crowned with a shallow dome and having on one wall a rather pretty plaster medallion of Queen Victoria as a young woman. There were three men and two girls working, and the sound of feet outside was accompanied within by the tapping and click of typewriters, and the continual ringing of a telephone bell. The stationmaster himself often rang up a mysterious higher authority, active elsewhere. This power he approached rather as a mortal might attempt to speak to those who dwell on Olympus.

"Is Mr Williams there? I want to speak to Mr Williams Himself. It's the stationmaster. Yes, I said HIMSELF. Is that you, Mr Williams? The lawns are dangerously crowded, sir. I thought you might care to inspect them, and pass your opinion. You may think the gates should be shut." (It was the first time I had heard platforms referred to as *lawns*,[1] and this interested me. It must be, I think, a relic of days when platforms were open strips of grass). . . .

From his Olympian retreat the great Mr Williams gave the order to shut the gates of the station, and this was done, so that now two crowds roared and raved, one inside, the other outside and besieging the yellow bulk of Paddington. From the office, the noise they made sounded like a rough sea. After an hour the stationmaster told me that his deputy would take me over to the platform: it was impossible, he said, to reserve a carriage, but he hoped to be able to put me in one with only three other people, if it could be done. He explained the identity of the others, who included the wife of the Medical Officer at Swindon. Her I shall always remember; a short, stocky, tweed-clad, determined-looking woman, who was already seated on her box on the platform, reading a book while waiting, with such resolution that she did not look up when we were introduced but shook hands in the void, as it were, over the cover. I recognised at once the book she was reading – a novel of mine. I was interested – because it is seldom that an author catches a reader red-handed – and so I said to her, "That book is very familiar to me."

She cannot have heard my name, for she said, somewhat morosely, "You mean, you've read it?"

"No", I answered, "I mean I wrote it."

A strong expression of disbelief and disapproval clamped down on her face. She thought, I apprehended, either that I was not telling the truth or that I was boastful. When we got into the train, she read the book without a single pause for the whole of the journey, which took four and a half hours instead of two; nor did she smile once. At the same time it was gratifying to me as an author to note that the general atmosphere of holiday (far from being only four in the carriage, we were eight in the seats, with several children crawling under and over us) in no whit caused her attention to wander. People and children bumped and screamed, but she read grimly on. ⟨1944⟩

Sir Osbert Sitwell, *Queen Mary and Others* (1975), 51–4

[1] The large space behind the buffer-stops at Paddington had been known as "The Lawn" from very early days. The origin of the nickname is uncertain.

9

Organisation and Management

150.   PATRONAGE ON THE RAILWAYS

The system of patronage . . . was valued and carefully preserved by the directors, though limited usually only to the traffic grades and clerks. Its persistence probably had some effect on the continued prevalence of family connection in railway service into the twentieth century.

Patronage on the railways, as elsewhere, became prominent as soon as there were any considerable number of places to fill. . . . Directors nominated in rotation to all vacancies for the police, porters, clerks, and traffic grades generally. Prior to the opening of the York & North Midland an "election" of policemen, guards, and porters was carried out. When the Great Northern from Peterborough to Lincoln and the East Lincolnshire Railway were opened in 1848 the appointments were fully organised. Out of 135 appointments 110 were offered to the directors "in equal proportion as to pecuniary amount, or as nearly as from the number and nature of the appointments can be done, the chairman having double the number of the other directors". . . .

This system was still fully working in the sixties. In the staff character books on the London & South Western the name of the director who had nominated each member of the staff had to be entered. On the London & North Western vacancies for porters, police, clerks, and clerical apprentices were classed in districts, and the manager applied to the directors resident there for nominations. . . . It was probably not until the 1870s that, because of its inadequacy to deal with the greatly increased number of servants, the system began to be inoperative. The regulations on the London & North Western still provided for all vacancies in the traffic and clerical grades to be nominated by the directors, and in some cases every fifth nomination was at the disposal of the chairman. Special recommendation by a director could except a man from the general rules as to minimum stature of entrants. But by the end of the decade the system had become a formality. The directors signed blank nomination forms which were completed by the officials. ⟨1830–80⟩

P. W. Kingsford, *Victorian Railwaymen* (1970), 5–7

151. PASSENGER TRAFFIC IN SCOTLAND

The most distinctive features of Scottish passenger services were . . . the low fare structures and the emphasis on third-class provision. These came not simply from company benevolence (although the companies clearly wished their customers to think that they did), but from the relative poverty of the Scottish travelling public and the regrettable willingness of the well-off to save money by travelling in a class below that indicated by their social status. The railways were thus forced to build their passenger revenue on quantity rather than quality of travellers. Inevitably, Scottish companies led the eventually successful campaign to alter the government's passenger duty from a fixed sum per passenger to a percentage levy on gross passenger receipts, and then to remove the duty altogether from services which satisfied the conditions laid down for Parliamentary trains. Passenger fare levels were often considered with rather more care than goods rates, perhaps because of the belief, for which there was circumstantial evidence, that passenger traffic was more price-elastic than freight, which, it was felt, depended more on the general economic state of the country. One of the more important contributions of the Scots to the development of railways was their demonstration that satisfactory profits could be made, even in a time of depression, from the conveyance of large numbers of low-fare passengers. Although fares could go too low, as the Greenock discovered under the pressure of river competition, by 1844 most companies agreed with John Learmonth that the low-fare policy which had been forced on them actually had positive advantages. ⟨1831–44⟩

C. J. A. Robertson, *The Origins of the Scottish Railway System, 1722–1844* (1983), 314–15

152. THE INNOCENT RAILWAY

The Edinburgh & Dalkeith, more than any other early line, entered popular folklore. Its familiar and affectionate sobriquet of the "Innocent Railway" was not due, unless inaccurately, to the legend that no one was ever killed on it, but rather to an air of old-fashioned unreality which stood by the leisurely horse-drawn tradition long after it had been abandoned elsewhere. Robert Chambers, who coined the nickname, gently enjoyed himself at its expense: "by the Innocent Railway you never feel in the least jeopardy; your journey is one of incident and adventure; you can examine the crops as you go along; you have time to hear the news from your companions; and the by-play of the officials is a source of never-failing amusement". Its eccentricities reached Parliamentary notice when Lord Seymour's Select Committee of 1839 heard this reply from manager David Rankine: "How do you take your tickets on the Dalkeith Railway?" – "We do not use them, there are so many different places for lifting passengers; it is a very populous country; there are a great many villages; and we have always found that many persons would not tell, or did not make up their minds, where they were going, which causes great confusion in using tickets". In spite of, or perhaps even because of, its eccentricities, the minister of Dalkeith in 1844 was prepared to affirm that "few undertakings have contributed more to the commerce and health of the surrounding neighbourhood". ⟨1831–44⟩

C. J. A. Robertson, *The Origins of the Scottish Railway System, 1722–1844* (1983), 64–5

153. LOSING YOUR TICKET

On some other lines of railway [i.e. not those of the Great Western] the code of laws is totally unbecoming a liberal country, being apparently modelled on French or Russian police ordinances. The traveller may feel perfectly assured about his baggage, not a strap will be broken; he need suffer no anxiety about himself, for the carriage will not be left behind; but if he have any regard for the well-paid accountants of the company, let him look to his booking-ticket. Why, perhaps little Jacky has already sent the little bits of yellow-brown paper flying out of the coach window, or, after having paid your money, you have dropped the scraps in the yard. You had better have thrown away a bank-note or chewed an Exchequer bill; for you are now required to pay all the fares over again, while if, with the spirit of an Englishman, you resist such an imposition, you may be locked up all night with felons in a police cell, and condemned to pay a fine of £5 or £10. Take care how you go to meet your sick wife returning home late at night from the country, where she has been to recover her health; you must wait patiently until she has been hustled by the swell mob, and had her pocket picked in the confusion of arrival, and if you behave quietly, after peering in the faces of fifty individuals, you may see one carrying off your own baggage, or at last meet your wife sinking under the insults she has met with, or the fatigues she has endured. If she has lost anything, be careful how you go into the station to seek for it, because for that act you may also be dragged off to the police jail, and your wife and children after all their fatigues still go on their way unattended. These are cases which the daily police reports have repeatedly confirmed, and they are but small parts of an abuse which is as derogatory to the privileges of our country as it is disgraceful to those who have obtained it. ⟨1839⟩

[James Wyld] *Great Western Railway Guide* (1839), 1–3

154. A WAY TO DEAL WITH FARE-DODGERS

Joseph Pease, examined by the Commons Committee on Railways in 1839, stated that the Stockton & Darlington company's practice was to collect tickets at the start of the journey.

Do you find passengers take the short ticket, and travel all the distance?

Pease. – We have found that but on one or two occasions; to remedy it, we have got them into a separate coach, drawing the bolt between the coach and the engine; and as they all agreed they were going half way, we left them to walk home, and that has cured it. ⟨1839⟩

Parliamentary Papers, 1839, x. 332

155. LOCKING CARRIAGE DOORS

A terrible accident on the railway between Paris and Versailles occurred on 8 May 1842. The train caught fire, and some fifty-five passengers were burnt alive. None of them could climb out, for they had all been locked into their compartments by the railway officials. Sydney Smith then waged a campaign against the Great Western company, which followed that French practice, in three letters to the Morning Chronicle.

Sir,

Since the letter upon railroads, which you were good enough to insert in your paper, I have had some conversation with two gentlemen officially connected with the Great Western. Though nothing could be more courteous than their manner, nor more intelligible than their arguments, I remain unshaken as to the necessity of keeping the doors open.

There is, in the first place, the effect of imagination, the idea that all escape is impossible, that (let what will happen) you must sit quiet in first class No. 2, whether they are pounding you into a jam, or burning you into a cinder, or crumbling you into a human powder. These excellent directors, versant in wood and metal, seem to require that the imagination should be sent by some other conveyance, and that only loads of unimpassioned, unintellectual flesh and blood should be darted along on the Western rail; whereas, the female *homo* is a screaming, parturient, interjectional, hysterical animal, whose delicacy and timidity monopolists . . . must be taught to consult. The female, in all probability, never would jump out; but she thinks she may jump out when she pleases; and this is intensely comfortable.

The truth is – and so (after a hundred monopolising experiments on public patience) the railroad directors will find it – that there can be no other dependence for the safety of the public than the care which every human being is inclined to take of his own life and limbs. Every thing beyond this is the mere lazy tyranny of monopoly, which makes no distinction between human beings and brown paper parcels. . . .

The directors and agents of the Great Western are individually excellent men; but the moment men meet in public boards, they cease to be collectively excellent. The fund of morality becomes less, as the individual contributors increase in number. I do not accuse such respectable men of any wilful violation of the truth, but the memoirs which they are about to present will be, without the scrupulous cross-examination of a committee of the House of Commons, mere waste paper. . . .

We have been, up to this point, very careless of our railway regulations. The first person of rank who is killed will put every thing in order, and produce a code of the most careful rules. I hope it will not be one of the bench of bishops; but should it be so destined, let the burnt bishop – the unwilling Latimer – remember that, however painful gradual concoction by fire may be, his death will produce unspeakable benefit to the public. Even Sodor and Man will be better than nothing. From that moment the bad effects of the monopoly are destroyed; no more fatal deference to the directors; no despotic incarceration, no barbarous inattention to the anatomy and physiology of the human body; no commitment to locomotive prisons with warrant. ⟨1842⟩

Sydney Smith, *Works* (1869 ed.), 792–4

156. S.O.S.

Let me beg of you to send another person here as soon as possible. I have a quantity of goods here that I know no more what to do with than a child. It is no use for me to attempt to do it for I cannot, therefore please send some person here in the morning. ⟨1846⟩

From William Hambleton, in charge of Navigation House station on the Taff Vale Railway, to George Fisher, manager of the company, 28 September 1846: Public Record Office, RAIL 1008/120

157. A MUNICIPALITY'S DISLIKE OF SUNDAY TRAINS

The Town Council of Bedford having been constituted the conservators of the peace and order of the borough, and considering that such peace and order and indeed the general security of the property and the social comfort of the inhabitants depend more upon their own religious and moral habits than upon the most perfectly organised system of police, and that nothing tends to promote and strengthen such religious habits as the sacred observance of the Sabbath, have remarked with regret that the London & North Western Railway Company have lately increased the number of trains on the Sabbath from one train up and one down to two up and two down; and as the Town Council consider that the present number of trains is more than sufficient for the wants of the neighbourhood they respectfully request that the said railway company will discontinue two of the said trains and make arrangements that the starting and arrival of the others may not disturb the town during the usual hours of divine service. ⟨1847⟩ 　　　Bedford Town Council, Minute of 9 February 1847: Bedfordshire Record Office

158. COMPETITORS WATCH EACH OTHER

(a)

Withdraw the man who has been peeping from the top story of your Botany Bay warehouse in Water Street [Manchester] during the last two months at every train of [the] London & North Western and Lancashire & Yorkshire companies to and from Liverpool, and counting the wagons. Send him to me and he shall see the books which will be much more information for you. ⟨1851⟩   Braithwaite Poole (LNW Rly.) to Fereday Smith (Bridgewater Trust, controlling Bridgewater Canal), 28 May 1851: F. C. Mather, *After the Canal Duke* (1970), 219–20

(b)

This Barry competition for the Cardiff–Pontypridd traffic was at one time a sufficient source of anxiety to the Taff Vale management for them to arrange for the young son of the Pontypridd (Taff Vale) stationmaster to be furnished each Monday morning with cash from the booking-office till, wherewith to visit Pontypridd (Barry Railway) station on his way to a nearby school and buy a single ticket to Cardiff. On his return from school the unused ticket was solemnly put in an envelope and forwarded to the Taff Vale Railway head office at Queen Street, Cardiff, where the serial number of the Barry ticket was checked against that bought the previous Monday, thus enabling a continuous record to be kept of the rival concern's carryings. ⟨c.1900⟩   D. S. Barrie, *The Barry Railway* (1962), 192–3

159. SABBATH TRAVELLING

"I fear there is a great deal of Sabbath travelling here", said he [Mr Slope]. "On looking at the 'Bradshaw', I see that there are three trains in and three out every Sabbath. Could nothing be done to induce the company to withdraw them? Don't you think, Dr Grantly, that a little energy might diminish the evil?"

"Not being a director, I really can't say. But if you can withdraw the passengers, the company, I dare say, will withdraw the trains", said the doctor. "It's merely a question of dividends." ⟨1857⟩

Anthony Trollope, *Barchester Towers* (new World's Classics ed.), 37

163. SEIZED FOR DEBT

The misfortunes of the companies included troubles with their creditors, some of whom got tired of waiting. On 10 November 1870 an Athenry & Ennis Junction Railway train was seized for debt by the County Clare sheriff, who agreed to allow the train to proceed with a posse of bailiffs on the footplate. Some days later the same train was seized at Gort by the County Galway sheriff, whose men drove the Clare officers from the engine and impounded the train. The company's officials had to rush around for transport to bring the passengers and mails from the stranded train to Ennis. The sequel was an Irish comedy, for it was found that the coaches were still the property of a finance company, and had to be handed back; but as the locomotive was owned by the Athenry & Ennis Junction Railway it was put up for sale; the only bidder was the Athenry & Ennis Junction Railway, which bought back its own engine. ⟨1870⟩

K. A. Murray and D. B. McNeill, *The Great Southern & Western Railway* (1976), 126

164. EPITAPH ON THE BRISTOL & EXETER RAILWAY

Here lies, from malediction free,
The niggard, grasping B. and E.;
High fares and bad accommodation
Made it renowned throughout the nation;
In life its customers it bled,
And o'er its grave no tears are shed,
Save such as kind folks will be venting
When their foes die without repenting.
Bath 20 October [1875].   JUBILATE
⟨1875⟩

Anonymous. Printed on black-bordered card.
Public Record Office, RAIL 1014/3/16

165. FROM AN ALPHABET OF RAILWAY MANAGEMENT

. . . O stands for Officers sleepy or drunk
P is the permanent way which has sunk
Q is the Quagmire o'er which it had past
R is the Rails which were wearing out fast
S is the Signals which Drivers don't mind
T is the Time some 2 hours behind. . . .
⟨? 1876⟩

Squib on the back of a paper concerning accident
claims on the Caledonian Railway, February
1876: Scottish Record Office, BR/CAL/4/171

166. TIGER-SHOOTING IN NORTHAMPTONSHIRE

On the 10th of July 1877 the stationmaster at Weedon, on the London &
North Western, was informed that a tigress had not only travelled on the
line but, moreover, had made its escape. She was somewhere, he ascertained, between Wolverton and Rugby, and she was prowling about at
large. The stationmaster thereupon gathered some friends and, with some
officers from the Weedon garrison, went off on an engine in search. The
tigress was discovered near the line, having been watched from a tele-
graph-box by a porter who had sighted her. A number of country people
acted as beaters, and she was at length dispatched after receiving no less
than eight rifle bullets, besides several charges of small shot. She belonged
to Mr Jamrach, of Ratcliff Highway, and had been forwarded from Broad
Street in what is called a "low-sided junction wagon". While at large she
had killed and partly eaten two sheep. ⟨1877⟩

F. S. Williams, *Our Iron Roads* (5th ed., 1888), 410–11

167. HAUGHTY RAILWAY DIRECTORS

*Presiding at a Mass Meeting on the Want of Railway Accommodation to
Blackpool, the Mayor gave his view of the directors of the Lancashire &
Yorkshire Railway, which was chiefly responsible for the service provided
to the town.*

My own opinion of them is not a good one, for although I have tried many times to come face to face with them, I have always been unsuccessful. I now regard them almost in the light of sacred personages – gentlemen who should be held in such reverence as the Tycoon of Japan or the Emir of Thibet. ⟨1882⟩ Printed report of the meeting, 29 September 1882: copy in
North Yorkshire Record Office, Northallerton: ZOP

168. FOG AT CHRISTMAS

Another very trying period of fog for those engaged in working railway traffic in and near London occurred at Christmas, 1891, and will not readily be forgotten by those whose business it was to encounter and overcome the difficulties it entailed. About 10 a.m. on Sunday, December 20, in that year, a dense fog descended over the metropolis and lasted, practically without intermission, until 8 o'clock on the evening of Christmas Day. The fog at times was so intense that a man standing at the foot of a signal-post 15 or 20 feet high could not see the light in the signal lamp, and men standing but a few yards apart could not see each other. A shunter, standing on a pair of rails, could not tell whether it was a main line or a siding, and could only ascertain this by following the rails and seeing where they led him. Under such conditions as these, it seems almost incredible that it was possible to carry on the working of a railway at all, much less to cope with the exceptionally heavy traffic of Christmas week, and yet it was done, and done successfully, for, during those four days, at Euston station, alone, three hundred trains were made up and dispatched, and 15,000 passengers, with their luggage, besides 40,000 parcels, were got away, all this being accomplished in the blinding fog without the smallest mishap of any kind occurring. At such a time, it is not too much to say that every man engaged in the service incurred great risk whenever he went on duty, and it speaks highly for the courage, discipline, and devotion of the staff that the work was carried on at all in such a state of things, and did not absolutely come to a stand. ⟨1891⟩

Sir George Findlay, *The Working and Management of an English Railway* (6th ed., 1899), 219–20

169. THE BOARD OF A GREAT RAILWAY

In this period there had opened the prospect of another sort of life, much more congenial to my wife and to me than politics and London.

In 1898 I had been elected to the Board of the North Eastern Railway

Company. In mileage and gross receipts and in financial strength combined the North Eastern ranked among the four greatest British railways. The work was interesting; the conditions under which it was done were exceedingly pleasant and congenial. The full Board consisted of twenty members; twice a month they assembled, generally at York, on a Thursday, and remained till after the Board meeting on Friday, working in committees on Thursday and spending the evening together. In this way they got to know each other well, and for all the time they were at York they were in the atmosphere of the business of the railway. The Board included some of the ablest and most experienced and soundest men of business in the country; the meetings were always interesting, as well as pleasant. The railway was a great separate organisation, playing a great part and spending large capital in the development of the prosperous industrial area of the North-East of England from the Humber to the Tweed, on which our whole interest and attention were concentrated.

Only twice in the year did the railway business take me to London; the other meetings were all at York or Newcastle. The North Eastern Railway no longer exists as a separate institution, and many things have changed since those easier and simpler days. In 1898 Sir Matthew Ridley was Home Secretary, and yet retained a seat on the Board and attended our meetings, and his doing so was taken as a matter of course; he himself was the last person to do anything that bordered on inconvenience or impropriety. But it would be out of the question for a Home Secretary to sit on a railway board today. In 1902, not long after his retirement from the Government, Lord Ridley (as he had then been made) became Chairman of the North Eastern Railway. He died suddenly in 1904 – a great loss to our district, for he was a man of ability, whom everyone trusted. I was chosen to succeed him. The year 1905 was one of the happiest of my life; the work of chairman of the railway was agreeable and interesting, but it left in those days plenty of leisure. There were many days spent at home, in the Itchen valley, or in Scotland. If only I could be free altogether from politics, there was the prospect of permanent and interesting work with income sufficient for all we needed, and a more constant home and country life than we had yet enjoyed. Life, which had been very pleasant since 1895, promised to become more pleasant and settled still. It was not to be. ⟨1898–1905⟩

Lord Grey of Fallodon, *Twenty-Five Years*
(1928 ed.), i. 116–18

170.   THE SISTERS BLAZEK

On Monday last the officials at the Great Northern King's Cross terminus were called on to solve a unique problem relating to the conveyance of passengers. The question was whether two twin sisters, who had travelled from Edinburgh to London, were entitled to journey on one ticket only. At first sight the solution appears obvious, as both the young ladies were over thirty, but the matter was complicated by the fact that the Sisters Blazek, as they are called, are joined together after the manner of the celebrated Siamese twins. They declared that they had hitherto always taken one ticket only and had never been asked to pay a second fare, thus sadly perplexing the station staff, as the Clearing House classification does not furnish any information on the point. Eventually the officials satisfied themselves by taking the name and address of a male companion. As one half of the twins also travelled with her baby, the partnership seems to have derived the utmost possible value out of its single railway ticket. ⟨1911⟩

Railway Gazette, 15 (1911), 51

171. RURAL TRANSPORT IN SCOTLAND

It could still be assumed in 1919 that the extension of transport facilities would be based primarily on railways.

We take the broad view that there is a national duty to provide every community with reasonably convenient means of communication. The fact that people have settled in isolated districts implies no fault on their part. . . .

A motor service for goods . . . is the natural pioneer of the railway. From this point of view motor transport in these regions might be described as a rudimentary form of branch line. It develops traffic, and when a time arrives at which the increased volume of that traffic has become greater than can be handled economically by this method, the railway extension follows naturally and necessarily. . . .

Taking the railways as a whole, we are satisfied that the capital cost will have to be met from public funds, and that in most cases not more than a return sufficient to cover working expenses can be looked for. The position, however, is put in a different light if we look on the whole system of transport in the country as unified and managed on the same principles as those on which the postal service is conducted. Then the provision of railways for agricultural districts will take its place as making good a defect in the whole system as it has been handed on to us from an earlier generation. ⟨1919⟩   Report of the Rural Transport (Scotland) Committee

Parliamentary Papers, 1919, xxx. 83–7

172.   THE JOYS OF AMALGAMATION

We arrived early next morning at Dorchester where it had been decided that the Southern should take over both stations, as we had the largest traffic. Led by Cox [Traffic Manager of the Southern Railway] and Nicholls [Superintendent of the Line of the Great Western], we tumbled out of the saloon to be met by the local stationmaster, the inevitable red rose in his button-hole, with his staff of three lined up behind him. Cox, who liked public speaking (in fact could rarely be stopped), gave a dissertation on the new duties of the joint stationmaster acting for both companies, and told him that everything depended on him and both staffs forgetting the past and thinking only of making the unified Southern and Great Western a useful part of the town. . . . Then it was Nicholls' turn and he was as brief as Cox had been long-winded. Shaking the stationmaster warmly by the hand, he said, "Well, stationmaster, you know what you've got to do". The answer came quickly: "Yessir, now we'll give these Great Western buggers 'ell". So much for the joys of amalgamation. ⟨c.1935⟩

Sir John Elliot, *On and Off the Rails* (1982), 44

173.   A DANE'S VIEW OF THE LONDON UNDERGROUND SYSTEM

A foreign architect may well feel disappointed on discovering that he can hardly find examples of architecture [in London] which is truly suited to the times but finds everywhere the same shallow and conventional type of *façade* covered with details which have lost all interest hundreds of years ago, and are now merely repeated mechanically to suit the taste of some mercantile magnate. Later, however, he will find out that there is another and more modern world literally beneath all this stale architecture – that is the London Underground Railway.

At Piccadilly Circus there is an excellent illustration of what the Underground has done for modern civilisation. After experiencing annoyance at the bad taste shown by prominent architects in the rebuilding of the Quadrant, one need only vanish down the stairways leading to the Underground and one finds oneself amidst surroundings which are different and far more refined. There down below lies the Underground railway station. It is planned as a large oval with exists and entrances all round it leading to the street. The escalators in the middle take people to and from the subways which lie deep down under the ground – so far down that they can be laid in any direction quite independently of the houses above. This subterranean station is a thoroughfare with splendid shop-windows along the sides of it and is always filled with people. In the morning it is like a turbine grinding out human beings on all sides. In the evening it sucks them in again, through the circle and down the escalators to the rushing stream of trains. The architects who have designed it have done the right thing in the right way. Everything is made of a smooth material easy to clean and always looking neat and orderly. And that is in reality one of the most important points in a problem of that kind. Nothing on earth is as dirty and depressing as the "real" London stations. Everything seems to be coated with soot, and the old-fashioned edifices with their many grooved spaces of brick wall, their gimcrack ornamentation and the iron framework of the roofs, seems made on purpose to collect the dust. It would be an absolute impossibility to clean them. No one could ever feel attracted by the stations which are a necessary evil, a filthy connecting link with the journey. On the other hand, it is a pleasure to go down into the stations of the Underground, bright clean and orderly as they are. It is all carried out in the same sober style. The tunnels have no ornamentation or decorated mouldings. The walls are covered with glazed tiles as easy to clean as those of a bathroom. The stream of people passes through the smooth tubular channels and down the escalators. The trains themselves, with their long, red cylindrical bodies, rush through the "tubes" like a serpent shooting through the earth at great speed until they stop at one of the larger stations, which are also tubular. Here, there, and everywhere, posters and signboards are the only decoration. And the signboards are many. It is never necessary to ask the way, the stranger finds his way about on the Underground as easily as the Londoner. The problem of the signboards has been most energetically taken in hand. In 1916 the company communicated with an expert in lettering, Edward Johnston, and got him to design an alphabet to be used for all notices on the underground. It was to be so simple that there could be no possible doubt of the meaning, and it must be legible from a distance. He designed a really first-rate alphabet. . . . It represents the very quintessence of the Roman lettering. One can look at it year after year without growing tired of it. . . . The result of this is a refined and sure form of advertisement, for as soon as one enters the precincts of the Underground one is reminded of its presence by this concise typography. Any firm whose business is carried on in many different places might advertise in the same manner. . . . I can imagine someone saying that so large a company on so well founded a basis as the Underground might well behave generously and spend money on aesthetic aims, while, under other conditions, the strictest economy is necessary to make both ends meet. The proper answer to this would be that neither did the Underground pay until it got its far-sighted and broad-minded management. ⟨1937⟩

S. E. Rasmussen, London: the Unique City (1937), 343–53

174.   EUSTON SLEEPERS

It is curiously difficult to feel self-assured when ringing up a railway. To begin with, there is the feeling that one is not so clever as one's friends, who have Bradshaws on their well-kept bookshelves, through which they could flip confidently and find the right answer even if they wanted to go, on a Sunday, to Parkgate and Rawmarsh (Yorks.), calling at Yarmouth on the way; whereas one cannot, oneself, even read the main-line timetables posted up at stations. On these blank white sheets, as uncompromising as the Finance Act, there are always three dots, instead of a time, at the place one wants to go to; and some trains appear to leave places before they arrive there.

There is, however, an even more uneasy feeling – a feeling that in telephoning one has become an Unauthorised Person backstage of the railway. "Oh you want Passenger Inquiries", says a distant female voice in a tone which suggests that one has interrupted its owner from moving model trains with a rake over a huge table-map. Of course I want Passenger Inquiries. One of these days I shall bark into the phone, before they have time to say anything, "Now see here, about these demurrage charges on bulk tariff consignments. . . ."

There follows a long, hollow silence, punctuated by somebody making squeaky noises with a toy balloon, or by frantic clickings, like desperate machine-gun fire, as the call is transferred from the slick, sophisticated Post Office system to the heavy, ironclad telephones and tremendous alarm bells of the railway: it is easy to visualise the wires looped along black walls, through tunnels and warehouses, and indeed it would not be surprising if the calls were finally answered from one of those mysterious little sheds, just outside any big station, where men in shirtsleeves are always drinking tea by gaslight.

But I have never got so far backstage as I did last week, for I was answered immediately by a sepulchral, curiously dignified voice which simply said: "Euston Sleepers!"

I couldn't have been more awed if it had said: "Delphic Oracle, at your service" or "Vestal Virgins, good morning". So *that's* what they've got upstairs in that central hall at Euston, with its pillars and statues, the tutelary deities of British Railways. How extraordinary that we should not have guessed; for we have all been faintly troubled by the feeling that in some way Euston is more than a station. . . .

Fundamentally Euston is a temple, complete with Propylaeum (that arch thing is still called this) or Sacred Entrance. When we look at early prints of Euston, showing it in all the glory of cream stone against a Canaletto sky, it is easy to imagine the people coming through the Propylaeum with their gifts to the old railway gods. The houses that now huddle round Euston were a later development, as innkeepers and traders moved in to cater for the pilgrims.

It is right that railways should have deities, for they are a nation within a nation, with their curious lanes of private property stretching across our homely fields, their aloof stations brooding on the outskirts of our towns. . . .

The Seven Euston Sleepers (one for each of the six British Railways districts and one for London) are the gods of the quiet country stations, where no sound is heard but the wind in the telephone wires and occasional signal bells; of the silent cuttings through woods; of the motionless rows of carriages at depots; of the pregnant silence when the train stops in a tunnel. They are the silence at the heart of the solemn dance of public transport. ⟨c.1960⟩

Paul Jennings, *The Jenguin Pennings* (1963), 77–9

175. THE BEECHING PLAN

Dr Richard Beeching here expounds some of the principles that underlay his first report on "the reshaping of British railways".

It is, of course, the responsibility of the British Railways Board to shape and operate the railways so as to make them pay, but . . . it must be clearly stated that the proposals now made are not directed towards achieving that result by the simple and unsatisfactory method of rejecting all those parts of the system which do not pay already or which cannot be made to pay easily. On the contrary, the changes proposed are intended to shape the railways to meet present-day requirements by enabling them to provide as much of the total transport of the country as they can provide well. To this end, proposals are directed towards developing to the full those parts of the system and those services which can be made to meet traffic requirements more efficiently and satisfactorily than any available alternative form of transport, and towards eliminating only those services which, by their very nature, railways are ill-suited to provide.

The point at issue here is so important that it is worthwhile to emphasise it by expressing the underlying thought in a different way.

The profitability or otherwise of a railway system is dependent on a number of external influences which may change markedly from time to time, important among them being decisions affecting the freedom of use, cost of use, and availability of roads. For this and other reasons, it is impossible to plan the maximum use of railways consistent with profitability, for years ahead, without some risk that it will prove, in the event, that services have been over-provided and that overall profitability is not achieved. On the other hand, to retain only those parts of the existing system which are virtually certain to be self-supporting under any reasonably probable future conditions would lead to grave risk of destroying assets which, in the event, might have proved to be valuable.

Confronted with this dilemma, arising from the impossibility of assessing future conditions and future profitability very reliably, the Railways Board have put forward proposals for reshaping the system which are conservative with regard to closures and restrainedly speculative with regard to new developments, but which are all directed towards shaping the system to provide rail transport for only that part of the total national traffic pattern which costing and commonsense consideration show to have characteristics favourable to rail transport.

The plan is not carried to the stage where it purports to answer the question, "How much of the railway can ultimately be made to pay?". This answer will emerge only after experience has shown how much benefit springs from elimination of those parts of the system which are obviously unsound, and the extent to which the good parts of the railways' system and traffic can be improved by cost savings, better quality of service, better operating methods, and attraction of favourable traffic. Nevertheless, the firm proposals included in the plan are expected to lead to substantial improvements in the financial position. Perhaps even more important, they set a clear course for the railways, in a general direction which must be right and which can be followed with vigour without any danger of eliminating too much or of incurring grossly wasteful expenditure before the position can be reviewed.

The changes proposed, and their phasing, are certainly not too drastic if regarded as a means of correcting the present departure of the railways from their proper role in the transport system as a whole. It is recognised, however, that changes of the magnitude of those proposed will inevitably give rise to many difficulties affecting railway staff, the travelling public, and industry. The Railways Board will do all that it can to ameliorate these difficulties, consistent with its responsibility for making railways an efficient and economic component in the transport system, but the Board knows that it will not be able to solve all problems unaided. ⟨1963⟩

British Railways Board: The Reshaping of British Railways
(1963), 2–3

176. EPITAPH ON THE GOLDEN VALLEY RAILWAY

We too easily forget . . . how much of the railway system of England, not only the little backwaters like the Golden Valley, which might better have never been made, but much larger concerns, of real and lasting value to the community, were built at the cost of private persons and the unpaid or little-paid services of local directors, gentry and tradespeople: money and service for which there was no financial return, often serious loss. And even the Golden Valley performed a real service to the people of the valley in the days when shanks's mare or the horse were the only alternative means of travel. ⟨1964⟩   C. L. Mowat, *The Golden Valley Railway* (1964), 85

177. JARGON UNKNOWN HERE

Attention please. The London train due at 16.46 has just left Weymouth. There was a change of engines; that's why the train was delayed. ⟨1981⟩
Station announcement at Dorchester, 8 July 1981

178. WHO CARES?

The other Friday I caught the 6.18 p.m. [from Manchester to Birmingham]. It was composed of a decaying rake of Mark I stock. Neither of the platform-side doors in my coach would open. Half the strip lighting was defective. The seats were festooned with reservation tickets from the down journey which had not been removed and which caused enormous confusion to less wily passengers than myself. The train left fifteen minutes late. It dropped another seven minutes by Stoke. Shortly before Wolverhampton an agitated guard ran through the train shouting "Passengers for Wolverhampton change at Birmingham New Street". We then began an agonisingly slow diversion through the Black Country freight avoiding lines. No explanations were offered when we arrived at New Street. The following Sunday I took Peter train-spotting. We arrived at New Street at about 1.15. Not a single [television] monitor was working. The arrival and departure boards were empty. The printed timetables had no information about trains before 4 o'clock. The station was quite full. ⟨1989⟩
J. M. Bourne to the compiler of this book,
27 November 1989

10

Railway Men

179. GEORGE STEPHENSON'S BATTLE

The battle which Mr Stephenson fought for the locomotive would have discouraged most other men; but it only served to bring into prominence his sterling qualities. 'I have fought", said he, "for the locomotive single-handed for nearly twenty years, having no engineer to help me until I had reared engineers under my own care." The leading engineers of the day were against him, without exception; yet he did not despair. He had laid hold of a great idea, and he stuck by it. When the use of his locomotive on the Liverpool & Manchester line was reported against, and the employment of fixed engines recommended instead, Mr Stephenson implored the directors, who were no engineers, only to afford a fair opportunity for a trial of the locomotive. Their common sense came to his rescue. They had immense confidence in that Newcastle engine-wright. He had already made steadfast friends of several of the most influential men amongst them, who valued his manly uprightness and integrity and were strongly disposed to believe in him, though all the engineering world stood on the one side, and he alone on the other. His patient purpose, not less than his intense earnestness, carried them away. They adopted his recommendation, and offered a prize of £500 for the best locomotive. Though many proclaimed the Liverpool men to be as great maniacs as Stephenson, yet the result proved the practical sagacity of the directors and the skill of their engineer; but it was the determined purpose of the latter which secured the triumph of the locomotive. His resolution, founded on sound convictions, was the precursor of what he eventually achieved; and his intense anticipation was but the true presentiment of what he was afterwards found capable of accomplishing. ⟨1813–30⟩

Samuel Smiles, *The Life of George Stephenson* (1857), 477

180.   THE YOUNG BRUNEL

I made your father's acquaintance, rather characteristically, in an unfinished tunnel of the Coalpit Heath Railway; and when the shaft in which we were suspended cracked and seemed about to give way, I well remember the coolness with which he insisted upon completing the observations he came to make. Shortly afterwards I became, at his request, his assistant; and during the Parliamentary struggle of 1835, and the subsequent organisation of the staff, and commencement of the works of the Great Western, I saw him for many hours daily, both in his office and in the field, travelled much with him, and joined him in the very moderate recreation he allowed himself.

These two years, and the preceding year, 1834, were, I apprehend, the turning points of his life. His vigour, both of body and mind, were in their perfection. His powers were continually called forth by the obstacles he had to overcome; and the result of his examinations in the committee rooms placed him, in the opinion of the members of the legislature, and of his own profession, in the very first rank of that profession, both for talents and knowledge.

I wish I could convey to you even a tolerable idea of your father as he was in those years, during which I knew him intimately, and saw him often under circumstances of great difficulty.

He was then a young man, but in the school of the Thames Tunnel he had acquired a close acquaintance with all kinds of masons' and carpenters' work, the strength and cost of materials, bridge building, and constructions under water, and with the working of the steam engine as it then stood. It happened not unfrequently that it was desirable to accept the tender of some contractor for railway work whose prices upon certain items were too high, and then it became the engineer's business to go into the details and convince the contractor of his error. On such occasions Brunel would go step by step through the stages of the work, and it was curious to see the surprise of the practical man as he found himself corrected in his own special business by the engineer. Thus, I remember his proving to an eminent brickmaker who had tendered for the Chippenham contract that the bricks could be made much cheaper than he supposed. He knew accurately how much coal would burn so many bricks, what it would cost, what number of bricks could be turned out, what would be the cost of housing the men, what the cartage, and how many men it would require to complete the work in the specified time. The contractor was astonished; asked if Mr Brunel had ever been in the brick trade, and finally took and made money by the contract at the proposed figure.

In the case of the Maidenhead bridge, the contractor being alarmed at learning that the arch was the flattest known in brick, Brunel pointed out to him that the weight which he feared would crush the bricks would be less than that in a wall which he, the contractor, had recently built, and he convinced him by geometry, made easy by diagrams, that the bridge must stand. Knowledge of detail Brunel shared with the carpenter, builder, or contractor for earthwork, and he was their superior in the accuracy and rapidity with which he combined his knowledge, and arrived at correct conclusions as to the cost of the work and the time it would take to execute it. . . .

I never met his equal for sustained power of work. After a hard day spent in preparing and delivering evidence, and after a hasty dinner, he would attend consultations till a late hour; and then, secure against interruption, sit down to his papers and draw specifications, write letters or reports, or make calculations all through the night. If at all pressed for time he slept in his armchair for two or three hours, and at early dawn he was ready for the work of the day. When he travelled he usually started about four or five in the morning, so as to reach his ground by daylight. His travelling carriage, in which he often slept, was built from his own design, and was a marvel of skill and comfort. This power of work was no doubt aided by the abstemiousness of his habits and by his light and joyous temperament. One luxury, tobacco, he indulged in to excess, and probably to his injury. At all times, even in bed, a cigar was in his mouth; and wherever he was engaged, there, near at hand, was the enormous leather cigar-case so well known to his friends, and out of which he was quite as ready to supply their wants as his own. . . .

He possessed a very fine temper, and was always ready to check differences between those about him, and to put a pleasant construction upon any apparent neglect or offence. His servants loved him, and he never forgot those who had stood by his father and himself in the old Tunnel days of trouble and anxiety.

No doubt the exertions of those three years, though they laid the foundation, or rather built the fabric, of his reputation, also undermined his constitution, and eventually shortened his life. Everything for which he was responsible he insisted upon doing for himself. I doubt whether he ever signed a professional report that was not entirely of his own composition; and every structure upon the Great Western, from the smallest culvert up to the Brent viaduct and Maidenhead bridge, was entirely, in all its details, from his own designs. ⟨1834–40⟩

> G. T. Clark to Isambard Brunel, the engineer's son:
> I. Brunel, *The Life of Isambard Kingdom Brunel*
> (1870), 94–8

181.   BRUNEL'S MISTRUST OF "AUTHORITY"

Nothing I believe has tended more to distinguish advantageously the profession of engineering in England and in America – nothing has conduced more to the great advance made in our profession and to our pre-eminence in the most practical application of the science – than the absence of all *règles de l'art* – a term which I fear is now going to be translated into English by the words "conditions to be observed". No man, however bold, or however high he may stand in his profession, can resist the benumbing effects of rules laid down by authority. ⟨1848⟩

> I. K. Brunel to Douglas Galton, 13 March 1848: Bristol
> University Library, Brunel Collection, Letterbook 5,
> ff. 355–6

182.   ON THE TRAMP

A navvy's wife speaks:

Well, he was just middling steady, and us was main comfortable for most a year; and then 'twas wintertime coming, and they was working nothing but muck. Charley was tipping then, like he is here; and 'tis dreadful hard to get the stuff out of the wagons when 'tis streaming wet atop and all stodge under. Then, you see, he was standing in it over his boots all day long, and once – no, twice – when he draw'd out his foot, the sole of his boot was left in the dirt; new ones, too, for he had a new pair of 15s. boots every week. So he cudn't stand that long. One Saturday night he took out his back money, and said us wid tramp for Yorkshire; for he'd a work'd there and 'twas all rock, and beautiful for tunnels. I didn' know where Yorkshire was, but I hadn' never been twenty mile nowhere. 'Twas four year agone, and I wasn' but just seventeen year old, and I didn' like for to go; and 'twas then us began for to quarley so. He took his kit, and I had my pillow strapped to my back; and off us sot, jawing all along. Us walked thirty mile a day, dead on end; it never stopped raining, and I hadn't a dry thread on me night or day, for us slept in such miserable holes of places, I was afeard my clothes 'ud be stole if I took 'em off. But when us comed to Leeds, where Charley know'd a man as kep a public, if I lives a thousand years I shan't never forgit the fire and the supper us had that night. But 'tis a filthy, smoky place; and when I seen it by day, I says, Well, if this is Yorkshire, us had better a stopped where us was, dirt and all. And what a lingo they talk! – I cudn' for the life of me understand 'em; and I were glad that Charley cudn' git work he liked there. So us had three days' more tramp – just a hundred mile – to a tunnel. They was a rough lot there; and then us seen and done all sorts o' things I wish I'd never heard on.

⟨Early 1840s⟩   Anna Rebecca Tregelles, *The Ways of the Line*
                                        (1858), 79–80

183.   NAVVIES' NICKNAMES

The names of navvies are very suddenly given, and are almost immovable. . . . A gentleman – an engineer – once walked through his engine-shed and saw three men by the furnace, apparently asleep. He hurried towards them to see who they were, but that mysterious telegraph which is always at work when the master is about warned the men, and they ran off too quickly for him to get a sight of their faces. "Who were those?" he demanded of a man who was near the spot. Of course the man interrogated declared at first he did not know, but finding his superior very much in earnest, he admitted that he knew them; that they were the Duke of Wellington, Cat's Meat, and Mary Anne; preposterous as it may sound, he knew them by no other names. The nose of the first, the previous profession of the second, and the effeminate voice of the third, gained these attractive titles. ⟨1840s⟩   F. S. Williams, *Our Iron Roads* (5th ed., 1888), 141

184.   NAVVY'S SONG

I'm a nipper and a tipper,
I'm a navvy on the line.
I get me five-and-twenty bob a week,
Besides me overtime.

Roast beef and boiled beef,
An' pudden made of eggs,
An' in comes a navvy
Wi' a fine pair o' legs!
⟨1857–9⟩
Sung on the building of the line from Torquay to Paignton,
1857–9: *Transactions of the Devonshire Association*,
67 (1935), 389

185. THE COMMUNITY OF NAVVIES

Navvies at work hold themselves responsible for their sick and the burial of their dead; in addition to which they allow the contractor to stop out of their wages a penny or twopence a week, to ensure for them the services of a medical man. Any navvy overtaken with sickness during his employment is entitled to support from the *gang* in which he is working, the sum given being ten or twelve shillings a week, which is raised by an equal contribution from every man; the quota varying according to the number of sick, and the number of men belonging to the gang. But should one die, all the gangs unite, every man on that contract (that is, portion of work under one contractor) subscribing the sum agreed upon; and after all expenses are paid, the over-plus or back-money is spent in drink. These burials are often the cause of sending many of the men drinking for days; as if, whatever influence the death of their *mates* might have upon their minds, they were determined to drown it in drunkenness. But should there be among them a case, or cases, requiring special help, the remainder is often given to them. They subscribe in the same way to bury the wife, or child, of a navvy. Sometimes these subscriptions fall rather heavy, especially in bad weather or accidents, but I never heard any complaints, as they pride themselves in giving their dead a "hansum berrin". Sometimes in sickness the patient requires more attention than his landlady can give, in which case they send a man from the gang to wait upon him, doing his work amongst them; and in visiting their sick I have witnessed what excellent nurses these navvies make, almost as kind and gentle, as watchful and patient, as a mother. . . .

But this general clanship among navvies does not prevent the existence of particular friendships; every navvy has his inner circle of "mates", and as, from their improvident habits, they are generally "hard up" when out of work, these mates, should they meet in such circumstances, assist one another. For instance, a navvy "on the road", their phrase for seeking work, when he comes to the neighbourhood of a new line, or any large piece of excavation, goes down to the works to see if any of his old mates are working there. . . . And having found such a mate the tramp knows he is right for that night, and the morrow; for though the man in work may have no money, he will get "sub" from the ganger, and give his mate supper, a lodging, and a shilling, or more, ere he starts on the road again. Of course they must have some ale together; and the consequence in many of such meetings is that the man who would have continued soberly at his work but for the calling of his mate is sent on the "randy" for days. Sometimes, however, these mates are not found, and unless the man "on the road" can get employment he often suffers a good deal of privation, for their general appearance of robust health does not ensure them much sympathy from strangers, though they are by no means ashamed to ask it. . . .

Navvies are ever on the move, more so in the summer months, and by this means they get to know from one another wherever there is work, what is the rate of wages, and what accommodation there may be for lodging. Threepence a day more on any works will take a navvy scores of miles, and he will lose more time after it than the extra pay would make up if he stayed thrice as long as he generally does. But they take care that too many do not ask for work at such a place, as that will at once bring the wages down. The most foolish example of this wandering that I came across was of a man who travelled, with his wife and two children, all the way from Kent to Westmorland, for the sole reason that he had there heard men were earning fourpence a day more than he was getting; and shortly after he got there this was taken off. ⟨1858⟩

T. Fayers, *Labour among the Navvies* (1862), 10–13

186.   THE RAILWAY NAVVY:
A JUST APPRAISAL

The railway navvy, unlike his contemporary, the canal boatman, was not cut off from the rest of society by the nature of his work since on most lines the overwhelming majority of workers were either householders themselves or lodgers with the resident population. Those who in the nineteenth century declared that the railway labourers were a class apart, spoke from the standpoint of more lofty social groups. The working classes, undeterred by their awesome reputation, had no aversion to accepting navvies as temporary visitors to their communities and even homes, and to making their needs a new source of income. The makeshift encampments, the fount of much navvy legend, which sprang up not only in inaccessible parts of the country but also on any contract where dense concentrations of men had assembled, were, under the influence of more responsible contractors, transformed from the often ramshackle shanties of the 1840s to the respectable cottages of the better-organised contracts of the 1880s. With the exception of work which had to be carried out by skilled men, notably tunnel construction, sheer muscle power, the deployment of regiments of men armed with the most rudimentary equipment, reigned supreme on the contracts until the last twenty years of the century. It was a sign of the advent of radical changes for the habits and style of work of the navvy when, in 1879, excavators who had left their jobs in dock building under Logan & Hemingway at Grimsby to do harvesting, returned to find that the work had been finished by steam navvies.

Riots, randies, and disasters were no doubt all part of the scene, but the true picture of railway construction is not that of the harrying of the wretched Irish over the fields around Oakenshaw viaduct, or of Robert Stephenson and Richard Creed peering through a cloud of dust into the collapsed shaft at Watford. It is a variegated canvas which has as its centrepiece men from all the nationalities of the British Isles, who either through sheer necessity or by choice travelled across the country or came from a neighbouring field to engage in the grinding and mindless slog of shifting mammoth quantities of earth and rock. But the breadth and diversity of the composition also find space for many remarkable vignettes – for Charles Hemingway's employee, Obadiah Stafford, self-taught builder of skew bridges of exquisite proportions, and for Israel "Whistler Dick" Collins and his brother, Fred, who as lads ran away from home to lead horses on the Oxford Worcester & Wolverhampton, were paraded along with their fellow navvies to see floggings during the Crimean War, and who died at a ripe old age having become two of the most responsible and knowledgeable railway foremen in the country.

Many reviled and despised the navvy, but at least at the end of a long day he could look back and derive some satisfaction from the dramatic evidence of his handiwork – the great white scar torn through the chalk of the Berkshire Downs where they meet the Thames Valley on the route of the Great Western, or the towering walls of Talerddig rock cutting, Montgomeryshire. Although his life may have been devoid of any sense of higher purpose, the navvy had the distinction granted to few human beings of making an addition to the nation's economy, its railway network, which was amenable to change and progressive improvement and of abiding value to successive generations of his countrymen. ⟨1830s–1880s⟩

David Brooke, *The Railway Navvy* (1983), 168–9

187. DAILY DUTIES SPELT OUT

Policeman's report, Glasgow Paisley & Greenock Railway, 1842:

I hereby certify having inspected my beat before the first train, going by one line of rails and returning by the other, taking care that both lines were in exact gauge, that all gates were shut, and every obstruction removed.

Wherever any part was found in bad order, I called the attention of the foreman or inspector to it; and the proper signals were exhibited according to the state of the road, or while under repair. I have also carefully gone over all the embankments, bridges, fences, slopes, cuttings, and drains on my beat, and the result given above. ⟨1842⟩

Printed form, signed by the policeman concerned:
Glasgow Museum of Transport

188.   ENGINE-DRIVERS

(a)

Even in bright sunshine, to stand – like the figure-head of a ship – foremost on a train of enormous weight, which, with fearful momentum, is rushing forward faster than any racehorse can gallop, requires a cool head and a calm heart; but to proceed at this pace in dark or foggy weather into tunnels, along embankments, and through deep cuttings, where it is impossible to foresee any obstruction, is an amount of responsibility which scarcely any other situation in life can exceed; for not only is a driver severely, and occasionally without mercy, punished for any negligence he himself may commit, but he is invariably sentenced personally to suffer on the spot for any accident that from the negligence of others may suddenly befall the road along which he travels, but over which he has not the smallest control. The greatest hardship he has to endure, however, is from cold, and especially that produced in winter by evaporation from his drenched clothes passing rapidly through the air. Indeed when a gale of wind and rain from the north-west, triumphantly sweeping over the surface of the earth at its ordinary rate of say sixty miles an hour, suddenly meets the driver of the London & North Western, who has not only to withstand such an antagonist but to dash through him, and in spite of him to proceed in an opposite direction at the rate of say forty miles an hour – the conflict between the wet Englishman and Æolus, tilting by each other at the combined speed of a hundred miles an hour, forms a tournament of extraordinary interest. ⟨1849⟩   Sir Francis Head, *Stokers and Pokers* (2nd ed., 1849), 63–4

(b)

Of all men in the employ of railway companies there is not a class with which the public are so little acquainted, and yet in the coaching days the driver was the man whose society was most sought. Is it not astonishing that whereas the driver of a coach and four horses, value a few hundreds, and say twenty passengers, should have been a man, for the most part, from the middle class, the driver of a railway engine and train, with say one hundred passengers and so many thousands worth of property, should be from the lower orders? And, as an old coach driver once said, "When an accident happened to a coach, *there you were*; but if an accident happened to a railway train, *where are you?*" ⟨1860s⟩

H. A. Simmons, *Ernest Struggles* (1879), 61

189. BREAKDOWN MEN

The traffic of the Oxford Worcester & Wolverhampton Railway was worked from 1852 onwards by a contractor, C. C. Williams, who placed it under the supervision of an engineer, David Joy. Joy wrote reminiscences, based on diaries he kept at the time, which offer a lively record of this work.

Next was a bigger bother. No. 14, with George Benson taking the 9.35 p.m. down to Dudley, broke a trailing tyre just beyond Hartlebury. I had got to bed when the shed-man tickled my window with the usual long stick with the little bunch of wire at the end. Shed-man: "Engine off at Hartlebury". I: "Get No. 20 ready". I, to my housekeeper: "Richardson, coffee and toast, smart". Then I dressed and found the meal ready. Gulped it quickly, and slipped down to shed just below me, to find No. 20 crawling out of the shed with 20lb steam only. Joe Lester, my man, was there, also Adcock, general manager, shivering in the cold, and others. Joe said he could "pick her up", so we started with 20lb steam. . . . Before we were ten miles away, past Droitwich, we were running away like a bird. Arrived at the accident, found it an awfully narrow shave, the trailing tyre had broken through, but held in one big open ring hanging on to the engine, till she stuck in the longitudinal timbers, stopping all quietly, almost without shaking the passengers. The traffic department took them and handled them, and we tackled the engine and tender to get them out of the way; it was 12 midnight.

As usual, when I had laid my plans and got all away, I sent a deputation to the nearest "public" for cans of coffee, and bread cut thick, and butter. Men work best on such stuff on cold, dark nights; we had big fires, and really it was very jolly, but we did not get clear till dawn, about 5 a.m. Then I passed glasses of beer round and bundled all the men out into our breakdown train, to sleep till Worcester. That was all right, too. ⟨1854⟩

Railway Magazine, 23 (1908), 155

190. THE GREAT IRISH CONTRACTOR

It is rarely the case that a country owes more to an individual than Ireland owes to the memory of Mr Dargan. He was the true father of Irish railways. No contractor, no dozen contractors, in England ever filled such a position as he did in his own country. No doubt he built his own fortune, although even that proved to be of not much more enduring reality than much of the fair gold that was heaped up in tens and hundreds of thousands by so many English contractors, only to prove, in the hour of trial, to consist of withered leaves. But he was a man fair in his dealings with all – just to the companies that employed him, just to the men whom he employed. His enterprise and energy taught Irishmen to labour at home as they are wont to labour out of Ireland, and formed the mainspring of the Irish railways.

He was singularly modest and quiet, in abode, in dress, in manners; and not only so, but in his estimate of himself. An English engineer who had undertaken, somewhat too rashly, engagements in Ireland that threatened to prove too heavy for his strength, called on Dargan with reference to some interference which was desired on the part of the Lord-Lieutenant. The Irish contractor saw the point, saw what might be done, but confessed himself ignorant as to whether His Lordship could, or would, do what was requisite. "I came to ask you", said the Englishman, "if you cannot spare the time to go to Dublin with me, to write a letter to the Lord-Lieutenant, to say that you have talked over this matter with me, and that you strenuously recommend him to do what I ask, as it is of great importance to the prosperity, and even to the peace, of the country." "What!" said Dargan, opening his eyes in unaffected surprise. "Me! me write to the Lord-Lieutenant, me dear Sir! I daur not. I never took such a liberty in me life." ⟨1868⟩　　　F. R. Conder, *Personal Recollections of English Engineers*, republished as *The Men Who Built Railways* (1983), 165–6

191. CIVILITY TO PASSENGERS

(a)

The generally received opinion [is] that railway officers are offhand and discourteous in their manner. We know that, from the very nature of their occupation, their replies must be concise. Time will not admit of their being moulded into flowery or lengthened speech; still they need not partake so much of that harshness and bad grace which often characterise their delivery. ⟨1861⟩　　　*Handbook Guide to Railway Situations* (1861), 12

(b)

A Pullman's car from St Pancras transports you to your destination so easily, rapidly, and luxuriously that you scarcely feel to have travelled at all. The guards and porters on this line [the Midland] are so polite and attentive, and in most cases so nobly indifferent to "tips" that you wonder where they can have acquired such charming manners and such disinterested minds. . . . On the Midland passengers receive civil answers to their questions; are provided with footwarmers, or anything else they may ask for, without demur or delay; and are, on changing trains or reaching their journey's end, courteously assisted to find their luggage. This is more than could be said of all railways, as many could testify to their cost. ⟨1881⟩   Miss H. Tupper in *Mid-England* (1881), 302

192. PORTERS

(a)

The attendant porter [at Shoreditch station] who had called his cab, and undertaken the general conduct of his affairs with that disinterested courtesy which does such infinite credit to a class of servitors who are forbidden to accept the tribute of a grateful public. ⟨1862⟩
Mrs M. E. Braddon, *Lady Audley's Secret* (1862), i. 291

(b)

At Aspatria [Cumbria] . . . the discriminating porter . . . was accustomed to call out to the first-class passengers, "Aspatriah, change heah for Mealsgate"; to the second-class, "'Speattry, change 'ere for Mealsyat"; and to the third-class merely, "'Spatthry, git oot". ⟨Late 19th cent.⟩
Railway Magazine, 22 (1908), 329

193. AN OBSTREPEROUS PASSENGER

On several occasions during the early years at Silverton, my father [the stationmaster there] had trouble with drunken passengers. On one occasion a certain book salesman came to the station and called for a ticket to Exeter, for which he tendered 5d. The parliamentary fare being 7d, my father asked him for the other 2d. The man began to abuse him and got on to the line, and would have been killed by an express, but father jumped down and dragged him back just in time to save both their lives. The man then struck father in the face with his umbrella and swore tremendously. After some trouble father succeeded in placing him outside the station gate and locked him out. The man finally paid 7d for his ticket, and then threatened to kill father. Of course he was summoned and had to pay heavy fines. Father wrote regarding this case: "If I had caused the death of this man, I should have had to do at least twelve months' hard labour in one of Her Majesty's country mansions, and there would have been two and a half columns in the *Times*, the *Standard*, and the *Daily Telegraph*, expatiating on the carelessness of railway officials; but having saved his life at great risk of my own, I received as complete and satisfactory a blackguarding as it is possible to conceive." ⟨1870⟩

The Life of Roger Langdon. Told by Himself (1909), 78–9

194. OVERWORK

(a)

The Chief Inspector of Railways, Henry Tyler, refers to an accident at Lawton Junction on the North Staffordshire Railway, 26 September 1873.

The guard [who subsequently died] . . . had been nineteen hours on duty and was over fatigued, and omitted to apply his brake. The driver of the pilot engine was stated to have been confused by drink, after having been on duty for thirty-two hours. He was employed altogether for forty hours. The fireman had been asleep on the engine and was unfit for duty. ⟨1873⟩

Parliamentary Papers, 1874, lviii. 357

(b)

Thomas Dippie, signalman at Tayport south cabin on the North British Railway when a fatal accident occurred on 25 November 1881, was in custody and not examined by the inspector inquiring into the accident. He was over sixty, and had been thirty years in the railway service. Here are some of the inspector's comments.

At the time of the accident he had been on duty for nearly thirteen consecutive hours, while his daily work on weekdays, exclusive of the time he may have taken in walking to and from his home, would average over 15½ consecutive hours, even if the last train, the arrival of which he had to await, was punctual to the minute.

It is hardly too much to say it is a scandal that such an amount of work as is implied by these hours should be expected from any man upon whose vigilance depends the safety of the public, and who by a momentary act of forgetfulness may, as in this case, cause a fatal catastrophe, and I am glad to learn that since the date of this accident an improvement in this respect has been made at Tayport. ⟨1881⟩ *Parliamentary Papers*, 1882, lx. 295

195. SISTER DORA

Dorothy Pattison (always known as Sister Dora) worked at the Walsall Cottage Hospital from 1863 to 1878. It was not a general hospital but was intended for the treatment of casualties in industrial accidents. Many railway men were nursed by her there.

(a)

At the foot of the slope [below the Hospital] ran the railway, with a ceaseless clanking of goods trains carrying coal and iron ore. The noise did not appear to disturb Sister Dora; railways to her generation were an unqualified blessing, and a view over a railroad had inspired Neale's famous sermon, in which the signal "stretches out its arms, and by the sign of the cross directs the passing train". To the patients, especially the railwaymen among them, the passing trains were a free entertainment. Every engine and driver had its distinctive whistle, which they recognised, and the ward echoed with shouts of "Hullo, that's our Bill" or "There goes Jack!" Sister Dora nursed many railwaymen, and always expressed admiration for the masculine mysteries of gauges, boilers, signals, plates, and shunting. Drivers and firemen were among her favourite patients.
⟨1863–78⟩ Jo Manton, *Sister Dora* (1971), 224

(b)

December 28th, the first Saturday after Christmas, 1878, was a day of drizzling rain in the Black Country. Snow had fallen on the town of Walsall, briefly veiling the dense rows of houses; it had been pock-marked by soot and flying cinders, and was now melting into a grimy slush. The town, usually raucous with the shouts of market people and the distant thud of steam hammers, was strangely quiet. The shops were closed. Houses stood silent, with drawn blinds. From St Matthew's Gothic spire, crowning the steep and winding High Street of the old borough, the bells rang a muffled peal, as they had each day since Christmas Eve. The sound, said a hearer, struck a dull chill into every heart.

At two o'clock in the afternoon a procession called at a small house in Wednesbury Road. Eighteen railwaymen, engine drivers, porters, and guards, in their working uniform, bore a plain wooden coffin from the door to a plain hearse. Behind it followed a choir, strangely composed for that period of sectarian strife; robed choristers from the parish churches walked with singers from the Dissenting chapels, from Roman Catholic churches, from the Unitarian meeting house. After them came clergy of every denomination in the town, with two bishops on foot. The Mayor and Corporation of Walsall were there, a representative of the Member of Parliament, the Magistrates and members of the Hospital Committee. Yet this was not the funeral of some borough dignitary who had lived rich and successful, died full of honours and was now being escorted to an official grave. They were following the body of a woman who had come among them as a stranger, member of an Anglican religious order, only fourteen years before and who had died at forty-six, poor as the day she came. She had been beautiful and fascinating, gay and courageous, the friend of all present, yet separated by an invisible barrier from the values and conventions of their society. How far she stood outside appeared as they wound a circuitous route between gutters of grey slush, through crowded streets towards the Walsall Cottage Hospital for casualties from the mines and iron works of the district. ⟨1878⟩

> *Ibid.*, 15–16. The London & North Western Railway named an engine after Sister Dora; an honour shared with only two other nurses, Florence Nightingale and Edith Cavell

196.   PUNISHMENTS

These examples were appended to the working timetables of the Stockton & Darlington division of the North Eastern Railway (issued to the staff only, not to the public), as cautionary indications of penalties.

A booking constable has been fined for an irregularity with a parcel.

A driver has been fined for jerking passengers.

A porter has been heavily fined and severely reprimanded for being asleep on duty, and causing a serious detention to a train.

A fireman has been fined for ejecting water over a station agent. ⟨1876⟩

> Timetables, 1 May and 1 August 1876: Public Record Office, RAIL 972/1

197. SIGNALMEN

Few men deserve the sympathy of their fellow-countrymen better than the class of railway signalmen. Porters and guards are in contact with the public, and in many places their wages are by no means the largest part of their actual earnings. Even engine-drivers sometimes come in for an occasional tip, while in any case their wages – ninepence an hour as a rule after a few years' service – are calculated on a scale more liberal than is paid to any other class of workmen who are not skilled artisans, and have not been obliged to serve an apprenticeship. But with the signalman, as far at least as the public is concerned, it is out of sight out of mind. He works long hours at his anxious occupation for wages that are only moderate in amount. A single slip – one error after a million movements accurately performed – may bring about an accident, and lead to his dismissal from his post, leaving him of course unable to obtain employment from any other company at the only trade he knows, and to a great extent unfitted by the life he has led for other outdoor occupations. At best he cannot hope that his nerves will suffer him to continue in his box much after what in the upper classes would be called middle life. I am far from wishing to suggest that the great lines treat their men badly. Undoubtedly the wages they pay are sufficient not only to attract but to keep good servants. But if every railway company in England were to establish a signalman's superannuation fund, and to maintain it with only a trifling deduction from the men's pay on account of it, I cannot think that many shareholders would be found to grudge the outlay. ⟨1889⟩

W. M. Acworth, *The Railways of England* (1889), 307–8

198. TO A GREAT WESTERN BROADGAUGE
ENGINE AND ITS STOKER

So! I shall never see you more,
You mighty lord of railway-roar;
The splendid stroke of driving-wheel,
The burnished brass, the shining steel,
Triumphant pride of him who drives
From Paddington to far St Ives.
Another year, and then your place
Knows you no more; a pigmy race
Usurps the glory of the road,
And trails along a lesser load.

Drive on then, engine, drive amain,
Wrap me, like love, yet once again
A follower in your fiery train.

Drive on! and driving, let me know
The golden West, its warmth, its glow.
Pass Thames with all his winding maze;
Sweet Clifton dreaming in a haze;
And, farther yet, pass Taunton Vale,
And Dawlish rocks, and Teignmouth sail,
And Totnes, where the dancing Dart
Comes seaward with a gladsome heart;
Then let me feel the wind blow free
From levels of the Cornish sea.

Drive on! Let all your fiery soul,
Your puissant heart that scorns control,
Your burnished limbs of circling steel,
The throb, the pulse of driving-wheel,
O'erflood the breast of him whose gaze
Is set to watch your perilous ways,
Burn brighter in those eyes of vair,
Blow back the curly, close-cropped hair.
Ah! Western lad, would I might be
A partner in that ecstasy.

⟨1891⟩   Horatio Brown, *Drift* (1900), 3

199.   THE FRAME SHED AT SWINDON

The personnel of the frame shed is individual and distinct in a very marked degree. Most of the men seem to have been chosen for their great strength and fine physique, or to have developed these qualities after their admission to the work. The very nature of the toil tends to produce strong limbs and brawny muscles. It is certain that continual exercise of the upper parts of the body by such means as the lifting of heavy substances tends to improve the chest and shoulders, and many of those who are engaged in lifting and carrying the plates and sole-bars are very stout and square in this respect. There is a number of "heavy weights", and a few positive giants among them, though the majority of the men are conspicuous, not so much by their bulk, as by their squareness of limb and muscularity. A proof of the strength of the frame shed men may be seen in the success of their tug-of-war teams. Wherever they have competed – and they have gone throughout the entire south of England – they have invariably beaten their opponents and carried off the trophies.

There was formerly a workman, an ex-Hussar, named Bryan, in the shed, who could perform extraordinary feats of strength. He was nearly seven feet in height and he was very erect. His arms and limbs were solid and strong; he was a veritable Hercules, and his shoulders must have been as broad as those of Atlas, who is fabled to have borne the world on his back. It was striking to see him lift the heavy headstocks, that weighed two hundredweights and a quarter, with perfect ease and carry them about on his shoulder – a task that usually required the powers of two of the strongest men. This he continued to do for many years, not out of bravado, but because he knew it was within his natural powers to perform. Nothwithstanding his tremendous normal strength, however, he was subject to attacks of ague, and you might have seen him sometimes stretched out upon the ground quite helpless, groaning and foaming at the mouth. If he had been working in the shed recently, since the passing of the new Factory Acts, he would have been promptly discharged, for no one is kept at the works now who is subject to any infirmity that might incapacitate him in the shed among the machinery. Later on, when work got slack, Bryan was turned adrift from the factory, a broken and a ruined man. All his past services to the firm were forgotten; he was cast off like an old shoe. However valuable and extraordinary a man may have proved himself to be at his work, it counts for little or nothing with the foreman and managers; the least thing puts him out of favour and he must go.

The men of the frame shed are of a cosmopolitan order, though to a less extent than is the case in some departments. The work being for the most part rough and requiring no very great skill, there has consequently been no need of apprenticeships, though there are a few who have served their time as wagon-builders or boiler-smiths. They are not recognised as journeymen here, however, and so must take their chance with the rank and file. Promotion is supposed to be made according to merit, but there are favourites everywhere who will somehow or other prevail. The normal order of promotion is from labourer to "puller-up", from puller-up to riveter, and thence to the position of chargeman. Here he must be content to stop, for foremen are only made about once or twice in a generation, and when the odds on any man for the post are high, surprise and disappointment always follow. The first is usually relegated to the rear, and the least expected of all is brought forward to fill the coveted position. It may be design, or it may be judgment, and perhaps it is neither. It very often looks as though the matter had been decided by the toss of a coin, or the drawing of lots, and that the lot had fallen upon the least qualified, but there is no questioning the decision. The old and tried chargeman, who knows the scale and dimensions of everything that has been built or that is likely to be built in the shed in his lifetime, must stand aside for the raw youth who has not left school many months, but who, by some mysterious means or other, has managed to secure the favour and indulgence of his foreman, or other superior. Perhaps he is reckoned good at arithmetic, or can scratch out a rough drawing, though more than likely his father was gardener to someone, or cleaned the foreman's boots and did odd jobs in the scullery after factory hours.

Another reason for the selection of young and comparatively unknown men for the post of foreman is that they have a smaller circle of personal mates in the shed, and, consequently, a less amount of human kindness and sympathy in them. That is to say, they will be able to cut and slash the piecework prices with less compunction, and so the better serve the interests of the company. The young aspirant, moreover, will be at the very foot of the ladder, hot and impetuous, while the elder one will have passed the season of senseless and unscrupulous ambition. ⟨1911⟩

Alfred Williams, *Life in a Railway Factory*
(1984 ed.), 76–7

200. DISCIPLINE

When I first came on the railway I found the discipline was a damn sight worse than the Navy. The old drivers were absolute disciplinarians. Absolutely. They were tin gods. And there's very rarely you didn't find one with a beard and a clay pipe and a box of snuff. They were a type of person like this. They'd got a kind of complex that had crept into them that they were *the* people. They were that wrapped up in railways when they saw other people come in, we've got to watch what they do, separate to my job. That's how they were. It was a case that you'd got to get on duty fifteen or twenty minutes before your book time just for the sake of getting every-thing ready for the driver. Go and fetch his oil from the store. Fill his feeders, his small feeder, his long feeder, put 'em on the dishplate to get 'em nice and soluble, warm. And then he'd come along. He'd stand there with his food box and an old stone jar. Some used to have tea without milk and a lemon in it. And I think some of them used to have a drop of beer in it. That was the way of them. "Come on, clean up this, and have you wiped that there box?" You had to near enough lift him in the engine. They were autocrats.

In conversation they knew it all. They were full of consequence. But at the same time they were reliable. In those days if you ran by a signal there was nothing to tell you you had run by. The only thing you knew were the consequences of running by a signal. I did admire them that way. There used to be some good chaps. As a pass cleaner you'd get different types on different weeks. Now you'd find one driver perhaps he'd be interested in gardening; you'd find another one he was interested in religion. You'd find another one that was absolutely opposite. You used to talk about this and the other. It was education. I remember Sam Redfern, number one in the Co-op. Now he'd got a long ginger beard. He was a guard. Then there was another one we used to call Foxy Reynolds. He was a big Co-op man.

If I had my time over again I wouldn't choose anything else. It's not only the job, it's the variety. Every day was different. Then there were the conversations with these old drivers. Perhaps it would be a lovely starlit night and he was an astronomer and he used to show me this and show me that. They were educated for the simple reason the job had educated them. ⟨c.1910⟩   H. Edwards in D. Stuart, *County Borough: the History of Burton-upon-Trent, 1901–74*, (1975), i. 101–3

201. SERVICE UNGENEROUSLY REWARDED

The very name of the Railway Executive Committee[1] would hardly be recognised by the multitude; yet this body, which controlled the railways with such astonishing skill, did much to ensure our ultimate victory in the field. Its members paid the price. Two general managers of railways died through overwork in the war.[2] They received very little thanks or recognition and none at all from the Government, while the bounteous showers from the fountain of honour left them almost unsprinkled. This was especially the case in Scotland, and it is deplorable to have to record the fact that while thousands of persons received war honours very lightly won, not a single Scottish railway man has ever been selected for conspicuous honour for war work. ⟨1921⟩

E. A. Pratt, *British Railways and the Great War* (1921),
1165, quoting *The Times*, 15 August 1921

202. A RAILWAY OF CHARACTERS

The Merthyr Tredegar & Abergavenny line ... [was] a railway of characters as well as character; there was a signalman who on occasion could be seen gesturing and declaiming to his unresponsive levers, and might be suspected to be slightly "round the bend", but this was only Old Huw (or Trevor, or Bleddyn, or Ivor, or whoever) rehearsing his sermon for the devout of Bethel the following Sunday. Of drivers, Dunn recalled a

---

[1] A committee of general managers of leading railway companies, formed by the Board of Trade in 1912, to co-ordinate and control the work of the railways in the event of war.

[2] Sir Guy Calthrop of the Caledonian and Frank Potter of the Great Western.

certain "Mad Dai", whose appearance half out of the cab would cause waiting passengers to blanch, step back, and decide the next train would be better – a long wait, too. As one of this ilk told a colleague of mine, "Well, sir, you see, I came on to the railway to *drive* the trains, like". ⟨c.1930⟩

> D. S. M. Barrie, *Regional History of the Railways of Great Britain: South Wales* (1980), 79–80

203.   ORDER AND DESIGN

There were not many things that gave greater pleasure to Pick than seeing a railway track well looked after. . . . His interest in it was further stimulated by the discovery round about 1930 of a kindred spirit who was at work in the North Eastern Area of the LNER – as Pick's old company was now called. His name was John Miller. The civil engineer of a railway spends millions of pounds in the course of a year, and of all that money some two-thirds can go into the maintenance of track. Miller, who had more than 5000 miles of it to look after, was the first main-line engineer to organise its upkeep as a single concerted operation. Pick, when he was travelling on the line, would note with approval the wonderful precision of the top edge of embankments, of the edges of stone ballast and trim grass verge. To make sure that the perfect edge of ballast would stay perfect Miller would reinforce it with bigger stones, handpicked, tapped in with a heavy hammer. There was no path or plot without its clean, firm kerbing of some strong and lasting material. His electric cable gear, his mile posts and other indication posts, all his various pieces of lineside furnishing would be beautifully arranged. Wherever Pick might look he would note that order and design had been brought to the performance of some simple everyday task. One day, when he was telling me something about one of his journeys north, he said: "You know, when the train slows down to approach the Selby swing bridge I put away my papers. I always look forward to a sight of the Miller country". ⟨1930s⟩

> Christian Barman, *The Man who Built London Transport* (1979), 233–4

204.   HEROISM AT BIRKENHEAD

It is the night of the first big blitz on Merseyside. In one great dark area, 140 men of the Great Western Railway, all new to the task in hand, are fighting like heroes. At first alone and then with the help of outside fire services, they work for twelve hours, saving docks, ships, cotton, food and munitions of war.

Seven-thirty in the evening. Take a look at the scene; buildings covering acres by the side of the great docks, scores of railway lines crowded with wagons, shunting engines going to and fro, trains being dismembered and remade, goods discharging and loading. Through a clear evening sky come enemy planes, flying low. Below them lie these targets.

Some trains are already stabled for the night. Among these are wagons loaded with shells and bombs of all sizes, waiting to be transferred to barges and ships next morning. Other wagons carry tins of high-grade spirit, flares, daylight bombs and cordite fuses. Here and there tarpaulins cover depth-charges, most deadly and destructive of all loads.

It was our first blitz; sirens had sounded. I was in charge of one of the ammunition trains. Then the incendiaries came with a tearing sound and the pop-pop-popping of a "bread basket". We had received orders to back the train with the ammunition wagons away from the main shed and out to the main line, clear of the station. I knew that six of the wagons contained high explosives, anything up to 500-pound bombs.

I walked the length of the train to see that all was in order and now, for the first time, I noticed burning debris dropping from one of the H.E. wagons. I ran back to the engine, got a bucket of water and warned the driver not to move "Ammo wagon on fire!" and went back again with the water. I scrambled underneath the wagon, threw the whole lot upwards and got a good soaking for my pains, but it seemed to me that there must be fire inside.

Climbing on top of the wagon, I now found a small hole in the sheet, through which the incendiary had made its way. Seeing that it was burning furiously, I decided to throw the whole thing open; flames and smoke streamed out of the wagon. Looking down, I could see the wood inside burning fast and the incendiary, still blazing, jammed between two very big bombs.

I made a quick grab for the incendiary but failed to get it out. It was firmly fixed and the bombs were getting hot. I had my shunting pole with me, so I tried to wedge the bombs apart to retrieve the incendiary. After some agonising time, I managed to do this and threw it away down the line.

That was not quite the end of the truck fire. The wood was still burning and the bombs getting still hotter, so I got a stirrup pump working and sprayed the bombs and wood until the fire went out. To make all safe, I pulled the train under the water column and gave the wagons a good soaking. ⟨1940⟩   Account given by Norman Tunna, shunter at Birkenhead, of his actions on the night of 26 September 1940, for which he was awarded the George Cross: A. Stanistreet, *Brave Railwaymen* (1989), 43–4

205. SOHAM SAVED

THIS TABLET COMMEMORATES THE HEROIC ACTION
OF FIREMAN J. W. NIGHTALL, G.C. WHO LOST HIS
LIFE, & DRIVER B. GIMBERT, G. C. WHO WAS BADLY
INJURED WHILST DETACHING A BLAZING WAGON
FROM AN AMMUNITION TRAIN AT SOHAM STATION
AT 1.43 A.M. ON JUNE 2ND 1944. THE STATION
WAS TOTALLY DESTROYED AND CONSIDERABLE
DAMAGE DONE BY THE EXPLOSION. THE DEVOTION
TO DUTY OF THESE BRAVE MEN SAVED THE
TOWN OF SOHAM FROM GRAVE DESTRUCTION.
SIGNALMAN F. BRIDGES WAS KILLED WHILST ON
DUTY & GUARD H. CLARKE SUFFERED FROM SHOCK.

"BE STRONG AND QUIT YOURSELVES LIKE MEN"

⟨1944⟩   Memorial in Soham church, Cambridgeshire

206. RAILWAY RITUAL

The guard blew his whistle and waved his flag – how weighted with ritual
have the railways in their brief century become! – and the train crawled
from the little station. The guard walked alongside through the snowflakes, wistful for that jump-and-swing at an accelerating van that is the
very core of the mystery of guarding trains. ⟨1945⟩

Michael Innes, *Appleby's End* (1945), 1

207. RAILWAY LANGUAGE

Railway language seems a closed area to historians of the age of steam.
Who has recorded the engine-driver's breakfast – "two Woodbines and an
aspirin" – or the contents of the fireman's head, which, when devoid of the
daily racing information, showed "twenty inches of vacuum"? Who has
heard of the "fifty face man" whose word could not be trusted?

The footplate was a rich tapestry of nicknames and uncomplimentary
titles such as:

> *Abadan*: This was a driver who hoarded engine oil in hideaways
> around the shed.

The Desert Drivers: These were enginemen who had a permanent fear of running short of water in the tank or sand in the boxes.

The Whispering Baritone: Every shed had a loudmouth, a barrack-room lawyer; this was his title.

His Master's Voice: Generally an ex-footplateman turned foreman's assistant. A crawler, a sycophant.

Little Sir Echo: See above, for interchangeable term.

The Bugler: Before the steam whistle was invented drivers had bugles which they used to give warning of their approach. The Bugler was an excessive whistler.

Captain Hornblower: Another excessive whistler – especially during the night hours. ⟨1980⟩

Frank McKenna, The Railway Workers (1980), 236

208. THE ENCLOSED ORDER OF RAILWAYMEN

The observation that the railways are a monastic order of disciplined, committed enthusiasts is as much a *cliché* as the observation that the industry has suffered from political intervention. But it remains true that the "culture of the railroad", rooted in its nineteenth century domination of the transport system, has survived all attempts to tinker with the organisational structure, from the dismantling of the main-line companies in 1947 to the establishment of an organisation dominated on paper by corporate planning and the use of executive directors in 1970. Some would argue that it will survive the introduction of "sector management" and the privatisation drive of the 1980s. The "enclosed order of railwaymen" exhibits strengths in its loyalty and discipline, necessary qualities in an industry where operational safety is rightly emphasised. But it also encourages a close-knit group antagonistic to outsiders and hostile to new ideas. Some of the costs of this kind of management may be seen in the heavy reliance on commercial and marketing practices developed in the late nineteenth and early twentieth centuries, which became increasingly inappropriate to the post-war world, and in the courtroom atmosphere of much collective bargaining before the late 1960s. All this was cemented by the "traffic apprentice" system of management development, which gave an advantage to managers trained in the operating departments. The disciplined functioning of an industry brought up on rule books and elaborate procedures also encouraged the first chairmen, Hurcomb and Robertson, who were both from disciplined backgrounds themselves, to err on the side of being too deferential to their political masters. At times they appeared only too willing to place their heads under the cosh.

Whatever the reasons for the improvement in railway management in the 1960s, it is clear that the new ideas and the new faces introduced by Beeching, Shirley and others had a great impact, with all their imperfections. It was Shirley who set out to puncture the railways' overblown bureaucracy, with its numerous committees and its mass of paper-work, much of which was produced by administrators isolated from the selling function and therefore insensitive to the changing needs of customers.
⟨1948–70⟩   T. R. Gourvish, *British Railways 1948–73* (1986), 577–8

11

Railways and the Community

FIRST CLASS POLITENESS.

SECOND CLASS POLITENESS.

THIRD CLASS POLITENESS.

209. THE NEW POWER OF THE RAILWAYS

The steam railways' real significance lay in the fact that they could cater for both high-value and low-value traffic. Before the coming of these railways there was no such single form of transport capable of performing the twofold function. ⟨1830s and 1840s⟩

> T. C. Barker and C. I. Savage, *An Economic History of Transport in Britain* (3rd ed., 1974), 15

210. A PLANNED RAILWAY SYSTEM

A modern historian allows it is unfortunate that the State did not exercise more control over the planning of the railway system in its formative period in 1830–50, but explains that that would have been impossible in Britain then.

Such control could only have been imposed at the cost of an enormous delay in securing a national rail network. The government lacked the money, the trained men, and the administrative experience as well as the will to enter the uncharted field of state enterprise at that date. If private enterprise was sometimes wasteful, unscrupulous and careless, no other social agency could have undertaken successfully the great railroad expansion of 1830–50.   Norman Gash, *The Age of Peel* (1968), 16

211. EARLY WARNING OF THE CONSEQUENCES OF RAILWAY DEVELOPMENT

Railroads, without the slightest permanent advantage to the subscriber, or the public in general, will, in their efforts to gain ground, do incalculable mischief. If they succeed, they will give an unnatural impulse to society, destroy all the relations which exist between man and man, overthrow all mercantile regulations, overturn the metropolitan markets, drain the provinces of their resources, and create, at the peril of human life, all sorts of confusion and distress. If they fail, nothing will be left but the hideous memorials of public folly . . . in the shape of ruinous, rotting mounds, the objects at once of the disgust and ridicule of those who have sense to appreciate, and prudence to preserve, the order of things as it exists, in perhaps the highest state of civilisation England has yet known.

John Bull, 15 November 1835

212. HOLIDAY-MAKING IN GUERNSEY

This comment was passed in the second season after the opening of the railway between London and Southampton.

The journey to London [from Guernsey], by the Southampton railway, may now be accomplished in fifteen hours. This facility of communication, coupled with the recent insular improvements, attracts annually great numbers of visitors, every one of whom necessarily leaves some money in the island, and thus increases its commercial wealth. ⟨1841⟩

J. Duncan, *History of Guernsey* (1841), 269

213. POLITICAL POSSIBILITIES

At Windsor yesterday for a Council; almost all the Cabinet went together in a special train. A Whig engineer [i.e. driver] might have produced an instantaneous and complete change of government. ⟨1842⟩

From the diary of C. C. F. Greville, Clerk to the Privy Council: *The Greville Memoirs*, ed. Lytton Strachey and Roger Fulford (1938), v. 47

214. ENTERPRISES FOR THE CANAILLE

"Our family have always been against manufactories, railroads – everything", said Egremont.

"Railroads are very good things, with high compensation", said Lord Marney; "and manufactories not so bad, with high rents; but, after all, these are enterprises for the canaille, and I hate them in my heart."

"But they employ the people, George."

"The people do not want employment; it is the greatest mistake in the world; all this employment is a stimulus to population." ⟨1845⟩

Disraeli, *Sybil* (1845), chap. 14

215. HERE THE RAILWAY PAYS THE FARMERS' POOR RATES

They manage generally to relieve the farmers of all poor rates and parish taxes, by the heavy way in which the railways are rated. I hear in Huyton this has amounted to an absolution from all such rates by the general body, and the laying of almost the whole upon the railway. This makes the railway a great benefit to the lands through which it passes. ⟨1845⟩

C. P. Grenfell to the Earl of Sefton, 13 January 1845: Lancashire Record Office, DDM 6/2

216. RAILWAYS AND FOX-HUNTING

(a)

Gentlemen who, like Mr Assheton Smith, wished to represent their shires in the House of Commons and at the same time hunt their fox-hounds two or three days a week, soon learnt to approve a system which brought the best hunting countries within two or three hours' ride of the capital. ⟨1845⟩   J. C. Jeaffreson, *Life of Robert Stephenson* (1864), i. 279

(b)

A line of rails carrying but very few passengers, and none too many goods, was made some years ago from Blisworth to Stratford-on-Avon, with a view to demonstrating to casual travellers how sweet a valley runs across the heart of the Grafton and Warwickshire countries. Though the public fail to avail themselves in any numbers of the means of sight-seeing thus afforded, the railway still exists as a proof of enterprise, and in full possession of a vale that had far better been left for the untrammelled use of fox and hounds and of men who ride after them. ⟨1892⟩

E. Pennell Elmhirst, *Fox-hound, Forest, and Prairie* (1892), 269

(c)

With reference to the hunting, a fair estimate of the landowners' attitude can probably be arrived at by trying to imagine the outcry that would be raised if anything were done to interfere with the amusements of the classes now in power, for instance if an attempt were made to seize football grounds in various parts of the country for use as landing places for public aeroplanes. ⟨1935⟩   Joan Wake, *Northampton Vindicated* (1935), 11

217. THE COMMUNITY'S INTEREST NEGLECTED

The tracing of the new routes of railways which were to join all the chief cities, ports, and naval arsenals of the island was a matter of the highest national importance. But, unfortunately, those who should have acted for the nation refused to interfere. Consequently numerous questions which were really public, questions which concerned the public convenience, the public prosperity, the public security, were treated as private questions. That the whole society was interested in having a good system of internal communication seemed to be forgotten. The speculator who wanted a large dividend on his shares, the landowner who wanted a large price for his acres, obtained a full hearing. But nobody applied to be heard on behalf of the community. The effects of that great error we feel, and we shall not soon cease to feel. ⟨1846⟩

> Macaulay, Speech on the Ten Hours Bill, 22 May 1846:
> *Speeches* (1854), 438

218.   SHOULD THE GOVERNMENT WARN THE PUBLIC?

The Prime Minister, Peel, writes to his Chancellor of the Exchequer, Goulburn, 21 and 27 August 1845:

Direct interference on our part with the mania of railway speculation seems impracticable. The only question is whether public attention might not be called to the impending danger, through the public press. . . . [He then considers the draft of an article for this purpose, sent to him by Goulburn, and replies on 27 August.] I have no alteration to suggest in the accompanying draft. I cannot think the insertion of it runs any risk of producing panic.

It is intended to produce a reasonable apprehension. The Governor [of the Bank of England] rather amuses me. He writes one day under the influence of great alarm, and seems to recommend some forcible intervention on the part of the Government. . . .

If the mischief which he apprehends is really at hand, there will be a panic with a vengeance. ⟨1845⟩

> C. S. Parker (ed.), *Sir Robert Peel* (1899), iii. 188–90

219.   RAILWAY MANIA IN SCOTLAND

28 November 1845. Britain is at present an island of lunatics, all railway mad. The patients are raving in the wildest recesses of the Highlands. The ultimate miracles of railways are obvious. We are not now thinking of such places as London and Edinburgh, or even of Europe. Imagination speculates on America, Asia, and even Africa. It hears the bell of a station at Pekin or Timbuctoo, and sees the smoke of the engine trailing along the valleys of the Rocky Mountains. Distance is diminished twenty-fold. The world is not half the size it was a few years ago. The globe is in the course of being inhabited as one city or shire, everything known to and everything touching everybody. The consequences of the whole human family thus feeling in each thread and living along the line cannot yet be foreseen fully, but there is no reason to doubt that on the whole the result must be good. It will give force to public reason, and thus give great advantages to civilisation over barbarism, and to truth over error.

But in *arranged* countries the change has intolerable present evils – at least in Britain, where the plethora of capital drives the new system on with regardless violence, and where self-interest combines all railway speculators into one corporation, which, with its bursting purse, defies resistance, and respects no feelings but its own. Even juries, our former shields, have been obliged to be superseded as the guardians of private interests, because it is found impossible to get fair ones; and Parliament itself, though it unguardedly conceded to injured parties the right of having their compensation adjusted by arbitrators, is itself to an alarming degree a company of railway owners. The outrages of these speculators are frightful. Their principle is that nothing must obstruct their dividends, which is expressed technically by saying that "the public must be accommodated". This being fixed, all that remains is to ascertain where a line of iron can be laid down horizontally. If the country were a desert, and nothing were to be considered but percentages and engineering, this might be all that required to be thought of; but in a *made-up* country it is the last thing that ought to be regarded. Taste seeks seclusion, and comfort seeks shelter, which implies no great elevation; but railways seek these too. The margin of a loch, the course of a stream, a gentle valley, a wooded plain – these are the railway pastures, for they imply flatness or a gradual rise; and therefore the long domestic happiness or care that may have been enjoyed or lavished upon them are scornfully disregarded. A human bird's-nest, a revered ruin, a noble castle, a poetical stream, a glorious wood, a dialled and urned bowling-green, the cottage where Burns was born, or the abbey where Scott lies buried, all the haunts of long-confiding affection, all the scenes over which taste and genius have lingered, all connected with localities that the heart cares for – what are these to a railway? Must not the public be accommodated? On this phrase the most brutal inroads are making every day, and in the most brutal spirit, on the most sacred haunts.

And the gamblers fancy that everything is compensated out of their fraudulent gambling purse. So it is sometimes. Chiefly when they deal with our poor lairds, who are often so insolvent that to have their places ruined for a few present pounds serves them for the hour. But where a respectable gentleman, a happy family, a widow contented with a comfortable though homely scene of a whole life's enjoyment, do not want their money, how are they treated? Trodden down, threatened with worse lines if they murmur, and defied to bear the expense of parliamentary resistance. The notion of these modern Huns is that everything (a very natural sentiment for them), even amenity, and the disturbance of old habits, can be valued in money. They have no idea that, independently of the loss of property, it is a heavier punishment than the Courts often inflict to be simply driven from Paradise. That helpless individuals should be sacrificed to Juggernaut is not so wonderful; but the apathy, or, which is more common, the treachery of public guardians is scandalous. Public beauty, recreation, or reverence seem to be absolutely abandoned. In addition to our Princes Street Gardens, the South Inch of Perth and the College of Glasgow are almost under sentence. That beautiful piece of verdure, the South Inch, was defended by all people who had no shares; but its destruction was worked by those who had, led on by the Town Council, the city Member, and commissioners from the Board of Trade. In Glasgow the voices of the few men of sense, who are in horror, are drowned by the howls of the selfish mob that is impatient for the sacrifice. The professors expect to gain chiefly by getting better houses, and even they are insensible to the value of age to an academic retreat. No one who lives in this iron age supposes that the Crown will interfere, or that Parliament will object. Yet it is one of the most academical edifices in Scotland, and all the better for being in the heart of a crowded population. This deepens its contrast. The very silence of either of the two quadrangles, when a person (with a soul) turns into them from the roaring street, inspires thought and study. The hall, with its massive, wide marble hearthstone and excellent proportions, is one of the best apartments in Scotland. . . . There is a grey stone image, something like a leopard, perched on one of the pillars of the great outer stair leading up to the hall. It has sat with its fore-legs up and its pleased countenance, smiling graciously on many generations of teachers, and students, and strangers. The head of this single creature is more worth preserving and consulting than the heads of all the living professors. ⟨1845⟩

Journal of Henry Cockburn (1874), ii. 129–33

The carrying of the railway through the Princes Street Gardens in Edinburgh had been authorised by Parliament, against strong opposition, in 1844. The sale of the College in Glasgow to a railway company did not go through at this time, but it was effected in the 1860s; Cockburn discounts too airily the disreputable character of the district in which it was situated. The admirable citizens of Perth who opposed the building of a station on the South Inch did in fact triumph over their MP and Town Council, as well as over the Board of Trade, and the station had to be built on another site further to the west.

220. WHO CAN BE EXEMPT?

(a)

Queen Victoria: "Tell me, oh tell me, dearest Albert, have *you* any railway shares?" ⟨1845⟩   *Punch*, 9 (1845), 182

(b)

Lord Derby had lent money freely to railway companies, at reasonable rates of interest. But when in September 1847 his agent asked for the repayment of part of what was owing from the Manchester & Leeds, he got a chilly answer.

In reference to your intimation that you will require £20,000 between this and Christmas I am requested to state that in the present extraordinary state of the money market our committee do not feel warranted in making you any positive promise, although they will endeavour to do what they can, hoping that some improvement will take place before that time. ⟨1847⟩   Peter Eckersley to Richard Earle, 14 September 1847: Lancashire Record Office, DDK 661/1/26

(c)

Yet prudence, steadily maintained, might prevail, as it did with Brunel.

I stick to my rule – of making what I can by engineering and not trusting myself in speculation. ⟨1851⟩   Brunel to Charles Geach, 27 August 1851: Bristol University Library: Brunel Collection, Letterbook 8, fol. 228

221. WISE IN TIME

I thought you would wonder how we were getting on, when you heard of the railway panic, and you may be sure that I am very glad to be able to answer your kind inquiries by an assurance that our small capital is as yet undiminished. The York & North Midland is, as you say, a very good line; yet, I confess to you, I should wish, for my own part, to be wise in time. I cannot think that even the very best lines will continue for many years at their present premiums; and I have been most anxious for us to sell our shares ere it be too late, and to secure the proceeds in some safer, if, for the present, less profitable investment. I cannot, however, persuade my sisters to regard the affair precisely from my point of view; and I feel as if I would rather run the risk of loss than hurt Emily's feelings by acting in direct opposition to her opinion. She managed in a most handsome and able manner for me when I was in Brussels, and prevented by distance from looking after my own interests; therefore I will let her manage still, and take the consequences. ⟨1846⟩

Charlotte Brontë to Miss Wooler, 30 January 1846:
Mrs Gaskell, *Life of Charlotte Brontë* (Penguin ed.), 289

222. GEORGE HUDSON'S FALL

Gladstone left a copy of these verses among his papers, in his own handwriting. They are probably his own composition.

What's the news upon Change, what's the talk of the town?
'Tis that Hudson was up and that Hudson is down.

He bamboozled the mob, he astonished the quality,
He led both through the quagmire of gross immorality,

But still, there's a maxim, both famous and true,
Give the Devil, nay even give Hudson, his due. . . .

How many thousands that counted their gains
Were miniature Hudsons, excepting the brains!

Who I ask were the Shareholders, greedy of gold,
That bought when he bought and that sold when he sold?

What were the meetings, assemblies of geese
That besought him to buy, or that begged him to lease?

They who lost by the game, every man of them squeaks;
But the winners, how is it no one of them speaks?

Nay both loser and winner foul harm on him cries,
And each piously turns up the whites of his eyes.

The world with its vices is cruel I wis,
But the world in its virtue, God save me from this!
⟨1849⟩   British Library: Add. MS. 44744, fol. 183

223. CLASS DISTINCTIONS

(a)

Though the word "class" has been in use from time immemorial, yet we question much whether the British public had a full practical comprehension of its import till the invention of the rail. John Bull, we believe, knows something about higher, middle, and lower classes; to have attempted any further sub-division would have been offensive alike to his dignity and humanity. It was left for the rail, at once his slave and his master, to teach him a different arrangement. There is your state-carriage, for example, into which no foot less vulgar than royalty dare enter; your first class, with its *coupés* and chairs as elegant and inviting as cushions and velvet can make them; your second class – a little harder in their features, to be sure, but still snug and clean; your third class, in which one shares, in common with some dozen or two, the luxury of a deal seat; and lastly, your fourth class, where seat and covering are alike denied, and where men, women, and children are packed like the cattle which follow on the trucks behind. These humiliating distinctions are but too fully adopted in the ordinary affairs of life. The draper has his fourth-class cloths, the grocer his fourth-class teas; this park is only open to first-class visitors, that common is set aside for the recreation of the working classes – in other words, for classes three and four of the rail. Mr Do'em opens an academy for gentlemen's sons only, meaning thereby class one; and the church, in her charity, sets aside a few rough dingy pews for the use of class four; as if, forsooth, calico could not worship with silk, or moleskin with "superfine invisible". These artificial and absurd distinctions are certainly not to be wholly attributed to the rail; but the rail has done, and is doing, much to disseminate and perpetuate the principle. There are, however, less offensive, nay positively amusing applications of the distinction. Thus the public has its first-class authors, as at Lloyd's they have their first-class vessels: the mechanic talks of a first-class wife, as well as of a first-class tool; and we have even heard a friend go so far as to speak of a fourth-class sermon. ⟨1846⟩   *Chambers' Edinburgh Journal*, 6 (1846), 194

(b)

As he left Leeds in the second-class railway carriage for London, he thought over the result of his visit with considerable satisfaction.

He had left Leeds at ten, and Mr Moulder had come down in the same omnibus to the station, and was travelling in the same train in a first-class carriage. Mr Moulder was a man who despised the second class, and was not slow to say so to other commercials who travelled at a cheaper rate than he did. "Hubbles and Grease", he said, "allowed him respectably, in order that he might go about their business respectable; and he wasn't going to give the firm a bad name by being seen in a second-class carriage, although the difference would go into his own pocket. That wasn't the way he had begun, and that wasn't the way he was going to end." He said nothing to Mr Dockwrath in the morning, merely bowing in answer to that gentleman's salutation. "Hope you were comfortable last night in the back drawing-room", said Mr Dockwrath; but Mr Moulder in reply only looked at him.

At the Mansfield station, Mr Kantwise, with his huge wooden boxes, appeared on the platform, and he got into the same carriage with Mr Dockwrath. He had come on by a night train, and had been doing a stroke of business that morning. "Well, Kantwise", Moulder holloaed out from his warm, well-padded seat, "doing it cheap and nasty, eh?"

"Not at all nasty, Mr Moulder", said the other. "And I find myself among as respectable a class of society in the second class as you do in the first; quite so – and perhaps a little better", Mr Kantwise added, as he took his seat immediately opposite to Mr Dockwrath. "I hope I have the pleasure of seeing you pretty bobbish this morning, sir." And he shook hands cordially with the attorney. ⟨1862⟩

Anthony Trollope, *Orley Farm* (old World's Classics ed.), i. 154–5

(c)

When the Midland Railway announced its intention of providing only two classes of accommodation for its passengers, first and third, there were numerous protests from its competitors who, for various reasons, did not wish to follow its example. Some people argued that the Midland was here disregarding a social law, universally established. A Times *leader said exactly that.*

By universal admission, there are, roughly speaking, three classes in all societies, and the existing arrangement of railway carriages appears to correspond very closely with the ordinary habits of life. ⟨1874⟩

The Times, 12 October 1874. It took fifty years for the Midland's practice to become established throughout Great Britain, and even then some exceptions remained

224. ICHABOD

Ferrybridge was a few years ago a place of great importance, being situated upon the Great North Road and having an immense coaching traffic passing through it daily, to the number of between twenty or thirty. The inns being of the first description, and an immense number of post-horses being kept, the nobility in passing to and from the north availed themselves of its excellent accommodations and stopped here during the night, which gained it a character of being one of the first posting towns in the kingdom; but since the opening of the York & North Midland Railway the traffic has been entirely diverted. ⟨1848⟩

> G. F. Copley, *Guide to the Wakefield Pontefract & Goole Railway* [1848], 48

225. THE MARINE METROPOLIS

This once famous resort of royalty and fashion [Brighton] may now, through the literal as well as metaphorical levelling of the railroad, be fairly entitled to the appellation of the Marine Metropolis. Merchants who formerly made Dulwich or Dalston the boundaries of their suburban residences now have got their mansions on the south coast and still get, in less time, by a less expensive conveyance, to their counting-houses in the City. Excursions are now made with greater facility, and possibly more enjoyment, to Brighton than would have, a few years back, sufficed for the commonplace pilgrimage to Hampton Court. ⟨1848⟩

> E. L. Blanchard, *Adams's Illustrated Descriptive Guide to the Watering-Places of England* (1848), 95–6

226. WILL TOWNS CHANGE PLACES?

(a)

Railways have set all the Towns of Britain a-dancing. Reading is coming up to London, Basingstoke is going down to Gosport or Southampton, Dumfries to Liverpool and Glasgow; while at Crewe, and other points, I see new ganglions of human population establishing themselves, and the prophecy of metallurgic cities which were not heard of before. Reading, Basingstoke, and the rest, the unfortunate Towns, subscribed money to get railways; and it proves to be for cutting their own throats. Their business has gone elsewhither; and they – cannot stay behind their business! They are set a-dancing, as I said; confusedly waltzing, in a state of progressive dissolution, towards the four winds; and know not where the end of the death-dance will be for them, in which point of space they will be allowed to rebuild themselves. That is their sad case. ⟨1850⟩

> Thomas Carlyle, *Latter-day Pamphlets* (1858 ed.), 229

(b)

The writer of this letter is urging the extension of the railway north of Aylesbury.

It appears to me to be a question of the last importance to Aylesbury and its inhabitants that these nine miles should be completed. . . . Already the transmission of letters to Quainton and other villages has been removed from Aylesbury to Winslow [where a station had been opened in the preceding month], and with the letters will go the traffic and perhaps the market also, and we shall have Winslow and Aylesbury changing places. ⟨1850⟩ G. Pigott to A. Tindal, 13 June 1850: Buckinghamshire Record Office, D/TL/46/B2

227. PETERBOROUGH

Peterborough presents an instance of a city without population, without manufactures, without trade, without a good inn, or even a copy of the *Times*, except at the railway station; a city which would have gone on slumbering to the present hour without a go-ahead principle of any kind, and which has nevertheless, by the accident of situation, had railway greatness thrust upon it in a most extraordinary manner.

Peterborough is one of the centres from which radiate three lines to London [together with four going in other directions]. . . . There is, therefore, the best of consolation on being landed in this dull inhospitable city, that it is the easiest possible thing to leave it. ⟨1851⟩

Samuel Sidney, *Rides on Railways* (1851), 61

228. TAKING TRADE AWAY

(a)

As regards the advantage this Rail will be to the trade of Horncastle – can you for a moment suppose that its trading establishments, such as grocers, linendrapers, ironmongers, chemists, etc. are of that quality and consideration to tempt parties living at a distance, say Boston or Lincoln, to come to Horncastle by rail to make purchases? or don't you rather think it more probable that the few independent people living in Horncastle and neighbourhood would take advantage of the rail to go to Boston or Lincoln, where there is most certainly a better, larger, and cheaper assortment of goods for sale, to make their purchases, instead of Horncastle? . . . Ask the tradesmen of Alford, Market Rasen, or any other small market town how much their rail has benefited or rather injured them? The fact is that this proposed railway would be for the benefit of Boston and Lincoln, and the damage of the trade of Horncastle! ⟨1853⟩

> Flysheet letter from "Fairplay" to the Provisional
> Committee of the Horncastle & Kirkstead Junction
> Railway: Lincolnshire Record Office, 2TP 3/1/1

(b)

Every railway takes trade from the little town to the big town, because it enables the customer to buy in the big town. ⟨1866⟩

> Walter Bagehot, *The English Constitution*, chap. 5:
> *Collected Works* (1965–86), v. 310

229.   RAILWAY PICKPOCKETS

This is the same class of persons who pick pockets on the public street as already observed. They often visit the various railway stations and are generally smartly dressed as they linger there – some of them better than others. Some of the females are dressed like shopkeepers' wives, others like milliners, varying from nineteen to forty years of age, mostly from nineteen to twenty-five; some of them attired in cotton gowns, others in silks and satins.

At the railway stations they are generally seen moving restlessly about from one place to another, as if they did not intend to go by any particular train. There is an unrest about the most of them which to a discerning eye would attract attention.

They seldom take the train, but dangle among the throng around the ticket office, or on the platform beside the railway carriages on the eve of the train starting off, as well as when the train arrives. When they see ladies engaged in conversation they go up to them and plant themselves by their side, while the others cover their movements. There generally are two, sometimes three of them in a party. They place themselves on the right-hand side of the ladies, next to the pocket, and work with the left hand. When the ladies move, the thieves walk along with them.

The female pickpockets generally carry a reticule on their right arm so as to take off suspicion, and walk up to the persons at the railway station, and inquire what time the train starts to such and such a place, to detain them in conversation and to keep them in their company.

The older female thieves generally look cool and weary, the younger ones are more restless and suspicious in their movements. They sometimes go into first and second-class waiting rooms and sit by the side of any lady they suppose to be possessed of a sum of money, and try to pick her pocket by inserting their hand, or by cutting it with a knife or other sharp instrument. They generally insert the whole hand, as the ladies' pockets are frequently deep in the dress. They often have a large cape to cover their hands, and pick the pocket while speaking to the lady, or sitting by her side. The young pickpockets are generally the most expert.

They seldom take the brooch from the breast, but confine themselves to picking pockets.

After they take the purse, they generally run to some by-place and throw it away, so that it cannot be identified; sometimes they put it into a water-closet, at other times they drop it down an area as they pass along.

After taking the purse, the thief hands it to her companion and they separate and walk away, and meet at some place appointed.

They occasionally travel with the trains to the Crystal Palace and other places in the neighbourhood of London, and endeavour to plunder the passengers on the way. Frequently they take longer excursions – especially during the summer – journeying from town to town, and going to races and markets, agricultural shows, or any places where there is a large concourse of people. Unless they are detected at the time they pick the pocket, they seldom leave any suspicion behind them, as they take care to lodge in respectable places, where no one would suspect them, and have generally plenty of money.

A considerable number of the male thieves also attend the railway stations, and pick pockets in the railway trains. They are generally well dressed, and many of them have an Inverness cape, often of a dark colour, and sometimes they carry a coat on their arm to hide their hand. There are commonly two or more of them together – sometimes women accompanying them. ⟨1862⟩

Henry Mayhew, *London Labour and the London Poor* (1862), 310

230. PROGRESS IN THE LAKE DISTRICT

We have no fear of injury, moral or economical, from the great recent change – the introduction of railways. The morals of rural districts are usually such as cannot well be made worse by any change. Drinking and kindred vices abound wherever, in our day, intellectual resources are absent: and nowhere is drunkenness a more prevalent and desperate curse than in the Lake District. Any infusion of the intelligence and varied interests of the townspeople must, it appears, be eminently beneficial: and the order of workpeople brought by the railways is of a desirable kind. And as to the economical effect – it cannot but be good, considering that mental stimulus and improved education are above everything wanted. Under the old seclusion, the material comfort of the inhabitants had long been dwindling; and their best chance of recovery is clearly in the widest possible intercourse with classes which, parallel in social rank, are more intelligent and better informed than themselves. . . .

The best, as well as the last and greatest change in the Lake District is that which is arising from the introduction of the railroad. ⟨1855⟩

> Harriet Martineau, *Guide to the English Lakes*
> (1855), 141–4

231. RAILWAYS AND PRIZE-FIGHTING

County magistrates had intervened to stop prize-fights with ungloved fists, in accordance with a judgment of 1826. But the speed of railway communication allowed meetings for such purposes to be held near the border of one county and then, on the approach of the police, to be transferred to another: as in Kent on 20 September 1859.

A special train belonging to the South Eastern Railway Company passed through the county containing a large number of people intent on getting off one or two prize fights in some locality unguarded by the police. The train was stopped in the parish of Leigh, in the Tonbridge division, but owing to the extreme zeal, vigilance, and alacrity shown by Superintendent Danes and the constables of that division, the peace in the County of Kent was preserved and the train proceeded to Etchingham in the County of Sussex, where one or two prize fights took place. ⟨1859⟩

> Chief Constable's report to the magistrates, 25 October 1859: Kent Archives Office, Q GB 41 (bundle B). Railway companies were statutorily forbidden to run special trains to prize fights in 1868

232. SUBURBAN DEVELOPMENT

It was announced [in May 1860] that a free first-class ticket valid for ten years would be granted to anyone building a "villa" of the annual poor-law valuation of £25 or over, within one mile of any of the stations between Belfast and Carrickfergus and to Londonderry or Coleraine for houses at Castlerock. Plans had to be submitted to the railway's engineer for approval *before* building commenced. Later the scheme was extended to include the entire Larne line when the extension was opened, and similar arrangements were made for second-class free travel for houses with a somewhat lower rateable value. This villa ticket system was the means of developing considerably such suburbs of Belfast as Whiteabbey, Jordanstown, Greenisland, and also Castlerock, but above all it was largely responsible for the rise of Whitehead from very meagre beginnings.[1] ⟨1860⟩   J. R. L. Currie, *The Northern Counties Railway*, (1973), i. 108

233.   THE RAILWAY IN WARFARE

William Bridges Adams develops here some of his ideas about the use of railways in national defence. Though his plan for lines to be built encircling London was never carried out, he was one of the earliest advocates of the railway-moved gun and the armoured train, which were used extensively in war in the later nineteenth century and the twentieth.

For the purpose of defending a country, railways might most advantageously be used for practical fighting purposes. Supposing that a railway were made in a line parallel to the coast, with a parapet embankment, no troops could get inland without crossing it; and supposing that the opposing troops, riflemen and artillerymen, were carried on moving forts along the line, the invaders could be destroyed at will, unless we suppose vessels to lie close to the shore to support them. . . . A moving fort on a railway, as compared with a stationary fort, has the same advantage that a vessel has on the water, and the invading enemy, to be on a par with the invaded, must bring batteries of railway artillery with him. And that artillery must be at least of the same weight and range as the artillery of the defenders. . . .

The most economical method of using artillery is to mount it on rail platforms instead of on fixed forts or batteries, because by this process one gun becomes the equivalent of many. The obvious advantage is that an ordinary enemy can actually be pursued by the fort, instead of being permitted to move round it at a distance. The invading army would experience a difficulty of the same kind after landing as before landing – land ships, instead of water ships, carrying the heaviest projectiles at the longest ranges. And bodies of riflemen, or other accurate shooters, might be practically formed into the equivalent of cavalry, to meet any attempt to storm the line of rail, by placing them in plated wagons, shot-proof and loop-holed. . . .

[The invaders might] have to encounter a circular railway, a line much

[1] On that see further in 250.

needed for connecting the radial lines, and forming a parallel around London as a centre. A fifteen-miles' radius would take in, or approach, Gravesend, Tilbury, Epping, St Albans, Uxbridge, Windsor, Epsom, and Reigate. . . . An inner circle would be about an eight miles' radius from the Post Office, and would take in, or approach, Harrow, Barnet, Romford, Woolwich, Sydenham, Croydon, Wimbledon, and Staines. The outer circle would be about ninety miles in length, the inner fifty miles, and they would be connected by all the radiating lines from London, which they would intersect, passing under or over them, or communicating with them. . . .

The attack on London would be a question of regular siege, with the first parallels to be opened at five miles' distance from the outside circular line, and with the necessity for a steam railway thoroughly defended. . . . The soldiers manning the circular lines of railway would be the volunteers, whose playground they would become, and who would know every inch of their defences. The machinists would be the general railway operatives and engineers, ready to keep the whole in repair in case of damage. . . .

The war in America has demonstrated beyond doubt that victory belongs to heavy and accurate artillery capable of rapid movement. Forts and armies have fallen down before the fire of gunboats. Had the Confederates possessed gun-wagons on rails, they would have had the same advantages on land that the Federals have had on water. There is less difficulty in clothing a railway wagon in plate-armour than a gunboat on water, and the nation that wilfully ignores this modern element in war will have to deplore the oversight when occasion shall arise for its use, and perchance too late. Even as the railway has superseded the canal, so will the railway artillery, moved by steam, supersede all that has hitherto been moved by horse power.

The heroic William Peel, both in the Crimea and in India, carried his great ship guns ashore and marched at the head of his sailors, who drew them to the siege of strongholds. Greater guns than his, with the sailors riding on them instead of drawing them, on iron instead of earthen roads, must be the rule of the future. ⟨1862⟩

W. B. Adams, *Roads and Rails* (1862), 332–53. For another similar plan see no. 253

234.   HAVE YOU A STATION NEAR BY?

Palmerston is speaking, at Bradford:

Formerly, when a gentleman asked a friend in London to come down to him in the country, the friend came with things to last him for a fortnight or three weeks, and took perhaps a week on the journey. Now, if one gentleman meets another, say in St James's Street, he says "I shall have some good shooting next week. Will you come down to me and spend a few days?" His friend replies, "Oh by all means. I shall be charmed. What is the station nearest your house?" The first speaker rejoins, "Why, I am not very well off at present in regard to railway communication – the nearest station is sixteen miles from my house. But it is a good road. You will get a nice fly, and you can come very well." Upon this the invited guest says, "Did you say it was Tuesday you asked me for?" "Yes", says the country gentleman, "I think you told me you were free". "The fact is", answers the friend, "I have a very bad memory, and now I think of it I am very sorry, but I have a particular engagement for that day – some other time I shall be happy to go to you." And so away he goes, and offers himself as a visitor to some other friend, who has got a station within one or two miles of his house. ⟨1864⟩

Walter Bagehot, *Collected Works* (1965–86), iii. 280–1

235. SOCIAL REVOLUTION IN WALES

At Llanrwst we dined, and got back here [Llandudno] by the train a little after eight o'clock. The people travelling about in Wales, and their quality, beggar description. It is a social revolution which is taking place, and to observe it may well fill one with reflexion. ⟨1864⟩

Matthew Arnold to his mother, 20 August 1864:
Letters (1895), i. 236

236. NATIONALISATION ADVOCATED
IN THE 1860s

"Little to pay for locomotion, and that little *known*": this is the rule for augmenting the amount of locomotion, and for increasing its yield. The railway companies never will – never can – try this great experiment, and the government might and could; and this is a great reason why the government ownership of the railways would be more useful to the public than a private ownership.

But though it is the most conspicuous, and perhaps the most forcible reason, it is not the only reason. The division of *jurisdictions* in the railway kingdom is an inconvenience, like the separation of political states. You often cannot get out of one into the other. If one company own an arc, and another the chord of that arc, and you happen for any other purpose to get on the line of company No. I, you will have to go by its curve; you will never get on to the line – the straight line – of company No. II. The trains will "dodge" you: the train you want to go by in the adverse jurisdiction will have just gone whenever you happen to arrive, and it will be pleasanter to go at once the long way round, than three hours hence to begin the straight journey.

Goods are driven about in the same arbitrary and capricious way as persons. Every line tries to keep every man and everything as long as it can, and to get the most out of him, even by compelling him to travel twice the distance that he need. Parliament felt this difficulty acutely some years ago, and gave a power to a court of law – the Court of Common Pleas – to interfere in such cases. But Lord Campbell justly said at the time that no judge could adjust a timetable. . . . The Court of Common Pleas has never effectually exercised its powers, and never will. The remedy provided by Parliament has failed, but the evil to be remedied remains. As long as there are separate realms with hostile interests in the railway world, all prescriptions will fail. The substitution of a single owner for this infinity of owners is the sole effectual cure.

Again, the present railways injure the working class of large towns by the construction of their works, but do not benefit it by their administration, at least not equally or as much as they might. A railway has to go through a poor suburb of a big town, through the working-class quarter: it demolishes the houses, already too full; it increases the compression, already too great. But though it pulls down the old dwellings of labourers, it does not take them to new dwellings. Lord Derby presented a resolution to the House of Lords compelling railways near large towns to have a cheap working-class train, night and morning, suitable for daily labour. But with the present management we have no such train. We are not likely to see such a resolution turned into an Act of Parliament in the face of many resisting companies. We are not likely to see such an Act fairly worked by these companies. But the government, if they owned the railways, might give the working class their share in the benefits of quick locomotion, though it will never get it from others.[1] ⟨1865⟩

Walter Bagehot in the *Economist*, 7 January 1865:
Collected Works (1965–86), x. 449–50

237.   RAILWAY PROPERTY DISCREDITED

During the financial panic of May 1866 bank rate was raised to 10%. It was then lowered cautiously, until by July 1867 it had come down to 2%. But cheap money produced no immediate revival of commercial activity.

[1] Such trains were already being "fairly worked" when Bagehot wrote (though not under statutory compulsion) on the Metropolitan Railway. The first to be run in compliance with an Act of Parliament were started between Ludgate Hill, Brixton, and Victoria six weeks after this article of Bagehot's was published. Here – for once – he proved a false prophet.

The depreciated value of the shares even in the soundest railway undertakings, and the difficulty which some of these companies experienced in renewing their debentures even on very advanced terms, testified that to them at least money was anything but cheap and the supply of capital by no means abundant. . . . With regard to railway companies in particular, a new cause of distrust was added to those which had already seriously affected their standing in the confidence of the public and depreciated the value of their shares. Fresh disclosures were made of irregularities and unsoundness in the accounts of some of these undertakings, which not only produced an enormous collapse in the prosperity of those companies but threw a discredit over railway property in general, and involved all railway management more or less in the general suspicion. The discovery that the Brighton Railway Company, hitherto supposed to be one of the most prosperous of these concerns, had been carrying on a delusive financial system; that the accounts of the North British had been deceptively manipulated; that the Great Eastern and Great Western were in serious financial straits, and that the London Chatham & Dover was in a state of utter insolvency, cast an atmosphere of distrust and discredit over all railway property. ⟨1867⟩   *Annual Register*, 1867, 202–3

238. RAILWAYS AND TEMPERANCE

A combination of social forces and temperance pressure severely curtailed the drinkseller's importance as provider of local meeting places during the Early Victorian period. The greatest blow came, not from the temperance reformers, but from the railway. Although some early railways used inns as stopping places, their role was soon taken over by railway stations. As the railway prospered after the 1840s, so the drinking place declined; as the railway declined in the twentieth century, so the drinking place partially revived.

There was almost as close a kinship between the railway and the temperance reformer as between horse-drawn travel and the publican. In no place was the teetotal orator made less welcome than in the coaching village. Both the railway and the temperance society constituted a threat to the agricultural interest; temperance reformers invested in early railways, regarded them as a beneficent social and political influence, were employed on them, were encouraged by the railway companies, and travelled conspicuously on their trains. . . .

Early railway promoters did not always recognise the likely effects of the new form of transport on public sobriety, or that the reduced exhaustion of travel would also reduce the need for intoxicants. Their stations therefore provided drink facilities at least as lavish as those to which road travellers had been accustomed. Most early railway stations had sections assigned to the sale of intoxicants, or at least had their "Railway Arms" nearby. Early railway travellers set off well fortified with bottles of spirits, and even in the 1870s they frequently treated railwaymen with drink. Yet with all these qualifications, the railway probably did more for temperance in the nineteenth century – the gaslamp more for morality – then either the temperance movement or the Vice Society. ⟨1840s–70s⟩

Brian Harrison, *Drink and the Victorians* (1971), 334–6

239. THE MORETONHAMPSTEAD BRANCH

After the railway came [in 1866] the trains proclaimed the hours, as most knew the timetables approximately, calling the 8.19 the 8, the 11.37 the 12, etc. – odd minutes did not count. As the trains upon this branch were "mixed", partly passenger and partly goods, there generally was some shunting to be done; but this caused no delay, as the timetables allowed for it. If there was no shunting, the train just waited at the station till the specified time was up. The driver of the evening train would often give displays of hooting with the engine whistle while he was stopping here, and would stay on over time if the owls were answering back.

The engines on this branch were quite unequal to their work, and there were no effective brakes then. Coming down the incline here, trains often passed the station; and passengers had to walk from where their train had stopped. My grandfather writes to my father, 12 March 1867, "On Saturday we had a runaway on the rails. The train passed here at four o'clock with two carriages, two trucks, and a van, and could not get on further than Sandick road, so unhooked the trucks and was not careful to secure them, and they went off and passed the station full 40 miles an hour. I was at the stile when they passed. Luckily did no harm and stopped at Teigngrace, and the engine came back and fetched them". . . .

When it was a novelty here, our line had great attractions for young men and boys, and many of them left their work upon the land. I lost sight of one family for thirty years or more, and on inquiry I found their history was this – "Well, one of'n went on the line, and he become a stationmaster; and 'nother, he went on the line, and he become a ganger; and t'other, he were a-runned over by a train, and so, as us may say, they was all connected with the railway". ⟨c.1870⟩

Cecil Torr, *Small Talk at Wreyland* (1918–23), iii. 12–13

240. WILTSHIRE DIVIDED

This county is divided into two almost completely separate portions by the long range of somewhat bleak downs which run almost due east and west. Before the new railway [the Swindon Marlborough & Andover] was opened in 1881, the traveller in North Wilts who wished to visit South Wilts usually hired a trap or a farmer's cart, for other convenient means of communication did not exist. If he insisted on travelling by rail he could do so, either by going to Reading towards the east and doubling back along a railway some miles to the south of the downs parallel to his former route, or by performing a similar circuitous journey in the opposite direction via Holt Junction near Trowbridge. And all this only took him through Mid-Wiltshire, for it required similar circuitous journeys via Basingstoke on the east, or Westbury on the west, to enable him to reach Salisbury. The trains over these routes were few and far between and of that slow variety which made the blades of grass in the fields appear nearly as far apart as quarter mileposts. ⟨1870s⟩

> E. L. Ahrons, *Locomotive and Train Working in the Latter*
> *Part of the Nineteenth Century* (1951–4), iv. 120

241. FAIR WAGES

Yes! the demands of the labouring classes are large as you say, but you will agree with me that they are entitled to a *fair* share of the general prosperity. I should be glad to see our office clerks getting some general advance and I intend to bring the subject up again. ⟨1871⟩

> E. S. Ellis, chairman of the Midland Railway, to W. H.
> Hodges, the company's accountant, 28 December 1871:
> Public Record Office, RAIL 491/962

242. THE CONISTON PEASANT

In old times, if a Coniston peasant had any business at Ulverstone, he walked to Ulverstone; spent nothing but shoe-leather on the road, drank at the streams, and if he spent a couple of batz [three pence] when he got to Ulverstone, "it was the end of the world". But now, he would never think of doing such a thing! He first walks three miles in a contrary direction, to a railroad station, and then travels by railroad twenty-four miles to Ulverstone, paying two shillings fare. During the twenty-four miles transit, he is idle, dusty, stupid; and either more hot or cold than is pleasant to him. In either case he drinks beer at two or three of the stations, passes his time, between them, with anybody he can find, in talking without having anything to talk of; and such talk always becomes vicious. He arrives at Ulverstone, jaded, half drunk, and otherwise demoralised, and three shillings, at least, poorer than in the morning. Of that sum a shilling has gone for beer, threepence to a railway shareholder, threepence in coals, and eighteenpence has been spent in employing strong men in the vile mechanical work of making and driving a machine, instead of his own legs, to carry the drunken lout. The results, absolute loss and demoralisation to the poor, on all sides, and iniquitous gain to the rich. ⟨1874⟩

John Ruskin: *Fors Clavigera*, Letter 44: *Works*, ed. E. T. Cook and A. Wedderburn (1903–12), xxviii. 129–30

243. BENEFITS CONFERRED BY A BRANCH LINE

Things had perhaps reached the lowest stage at St Ives [in Cornwall] about the year 1877, at which period mining was at a standstill, owing to the importation of cheap tin from the Colonies, and the pilchards had for several years seemed to shun the Bay of St Ives. On 24 May 1877 the new railway from St Erth on the main line, to St Ives, was opened, and the town soon began to receive the advance guard of the host of London visitors which has since invaded it. It is upon these visitors, the majority of whom belong to a wealthy class, that St Ives mainly depends for the support of its inhabitants. Great contrasts are observable in the condition of the town at present as compared with its state "before the railway". Previous to 1877 St Ives was hardly ever visited by tourists, and held but little communication with the outer world. Travellers drove from the junction, then called St Ives Road station, in a bus, which took a considerable time to perform the journey. The advent of this bus was looked forward to as a daily treat, the greatest interest being taken in the arrival of any stranger from "foreign parts". But now the many trains come in and go away without exciting much notice. Such goods as fish and early vegetables are now sent direct to the metropolis, greatly to the advantage of the townspeople; nor could the neighbourhood dispense with the large number of visitors who now come every year to circulate money in this remote watering-place. On the other hand, the fishermen and gardeners of the neighbourhood have not been benefited by the railway to the extent that they anticipated, owing to the reluctance of the Great Western Railway Company to moderate their charges. ⟨1877–92⟩   J. H. Matthews, *History of St Ives* (1892), 368

244. THE RAILWAY IN BIRMINGHAM

The railway system . . . has largely altered the centre of the town, especially through the station extensions of the North Western and Midland lines in the neighbourhood of New Street and Suffolk Street; while the Great Western has done much the same for the district including Monmouth Street, Snow Hill, and Livery Street. In each instance insanitary areas have been cleared, streets abolished, new thoroughfares opened, and leading lines of communications improved. To these railway extensions, involving the consequent development of purely local traffic, a large part of suburban Birmingham owes its progress. ⟨1880⟩

> J. T. Bunce, *History of the Corporation of Birmingham*,
> vol. ii. (1885), p. xxiii

245. THE RAILWAY IN THE VICTORIAN CITY

The direct effects of railway building are, after all, considerable enough in themselves to require no exaggeration. They profoundly influenced the internal flows of traffic, the choices of site and patterns of land use, the residential densities and development prospects of the central and inner districts of the Victorian city. . . . They manipulated local authorities, overloaded Parliament, wrecked or evaded attempts at bureaucratic control, monopolised for specialised uses large areas of urban land which are only partially being released again in the 1960s, cut great swathes through the cities as completely as a blitz. Admittedly the nature and timing of the outward expansion of residential housing depended partly upon the growth of demand factors in the economy; the location of that growth depended partly upon land ownership; but it was the railway which made feasible the widely-spaced clusters of villa residences which provided a Victorian nucleus for the more intensive development of many a dormitory suburb in the twentieth century. . . .

In many ways urban landowners were the most important single agents of change; more important than the railway managers, whose imagination and foresight could often be exercised only within very strict limits. The landowners profited at all stages of railway building, and probably exercised the greatest single influence upon the selection of central sites, upon the location and character of suburbs; and even exercised a lesser, though still considerable influence upon the costs of the service offered. . . .

If one bears in mind the large practical role in urban growth played by orthodox, horse-drawn transport, and the very broad limits within which growth was possible without steam locomotion – at least to the two million population total achieved by pre-railway London – the railways fall into a more modest perspective. To stress the subordination of railway building to these larger processes, and to underline the pre-eminent importance of property ownership and land value patterns, is not to diminish the importance of the railways, but rather to attempt to weave them into the more general texture of urban history. ⟨1837–1901⟩

J. R. Kellett, The Impact of Railways on Victorian Cities
(1969), 419–24

246. THE EXTENSION OF RAILWAYS IN THE LAKE DISTRICT

From Wordsworth's time onwards there was constant opposition to extending railways in the Lake District, and a Lake District Defence Society was formed for this purpose, at a meeting presided over by Matthew Arnold, in 1883. There were some responsible people, however, who looked on it rather coolly.

I am not much inclined to join the "Lake District Defence Society". I value natural beauty as much as most people – indeed I value it so much, and think so highly of its influence that I would make beautiful scenery accessible to all the world, if I could. If any engineering or mining work is projected which will really destroy the beauty of the Lakes, I will certainly oppose it, but I am not disposed, as Goschen said, to "give a blank cheque" to a Defence Society, the force of which is pretty certain to be wielded by the most irrational fanatics among its members.

Only the other day I walked the whole length of Bassenthwaite from Keswick and back, and I cannot say that the little line of rails which runs along the lake, now coming into view and now disappearing, interfered with my keen enjoyment of the beauty of the lake any more than the macadamised road did. And if it had not been for that railway I should not have been able to make Keswick my headquarters, and I should have lost my day's delight.

People's sense of beauty should be more robust. I have had apocalyptic visions looking down Oxford Street at a sunset before now. ⟨1886⟩

T. H. Huxley to his eldest son, 6 July 1886: Leonard
Huxley, Life and Letters of Thomas Henry Huxley
(1913 ed.), ii. 454–5

247. EMIGRANTS

The scenery, however, was not the only thing that impressed me that morning on Spey-side. As the train ran into Aberlour station, there was an unusual number of people and an unusual excitement on the platform, with an amount of luggage that even in August would have been considered respectable. The large square wooden boxes with their big printed labels, "Anchor Line – not wanted on voyage", soon told their own tale. It was a party of emigrants *en route* for New York; "going away", as the engine-driver phrased it with the pathos of simplicity. Not indeed as friendless outcasts, for the laird himself – who probably knew something as to the contents of those substantial boxes – had come down to see them off, and wrung their hands as he wished them God speed; and when, a moment afterwards, the train sped unconcernedly on its way, all along the line for several miles, at the door of every cottage, from which the blue wreath of peat smoke curling up showed there was someone at home, friends had gathered to wave their hands and wish them once more good-bye. ⟨1889⟩   W. M. Acworth, *The Railways of Scotland* (1890), 134–5

248. AN ENORMOUS INVESTMENT

I have been connected with the construction and management of all the railways now forming the Highland system since the commencement of the undertakings.

The sum subscribed by me was £357,142. . . .

In my opinion it would be unfair, after the sacrifices that were made in the construction of the Highland line, to sanction a competing scheme unless it were much more necessary in the public interest than this line is. Fort William is the only place calling for railway accommodation, and it is already well supplied by steamers from Oban, Glasgow, and Inverness. I believe that the population of the town is about 1600, and it is simply a Highland village without trade or manufacture. ⟨1889⟩

Proof of evidence submitted by the 3rd Duke of Sutherland in opposition to the proposed West Highland Railway, 1889; copy in Staffordshire Record Office, D593, P/33/12

249. COMMUTING

(a)

THIRTY BOB A WEEK

For like a mole I journey in the dark,
  A-travelling along the underground
From my Pillared Halls and broad Suburbean Park,
  To come the daily dull official round;
And home again at night with my pipe all alight,
  A-scheming how to count ten bob a pound. . . .
⟨c.1890⟩   John Davidson, *Ballads and Songs* (1894), 42

(b)

OUR SUBURB

He leaned upon the narrow wall
That set the limit to his ground,
And marvelled, thinking of it all,
That he such happiness had found.

He had no word for it but bliss;
He smoked his pipe; he thanked his stars;
And, what more wonderful than this?
He blessed the groaning, stinking cars[1]

That made it doubly sweet to win
The respite of the hours apart
From all the broil and sin and din
Of London's damnèd money-mart.
⟨1906⟩   Ernest Radford, *A Collection*
                   of Poems (1906), 60

(c)

The commuter – *l'homme moyen de notre époque*. The anti-hero of our age. More than the soldier, the nuclear physicist, the political prisoner or the starving child, he indicates where we've gone wrong. ⟨1984⟩
                   Tiresias [Roger Green], *Notes from Overground* (1984), 8

[1] Underground, old style (*Author's note*). The Metropolitan and District lines were electrified in 1905.

(d)

People ask why the Second World War produced so few War Poets. They see this as a perfectly natural and legitimate question. They expect poetry to have come out of that hell. It does not even occur to them to demand Commuter Poets. Few know that our hell exists. Fewer still expect to hear from it so much as a lost linnet singing. Commuting and war have this in common – they force people to come out into the open and make their private behaviour public. Cf. Henry Moore's studies of sleeping figures taking refuge in the underground. The Government ought to commission Train Artists, for, without some kind of record, posterity will never believe that this huge quiet disaster occurred. ⟨1984⟩ *Ibid.*, 195

250. SEASIDE RESORT

The little town of Whitehead [see 232] was growing by leaps and bounds, largely thanks to the villa tickets, the Belfast & Northern Counties Railway fulfilling many of the functions of a local authority. The 1899 Act gave the B & NC authority to build a promenade and landing stage at Whitehead and an agreement was signed with the Board of Trade on 21 January 1901 assigning the railway a portion of the foreshore. The promenade, some half a mile in length, bore tribute to its owners, since it was largely built of railway sleepers and lit by typical railway-style oil lamps. It gave the town a real tourist attraction and was the source of much pride to the company. The landing stage enabled pleasure boats to tie up.

It was also necessary to provide a beach, which was lacking. To overcome this deficiency Wise [the company's engineer], with his usual enterprise, imported sand by special train from Portrush and, to protect the new strand, groynes of old sleepers were built! A bandstand was built on the promenade ("Marine Parade" was its official title) and here on Waterloo night four or five bands provided the music and there was a display of what the Victorians called "pyrotechnics". Ladies' and gents' bathing places, with the usual boxes, completed the new facilities. . . .

Further north of Whitehead on the eastern coast of Islandmagee lies the region of high basaltic cliffs known as the Gobbins. They reach a height of 250ft and were then approachable only by water. . . . Wise set out to build a path which for long stretches was quarried out of solid basalt only a few feet above the sea. Steps were cut to reach the various levels and across ravines bridges were thrown; at one point two bridges connected a spectacular feature, the "Man o' War's Stack", to the main path, one of these tubular bridges being 70ft long. These and the other bridges were built at Belfast, then hauled out from Whitehead on barges and laboriously lifted into place.

The first section was completed in August 1902 in time for the visit to Belfast of the British Association. On 20 August a special train carried the members, who had elected Wise chairman for the visit, and the Northern Counties directors to Ballycarry, and thence they were led over the path by the engineer "whose skill ... has added so much to the success of the Northern Counties Railway". ⟨1899–1902⟩

> J. R. L. Currie, *The Northern Counties Railway*,
> (1973), i. 249–52

251. SOCIAL DIVISIONS

Every morning in my childhood the business men caught the 8.25 or the 8.50 or the 9.18 trains into Manchester. The times are graven in my memory. Anyone out early would see them hurrying to the station, one lot down the "back hill" – Dr Hopkinson from Ferns, Mr Schill from Croston Towers, Mr Bles from Underwood, Mr Lees from St Mary's Clyffe and Mr Pilkington from Firwood. And then there would be another stream down the "front" hill, the Macclesfield road; this would include Mr Crewdson from Springfield, Mr Worthington and his sons from Broomfield, Mr Roby and funny old Dr Wilde who was a distinguished scientist. At the station other streamlets would converge from roads which struck out into the plain from the village. In one of these would be found Mr Cobbett, a grandson of the great Tory-Radical pamphleteer.

The business men travelled, of course, in the first-class carriages, dividing easily into groups so that compartments were made up between more or less particular cronies. The young men who got together in this way made, I fancy, a boisterous journey; the elders probably read *The Times* or the *Morning Post*, but most frequently the *Manchester Guardian*. But I can only tell by hearsay, for any wife or daughter who had to go into Manchester by one of those trains always travelled third; to share a compartment with the "gentlemen" (we were taught never to call them just plainly "men") would have been unthinkable. Indeed, the ladies always avoided the business trains if they possibly could. It was highly embarrassing, a sort of indelicacy, to stand on the platform surrounded by a crowd of males who had to be polite but were obviously not in the mood for feminine society. ⟨c. 1900⟩   Katharine Chorley, *Manchester Made Them* (1950), 114–15

252.   TAKING THE TIME FROM THE TRAIN

These cottagers told the time by the smoke of the trains which passed in the valley. They got up by the milk train between four and five; they had breakfast by the paper train at half-past seven: the London express at half-past twelve was their dinner-bell. If they had a clock, they did not use it or even wind it up. ⟨1907⟩

> Edith Olivier, *Without Knowing Mr Walkley* (1939 ed.), 113. The cottagers lived in the neighbourhood of Salisbury race-course, south-west of the city

253.   A STRATEGIC RAILWAY

The attitude of Parliament and of British authorities in general has not been sympathetic to suggestions of strategical railways, even when proposals put forward have had the support of the War Office itself.

This tendency was well shown in connection with the Northern Junction Railway scheme which was inquired into by a Select Committee of the House of Commons in 1913. Under the scheme in question, a railway was to be constructed from Brentford, on the west of London, passing through Acton, Ealing, Wembley Park, Hampstead, and Finchley, and establishing connections with and between several of the existing main-line systems. In this respect it compared with those "outer circle" railway systems which, as a further result of the war of 1870–1, were expressly designed by the French government for the better defence of Paris. . . .

Strong opposition was offered, however, on the ground that the construction of the line would do "irreparable damage" to the amenities of the Hampstead Garden Suburb; and, after a sitting which extended over several days, the Committee threw out the Bill, the Chairman subsequently admitting that "they had been influenced very largely by the objection of the Hampstead Garden Suburb".

In 1914 the scheme was introduced afresh into the House of Commons, with certain modifications, the proposed line of route no longer passing through the Hampstead Garden Suburb, though near to it. One member of the House said he had collaborated in promoting the Bill because "he most earnestly believed this railway was of vital import to the mobilisation of our troops in time of emergency"; but another declared that the alleged military necessity for the railway was "all fudge", while much was now said as to the pernicious effect the line would have on the highly-desirable residential district of Finchley. In the result strategical considerations were again set aside, and the House rejected the Bill by a majority of seventy-seven. ⟨1913–14⟩   E. A. Pratt, *The Rise of Rail-Power in War and Conquest* (1915), 203–4

254. IRISH CATTLE FAIRS

Livestock traffic formed an important part of the freight workings. Much of it was contributed from the west of the province [of Ulster], often coming from the Sligo Leitrim & Northern Counties Railway into Enniskillen.

In connection with the periodic fairs that were held at various places, special livestock trains were run to each centre monthly, or in some cases fortnightly. In the area served by the Great Northern system there were about fifty such fairs held in the course of a month. Animals were generally walked in by their owners to the fairground in the early morning; after sale they were driven to the railway station for loading and dispatch by a train which had come in empty earlier in the day. In some cases one station's traffic was contributed by several neighbouring fairs; thus Carrickmacross derived traffic not only from its own fair, held on the second Thursday of each month, but from Bailieborough (first Monday of each month) and Shercock (second Tuesday of each month) as well. . . . The complexity of fair movements is obvious, and it was enhanced by the need to get the trains of stock on their way to catch cross-channel steamers. Not only had sufficient covered wagons to be provided to remove the estimated number of cattle, but in some cases additional accommodation had to be made available for the drovers. Thus in the 1939 Appendix:

> Cootehill Fair. Third Friday of every month. Stock to be forwarded by 1.20 p.m. mixed train. Clones to attach a Small Third Class Carriage to 11.10 a.m. ex Derry for Dealers returning from the fair. ⟨1930s⟩
>
> E. M. Patterson, *The Great Northern Railway of Ireland* (1986 ed.), 139–40

255. NIGHT MAIL

The Post Office Film Unit made a documentary film to show the sorting of letters in a mail train en route. When finished, it was felt to be incomplete, being concerned with technology alone and having nothing at all to say about the people who wrote and received the letters. Auden, who was then working with the Unit, was asked to write a poem to round the film off, supplying this deficiency. "We were experimenting", he said, "to see whether poetry could be used in films, and I think we showed it could."

I

This is the Night Mail crossing the Border,
Bringing the cheque and the postal order,

Letters for the rich, letters for the poor,
The shop at the corner, the girl next door.

Pulling up Beattock, a steady climb:
The gradient's against her, but she's on time.

Past cotton-grass and moorland boulder,
Shovelling white steam over her shoulder,

Snorting noisily, she passes
Silent miles of wind-bent grasses.

Birds turn their heads as she approaches,
Stare from bushes at her blank-faced coaches.

Sheep-dogs cannot turn her course;
They slumber on with paws across.

In the farm she passes no one wakes,
But a jug in a bedroom gently shakes.

II

Dawn freshens. Her climb is done.
Down towards Glasgow she descends,
Towards the steam tugs yelping down a glade of cranes,
Towards the fields of apparatus, the furnaces
Set on the dark plain like gigantic chessmen.
All Scotland waits for her:
In dark glens, beside pale-green lochs,
Men long for news.

III

Letters of thanks, letters from banks,
Letters of joy from girl and boy,
Receipted bills and invitations
To inspect new stock or to visit relations,
And applications for situations,
And timid lovers' declarations,
And gossip, gossip from all the nations,
News circumstantial, news financial,
Letters with holiday snaps to enlarge in,
Letters with faces scrawled on the margin,

Letters from uncles, cousins and aunts,
Letters to Scotland from the South of France,
Letters of condolence to Highlands and Lowlands,
Written on paper of every hue,
The pink, the violet, the white and the blue,
The chatty, the catty, the boring, the adoring,
The cold and official and the heart's outpouring,
Clever, stupid, short and long,
The typed and the printed and the spelt all wrong.

IV

Thousands are still asleep,
Dreaming of terrifying monsters
Or a friendly tea beside the band in Cranston's or Crawford's:
Asleep in working Glasgow, asleep in well-set Edinburgh,
Asleep in granite Aberdeen,
They continue their dreams,
But shall wake soon and hope for letters,
And none will hear the postman's knock
Without a quickening of the heart.
For who can bear to feel himself forgotten?
⟨1935⟩   W. H. Auden, *Collected Shorter Poems,*
                                   1927–57 (1966), 83–4

256.   A POOR BAG OF ASSETS

Let us look at the railway system now. It is in very poor shape. Partly that is due to the strain of six years' war; partly, but not wholly. Those dingy railway stations, those miserable, unprepossessing restaurants, all the out-of-date apparatus for sleeping and eating, make one ashamed as an Englishman when one is travelling abroad. . . . This railway system of ours is a very poor bag of physical assets. The permanent way is badly worn. The rolling stock is in a state of great dilapidation. The railways are a disgrace to the country. ⟨1946⟩

> Hugh Dalton, Chancellor of the Exchequer, in the House of Commons, 17 December 1946: Hansard, vol. 431, cols. 1808–9

12

*Railways
and the Imagination*

257. THE RAILWAYS' PRESENCE

The railways had in every sense a presence. Their very appearance kindled a kind of awe and sense of poetry that seems to have been shared by people of every class: steam, speed, controlled power, new sounds, spontaneous movement – there was an excitement here that communicated itself to the press, the board room, the stock market, the arts, and everyday speech in a way that was almost oblivious of the canals. In retrospect it certainly appears that their obsolescence was too readily taken for granted, perhaps even before their latent capacity had been realised. Yet it must be recognised that this tacit acceptance by the Victorians of a situation in which an asset of these proportions was allowed to waste before its time is strikingly modern in its approach. ⟨1830–60⟩

> H. J. Dyos and D. H. Aldcroft, *British Transport: an Economic Survey from the Seventeenth Century to the Twentieth* (1974 ed.), 213

258. THE SEEING EYES

The railway journey recounted here begins at Beam Bridge, a station west of Wellington in Somerset, opened on 1 May 1843 to serve as a temporary terminus of the line down from London and Bristol until that was continued to Exeter a year later. The young woman making it had travelled up from Plymouth by coach to join the train at this point.

The weather after Exeter got worse and worse; the wind began to bluster, the lightning changed from summer gleams to spiteful forks, and the roll of thunder was almost continuous; and by the time we reached Beam Bridge the storm was at such terrible purpose that the faithful guard wrapped me up in his waterproof and lifted me, literally, into the shed which served as a station. In like manner, when the train was ready, he lifted me high and dry into a first-class carriage, in which were two elderly, cosy, friendly-looking gentlemen, evidently fellows in friendship as well as in travel. The old Great Western carriages were double, held eight persons, four in each compartment, and there was a glass door between; which was on this occasion left open. The old gentleman sate with his face to the horses (so to speak) on my side, and one on the inside corner, opposite to me exactly. When I had taken off my cloak and smoothed my plumes, and generally settled myself, I looked up to see the most wonderful eyes I ever saw, steadily, luminously, clairvoyantly, kindly, paternally looking at me. The hat was over the forehead, the mouth and chin buried in the brown velvet coat collar of the brown greatcoat. I looked at him, wondering if my grandfather's eyes had been like those. I should have described them as the most "seeing" eyes I had ever seen. . . .

Well, we went on, and the storm went on more and more, until we reached Bristol; to wait ten minutes. My old gentleman rubbed the side window with his coat cuff, in vain; attacked the centre window again in vain, so blurred and blotted was it with the torrents of rain! A moment's hesitation, and then:

"Young lady, would you mind my putting down this window?"

"Oh no, not at all."

"You may be drenched, you know."

"Never mind, sir."

Immediately, down goes the window, out go the old gentleman's head and shoulders, and there they stay for I suppose nearly nine minutes. Then he drew them in, and I said: "Oh please let me look".

"Now you *will* be drenched"; but he half opened the window for me to see. Such a sight, such a chaos of elemental and artificial lights and noises, I never saw or heard, or expect to see or hear. He drew up the window as we moved on, and then leant back with closed eyes for I dare say ten minutes, then opened them and said:

"Well?"

I said, "I've been 'drenched', but it's worth it".

He nodded and smiled, and again took to his steady but quite inoffensive perusing of my face, and presently said it was a bad night for one so young and alone. He had not seen me at Exeter.

"No, I got in at Plymouth."

"Plymouth!!"

"Yes." I then said I could only save my friends trouble and anxiety by travelling up that night, and told simply the how it came to pass. Then, except a little joke when we were moving through a long tunnel (*then* the terror of "elegant females"), silence until Swindon, but always the speculative steady look. There we all got out and I got some tea and biscuits. When we were getting in (the storm by then over), they asked me if I had got some refreshment, and when I said tea, my friend with the eyes said: "Tea! poor stuff; you should have had soup."

I said tea was more refreshing, as I had not had anything since eight the previous morning. We all laughed, and I found the two cosy friends had had something more "comfortable" than tea, and speedily fell into slumber, until I watched the dawn and oncoming brightness of one of the loveliest June mornings that have ever visited the earth.

At six o'clock we steamed into Paddington station, and I had signalled a porter before my friends roused themselves. They were very kind – could they do anything to help me? – where had I to go to? "Hammersmith: that was a long drive." Then they took off their hats and went off arm in arm. . . .

The next year, I think, going to the Academy, I turned at once, as I always did, to see what Turners there were.

Imagine my feelings: –

"RAIN, STEAM, AND SPEED,
GREAT WESTERN RAILWAY, JUNE THE –, 1843"

I had found out who the "seeing" eyes belonged to! As I stood looking at the picture, I heard a mawkish voice behind me say:

"There now, just look at that; ain't it *just* like Turner? – whoever saw such a ridiculous conglomeration?"

I turned very quietly round and said:

"*I* did; I was in the train that night, and it is perfectly and wonderfully true"; and walked quietly away. ⟨1843⟩

Lady Simon, in John Ruskin, *Dilecta: Works*, ed. E. T. Cook and A. Wedderburn (1903–12), xxxv. 559–601

259.   RAILWAYS AND ARCHAEOLOGY

In consideration of the importance of the district with respect to both natural history and both British and Roman antiquities, and more especially at this time when the disturbance of the surface of the country in the formation of railroads is likely to bring to light specimens of interest in these departments of science, it is advisable to take immediate steps for the establishment of an institution in this town [Dorchester] containing a Museum and Library for the County of Dorset. ⟨1845⟩

> Resolution passed at preliminary meeting, 15 October
> 1845: G. Dugdale, *William Barnes of Dorset* (1953), 119

260.   RAILWAYS AND WILD LIFE

(a)

Cutting open rail-ways causes a change of vegetation in two ways, by turning up buried live seeds and by affording space and protection for the growth of transported seeds: so that it is often very difficult to determine to which cause the appearance or superabundance of a plant is attributable. ⟨1845⟩   J. D. Hooker to Darwin, July 1845: *Correspondence of Charles Darwin*, (1987), iii. 224

(b)

I wonder what most of the people who only knew him [John Stuart Mill] in connection with public meetings, would have thought if they had been like the mouse behind the curtain, when I, one day, as a youth, asked him in his room at the old India House about stations for rare plants along the Great Western Railway. He jumped from the four-legged stool on which he sat at his desk, with the words: "I'm your man for that!" and I still possess the list which he sent me afterwards in his own hand. ⟨c.1845⟩

> Mountstuart Grant Duff, *Out of the Past* (1903), ii. 27

(c)

Beyond the Yantle we come upon a line of railway, running down from Chipping Norton to join the main line to Worcester. The main railway is here joined by two subsidiary lines, the one coming from Chipping Norton and the other from Cheltenham over the Cotswolds. Paradoxical as it may seem, I do not hesitate to say that this large mileage of railway within a small radius acts beneficially upon our bird life. Let us see how this is.

In the first place, both cuttings and embankments, as soon as they are well overgrown with grass, afford secure and sunny nesting-places to a number of birds which build their nests on the ground. The Whin-chat for example, an abundant bird here every summer, gives the railway banks its especial patronage. . . . You may see a cock-bird sitting on the telegraph wires singing his peaceful little song, but unless you disturb his wife from her beautiful blue eggs you are very unlikely to find them in the thickening grass of May or June. And even if she is on the nest she will sit very close; I have seen an express train fly past without disturbing her, when the nest was but six or eight feet from the rails. The young, when reared, will often haunt the railway for the rest of the summer, undismayed by the rattle and vibration which must have shaken them even when they were still within the egg. . . . Even the station itself[1] meets with some patronage from the birds. In the stacks of coal which are built up close to the siding, the Pied Wagtails occasionally make their nests, fitting them into some hospitable hole or crevice. These, like all other nests found in or about the station, are carefully protected by the employees of the company. In a deep hole in the masonry of the bridge which crosses the line a few yards below the station, a pair of Great Titmice built their nest two years ago, and successfully brought up their young, regardless of the puffing and rattling of the trains, for the hole was in the *inside* of the bridge and only some six feet from the rails of the down line. A little coppice, remnant of a larger wood cut down to make room for the railway, still harbours immense numbers of birds; here for example I always hear the ringing note of the Lesser Whitethroat; and here, until a few years ago, a Nightingale rejoiced in the density of the overgrown underwood. ⟨1886⟩

W. Warde Fowler, *A Year with the Birds* (1886), 144–51

(d)

Before the railway [between Perth and Inverness] was made, people said it would frighten all game out of the valley, but it has not the slightest effect upon it, except that extinct animal the brown hare, which had a trick of using the line as a highway like the other natives, and when it met a train sometimes lost its life through indecision, as cats do in London.

I remember a partridge's nest with an incredible number of eggs, in the hollow between the two sleepers in the goods siding at Dalguise, where trucks were constantly shunted over the bird's head. It is common to see roe deer from the train, they lift their heads and then go on feeding. There are many in the wood at the back judging by their tracks, and yesterday I

---

[1] Kingham

flushed a pair of beautiful woodcocks on the spring head where we get our water at the edge of the wood. ⟨1892⟩

The Journal of Beatrix Potter, ed. L. Linder (1966), 260

261. STANDARD TIME

(a)

A traveller sets out by the express train on a journey of 250 miles from west to east; and, consulting his Bradshaw, he finds he shall be seven and a half hours on the road. Calculating distance and time, he finds he shall accomplish, including all stoppages, about 33 miles per hour. Returning home shortly, by the same train, he again refers to his Bradshaw, and he finds the journey from east to west is performed in about six and a half hours! – making the speed of travelling, including stoppages, about 39 miles per hour.

Now, both these announcements are false; and it is one of the consequences of keeping "local time". The speed of travelling is really the same in both directions, though very different by the timetable! Bradshaw is wrong, every way; the *time* is more than six and a half hours in one direction, and less than seven and a half hours in the other direction; the *speed* is more than 33 miles per hour from west to east, and it is less than 39 miles per hour from east to west; and thus are "facts and fallacies" intermingled in the most marvellous confusion. . . .

Emphatically, what we desire is, that when the great bell of St Paul's strikes ONE, every church clock in England, Scotland, and Wales, and Berwick-upon-Tweed, should strike ONE, also. We want that travellers from the east and from the west, meeting at some common centre (each with a timepiece in his pocket) should be able to keep their appointments, without first consulting the longitude or the parish clock. We want that those absurd discrepancies should cease, at present exhibited by Bradshaw's timetable, according to which your railway trains appear to move marvellously quick from east to west, and proportionately slow from west to east – while, in reality, both speed and time are the same in each direction. ⟨1847⟩   Henry Booth, *Uniformity of Time* (1847), 6, 9–10

Standard (i.e. Greenwich) time was accepted almost everywhere in England (except in Cornwall, then still unconnected to the main railway system) by 1852. Its spread throughout the rest of the island followed, though it was not until 1880 that the matter was settled by legislation. It was then declared that Greenwich time was to prevail in Great Britain, Dublin time in Ireland.

(b)

In consequence of instructions received from the General Post Office it is intended, on and after the first day of December next, to adopt LONDON TIME. Memorandum – London Time is in advance of local time 12 minutes at Carlisle, 15 minutes at Edinburgh, 17 minutes at Glasgow. ⟨1847⟩   Caledonian Railway time-sheet: Scottish Record Office

262.   AN APPRECIATIVE AMERICAN TOURIST

So complete is the system of English railways that four weeks judiciously appropriated, during the intervals of business or social engagements, will enable the American, in London, to visit and thoroughly explore a specimen, at least, of what is peculiar to the country; he may thus become acquainted with a large rural domain, a manufacturing district, an ancient castle, a watering place, and a venerable seat of learning; and these excursions will alternate profitably with metropolitan life. ⟨1853⟩

Henry T. Tuckerman, *A Month in England* (1982 ed.), 9

263.   GEORGE BORROW VISITS BIRMINGHAM

At Birmingham [New Street] station I became a modern Englishman, enthusiastically proud of modern England's science and energy; that station alone is enough to make one proud of being a modern Englishman. Oh, what an idea does that station, with its thousand trains dashing off in all directions, or coming from all quarters, give of modern English science and energy. My modern English pride accompanied me all the way to Tipton; for all along the route there were wonderful evidences of English skill and enterprise; in chimneys high as cathedral spires, vomiting forth smoke, furnaces emitting flame and lava, and in the sound of gigantic hammers, wielded by steam, the Englishman's slave. ⟨1854⟩

George Borrow, *Wild Wales* (1862), i. 15–16

264.   BEFORE RAILWAYS WERE MADE

We who have lived before railways were made, belong to another world. In how many hours could the Prince of Wales drive from Brighton to London, with a light carriage built expressly, and relays of horses longing to gallop the next stage? Do you remember Sir Somebody, the coachman of the Age, who took our half-crown so affably? It was only yesterday; but what a gulf between now and then! *Then* was the old world. Stage-coaches, more or less swift, riding-horses, pack-horses, highwaymen, knights in armour, Norman invaders, Roman legions, Druids, Ancient Britons painted blue, and so forth – all these belong to the old period. I will concede a halt in the midst of it, and allow that gunpowder and printing tended to modernise the world. But your railroad starts the new era, and we of a certain age belong to the new time and the old one. We are of the time of chivalry as well as the Black Prince or Sir Walter Manny. We are of the age of steam. We have stepped out of the old world on to "Brunel's" vast deck, and across the waters *ingens patet tellus*. Towards what new continent are we wending? to what new laws, new manners, new politics, vast new expanses of liberties unknown as yet, or only surmised? I used to know a man who had invented a flying machine. "Sir", he would say, "give me but five hundred pounds, and I will make it. It is so simple of construction that I tremble daily lest some other person should light upon and patent my discovery." Perhaps faith was wanting; perhaps the five hundred pounds. He is dead, and somebody else must make the flying machine. But that will only be a step forward on the journey already begun since we quitted the old world. There it lies on the other side of yonder embankments. The young folk have never seen it; and Waterloo is to you no more than Agincourt, and George IV than Sardanapalus. We elderly people have lived in that prae-railroad world, which has passed into limbo and vanished from under us. I tell you it was firm under our feet once, and not long ago. They have raised those railroad embankments up, and shut off the old world that was behind them. Climb up that bank on which the irons are laid, and look to the other side – it is gone. There is no other side. Try and catch yesterday. Where *is* it? Here is a *Times* newspaper, dated Monday 26th, and this is Tuesday 27th. Suppose you deny there was such a day as yesterday?

We who lived before railways, and survive out of the ancient world, are like Father Noah and his family out of the Ark. The children will gather round and say to us patriarchs, "Tell us, grandpapa, about the old world". And we shall mumble our old stories; and we shall drop off one by one; and there will be fewer of us, and these very old and feeble. There will be but ten prae-railroadites left: then three – then two – then one – then O! ⟨1860⟩ From W. M. Thackeray, "De Juventute": *Roundabout Papers* (Everyman ed.), 85–7

265. MUGBY JUNCTION IN THE BLACK HOURS

A place replete with shadowy shapes, this Mugby Junction in the black hours of the four-and-twenty. Mysterious goods trains, covered with palls and sliding on like vast weird funerals, conveying themselves guiltily away from the presence of the few lighted lamps, as if their freight had come to a secret and unlawful end. Half-miles of coal pursuing in a Detective manner, following when they lead, stopping when they stop, backing when they back. Red-hot embers showering out upon the ground, down this dark avenue, and down the other, as if torturing fires were being raked clear; concurrently, shrieks and groans and grinds invading the ear, as if the tortured were at the height of their suffering. Iron-barred cages full of cattle jangling by midway, the drooping beasts with horns entangled, eyes frozen with terror, and mouths too: at least they have long icicles (or what seem so) hanging from their lips. Unknown languages in the air, conspiring in red, green, and white characters. An earthquake, accompanied with thunder and lightning, going up express to London. Now, all quiet, all rusty, wind and rain in possession, lamps extinguished, Mugby Junction dead and indistinct, with its robe drawn over its head, like Caesar. ⟨1866⟩

Charles Dickens, from "Mugby Junction": *Christmas Stories* (Oxford Illustrated ed.), 476–7.

266. A FIERY CENTIPEDE

In the still evening air I hear a sound,
A roaring like a distant cataract,
It dies and dies away, and wholly ceases;
Suddenly and louder still it roars again
Along the valley and the wooded hill. . . .
Is it an earthquake gathering up its strength?
Again it dies away, yet keeps on muttering,
Till on a sudden bursting from the hills
And thundering like an alpine avalanche,
The railway train dashes along the line –
A fiery centipede, terribly beautiful,
More wonderful than any fabled dragon
Disgorging sulphurous smoke and clouds of steam,
The embodiment of swiftness and of power.

⟨1870⟩   James Hurnard, *The Setting Sun*
                              (1870), 42

267.   ALICE IN THE TRAIN

"Tickets, please!" said the Guard, putting his head in at the window. In a moment everybody was holding out a ticket: they were about the same size as the people, and quite seemed to fill the carriage.

"Now then! Show your ticket, child!" the Guard went on, looking angrily at Alice. And a great many voices all said together ("like the chorus of a song," thought Alice), "Don't keep him waiting, child! Why, his time is worth a thousand pounds a minute!"

"I'm afraid I haven't got one," Alice said in a frightened tone: "there wasn't a ticket-office where I came from." And again the chorus of voices went on. "There wasn't room for one where she came from. The land there is worth a thousand pounds an inch!"

"Don't make excuses," said the Guard: "you should have bought one from the engine-driver." And once more the chorus of voices went on with, "The man that drives the engine. Why, the smoke alone is worth a thousand pounds a puff!"

Alice thought to herself, "Then there's no use in speaking." The voices didn't join in this time, as she hadn't spoken, but, to her great surprise, they all *thought* in chorus (I hope you understand what *thinking in chorus* means – for I must confess that *I* don't), "Better say nothing at all. Language is worth a thousand pounds a word!"

"I shall dream about a thousand pounds to-night, I know I shall!" thought Alice.

All this time the Guard was looking at her, first through a telescope, then through a microscope, and then through an operaglass. At last he said, "You're travelling the wrong way," and shut up the window and went away.

"So young a child," said the gentleman sitting opposite to her (he was dressed in white paper), "ought to know which way she's going, even if she doesn't know her own name!"

A Goat, that was sitting next to the gentleman in white, shut his eyes and said in a loud voice, "She ought to know her way to the ticket-office, even if she doesn't know her alphabet!"

There was a Beetle sitting next the Goat (it was a very queer set of passengers altogether), and, as the rule seemed to be that they should all speak in turn, *he* went on with, "She'll have to go back from here as luggage!"

Alice couldn't see who was sitting beyond the Beetle, but a hoarse voice spoke next. "Change engines – " it said, and there it choked and was obliged to leave off.

"It sounds like a horse," Alice thought to herself. And an extremely small voice, close to her ear, said, "*You might make a joke on that – something about 'horse' and 'hoarse', you know.*"

Then a very gentle voice in the distance said, "She must be labelled, 'Lass, with care,' you know –"

And after that other voices went on ("What a number of people there are in the carriage!" thought Alice), saying, "She must go by post, as she's got a head on her –" "She must be sent as a message by the telegraph –" "She must draw the train herself the rest of the way –," and so on.

But the gentleman dressed in white paper leaned forwards and whispered in her ear, "Never mind what they all say, my dear, but take a return-ticket every time the train stops."

"Indeed I shan't!" Alice said rather impatiently. "I don't belong to this railway journey at all – I was in a wood just now – and I wish I could get back there!"

"*You might make a joke on THAT,*" said the little voice close to her ear: "*something about 'you WOULD if you could,' you know.*"

"Don't tease so," said Alice, looking about in vain to see where the voice came from; "if you're so anxious to have a joke made, why don't you make one yourself?"

The little voice sighed deeply: it was *very* unhappy, evidently, and Alice would have said something pitying to comfort it, "if it would only sigh like other people!" she thought. But this was such a wonderfully small sigh, that she wouldn't have heard it at all, if it hadn't come *quite* close to her ear. The consequence of this was that it tickled her ear very much, and quite took off her thoughts from the unhappiness of the poor little creature.

"*I know you are a friend,*" the little voice went on; "*a dear friend, and an old friend. And you won't hurt me, though I AM an insect.*"

"What kind of insect?" Alice inquired a little anxiously. What she really wanted to know was, whether it could sting or not, but she thought this wouldn't be quite a civil question to ask.

"*What, then you don't –*" the little voice began, when it was drowned by a shrill scream from the engine, and everybody jumped up in alarm, Alice among the rest.

The Horse, who had put his head out of the window, quietly drew it in and said, "It's only a brook we have to jump over." Everybody seemed satisfied with this, though Alice felt a little nervous at the idea of trains jumping at all. "However, it'll take us into the Fourth Square, that's some comfort!" she said to herself. In another moment she felt the carriage rise straight up into the air, and in her fright she caught at the thing nearest to her hand, which happened to be the Goat's beard. ⟨1871⟩

Lewis Carroll, *Through the Looking-Glass*
(Everyman ed.), 127–30

268.   A CHILD'S ALPHABET

Derbyshire is a lovely child's alphabet; an alluring first lesson in all that's admirable, and powerful chiefly in the way it engages and fixes the attention. On its miniature cliffs a dark ivy leaf detaches itself as an object of importance; you distinguish with interest the species of mosses on the top; you count like many falling diamonds the magical drops of its petrifying well; the cluster of violets in the shade is an Armida's garden to you. And the grace of it all! and the suddenness of its enchanted changes, and terrorless grotesque – Grotesque *par excellence*! It was a meadow a minute ago, now it is a cliff, and in an instant is a cave – and here was a brooklet, and now it is a whisper under ground; turn but the corner of the path, and it is a little green lake of incredible crystal; and if the trout in it lifted up their heads and talked to you, you would be no more surprised than if it was in the Arabian Nights. And half a day's work of half a dozen navvies, and a snuff-box full of dynamite, may blow it all into Erebus, and diabolic Night, for ever and ever. . . .

And there is yet this to be noted of the ghastly *precision* of the destroying force, in Derbyshire country, that it is in the very Eyes of it that the fiery brand is plunged. In almost every other lovely hill-district, and in all rich Lowland, the railway kills little more than its own breadth and a square mile or two about every station, and what it leaves is as good as what it takes. But in Derbyshire the whole gift of the country is in its glens. The wide acreage of field or moor above is wholly without interest; it is only in the clefts of it, and the dingles, that the traveller finds his joy, and *in* those clefts every charm depends on the alternate jut and recess of rock and field, on the successive discovery of blanched height and woody hollow; and, above all, on the floretted banks and foam-crisped wavelets of the sweetly wilful stream. Into the very heart and depth of this, and mercilessly bending with the bends of it, your railway drags its close-clinging damnation. The rocks are not big enough to be tunnelled, they are simply blasted away; the brook is not wide enough to be bridged, it is covered in, and is thenceforward a drain; and the only scenery left for you in the once delicious valley is alternation of embankments of slag with pools of slime. ⟨1884⟩

John Ruskin: Letter to the *Manchester City News*, 13 April 1884. *Works*, ed. E. T. Cook and A. Wedderburn (1903–12), xxxiv. 571–2

269. THE SUMMIT OF THE SETTLE &
CARLISLE RAILWAY

If anyone would like to contrast certain triumphs of men over outside Nature with certain failures to manage inside Nature, let him take a look some fine morning at those Westminster slums – not a stone's throw from the Houses of Parliament – where fate has rolled men into gutters, where rents kill modesty, and so dirt and disgrace are accepted good-humouredly as a matter of course – and then, turning his back on this, let him rattle up to St Pancras in time for the 10.35 express, and by five in the afternoon step out in romantic Westmorland. When he has had some food, he should retrace his steps by rail up the ascent to Hawes Junction. Strolling out there on the shadowy hills as the sun begins to set, he has come to a gathering of pure Nature, and he stands alone with an assemblage of mute mountain-peaks. A little later, having walked to the top of the watershed, where rivulets rustle down the rocks, as he waits in the shelter where the Ure and Eden rise together, except for the faint crackling of the limestone crags he can almost hear the moonlight fall upon the stillness. Beside him is the railway, a strange intruder, and Bow Fell looks down calm on this triumph over difficulties. Then there issues an earnest uproar from the milk-blue mist where Kirkby Stephen lies some miles lower down, and soon he sees three red lights diminishing past him till they vanish in the tunnel on the south. ⟨1884⟩   E. E. Foxwell, *Express Trains: Two Papers* (1884), 53–4

270. TRAIN-SPOTTING

I remember how long and carefully I used to wait behind the hedge to catch the wonderful names [of the engines] and store them up in my memory. How inexpressibly and mysteriously great some of those titles seemed to be to my boyish mind, even at that early age – Agamemnon, Hyperion, Prometheus, Ajax, Achilles, Atalanta, Mameluke; they fired my imagination and filled me with strange feelings of pride and joy. It was years before I came to learn who those lordly personages were – if they really ever were, that is – but I surely and certainly received an intimation of their august greatness at the time I first saw their names as a small boy about the farm. ⟨c.1885⟩   Alfred Williams, *A Wiltshire Village* (1912), 216–17

271. EXPRESS

(*From Liverpool, Southwards*)

We move in elephantine row,
  The faces of our friends retire,
The roof withdraws, and curtsying flow
  The message-bearing lines of wire;
    With doubling, redoubling beat,
    Smoother we run and more fleet.

By flow'r-knots, shrubs, and slopes of grass,
  Cut walls of rock with ivy-stains,
Thro' winking arches swift we pass,
  And flying, meet the flying trains,
    Whirr – whirr – gone!
    And still we hurry on;

By orchards, kine in pleasant leas,
  A hamlet-lane, a spire, a pond,
Long hedgerows, counter-changing trees,
  With blue and steady hills beyond;
    (House, platform, post,
    Flash – and are lost!)

Smooth-edged canals, and mills on brooks;
  Old farmsteads, busier than they seem,
Rose-crusted or of graver looks,
  Rich with old tile and motley beam;
    Clay-cutting, slope, and ridge,
    The hollow rumbling bridge.

Gray vapour-surges, whirl'd in the wind
  Of roaring tunnels, dark and long,
Then sky and landscape unconfined,
  Then streets again where workers throng
    Come – go. The whistle shrill
    Controls us to its will.

Broad vents, and chimneys tall as masts,
  With heavy flags of streaming smoke;
Brick mazes, fiery furnace-blasts,
  Walls, waggons, gritty heaps of coke;
    Through these our ponderous rank
    Glides in with hiss and clank.

So have we sped our wondrous course
  Amid a peaceful busy land,
Subdued by long and painful force
  Of planning head and plodding hand.
    How much by labour can
    The feeble race of man!
⟨1889⟩

William Allingham, *Life and Phantasy* (1889),
71–2. The poem includes material from an earlier
date, perhaps of the 1860s

272.   THE MAIL SERVICE IN NORTHERN SCOTLAND

Imagine a mail leaving Aberdeen at 3.30 a.m., and picking up and putting out its bags all along the route – in order that the fishermen of the Banff coast may find their Edinburgh and Glasgow letters awaiting them when they come down to breakfast. Yet more remarkable, imagine that from Inverness to Wick, through that "desert of silence", as Mr Foxwell appropriately terms Caithness, the Highland company hurries the mails faster than the Italian lines can convey the international special train to Brindisi, faster than the German and the Belgian governments, with the assistance of the *Chemin de fer du Nord*, can forward their passengers from Aix [i.e. Aachen] to Calais. Till some one can point out a better, I shall venture to believe that the combined rail and steamboat mail services to the western coast, and to Skye and the Lews, are unmatched in the world. ⟨1889⟩   W. M. Acworth, *The Railways of Scotland* (1890), 136

273.   THE DUKE OF SUTHERLAND'S FUNERAL TRAIN

Birnam. *26 September 1892*. Last night, between eleven and twelve, we thought we heard the special train taking the Duke of Sutherland on his long, last journey [from Dunrobin to Trentham]. Some people can see no sentiment or beauty in a railway, simply a monstrosity and a matter of dividends. To my mind there is scarcely a more splendid beast in the world than a large Locomotive: if it loses something of mystery through being the work of man, it surely gains in a corresponding degree the pride of possession. I cannot imagine a finer sight than the Express, with two engines, rushing down this incline at the edge of dusk. ⟨1892⟩

The Journal of Beatrix Potter, ed. L. Linder (1966), 267

274. DRAWING ENGINES

I have said before that from my earliest years I had always been fond of drawing engines and bridges and signals and tunnels. As time went on this enthusiasm was canalised more and more into the drawing of locomotives. Whether or no I was any good at it does not matter. The point is that I was always doing it and with progressively greater and greater attention to the details of structure and the technique of draughtsmanship. I knew little or nothing of mathematical drawing. I used rulers and compasses, but as regards measurements and proportion I went entirely by eye. I was very much concerned with the structure and movement and purposes of locomotives, because you can't make a good drawing of anything unless you know how it works and what it is for. This may be a "heresy" from the point of pure aesthetics but I wasn't interested in such things then and am only interested in them now in order to repudiate them. But what I was primarily concerned with then was locomotives as such, their character, their meaning. And as this character and meaning were manifest in their shape, it was their shape I was determined to master. I laboured under the spur of this enthusiasm for ten crowded years. I don't know how many hundreds of drawings I made. Perhaps it was not very many; for I could only do them in my spare time in the evenings and in holidays – on the breakfast-room table when the things had been cleared away and before the time came for the next meal to be laid. I suppose I was a pretty good nuisance, but my parents were proud of the result and encouraged me, and once or twice my drawings were even exhibited at school. I suppose I was training myself to be an engineer. I think I thought that all engineering was like that – an immense enthusiasm for engines – engines as beings. Engines pulled trains; they belonged to the Railway Company, they did things and served purposes. Their construction depended upon a vast amount of mathematical calculation and knowledge of physics. But, though I saw, though rather dimly, that I should certainly have to go into all that, it was the shape and character of the locomotive that really enthralled me. ⟨c.1895⟩   Eric Gill, *Autobiography* (1944 ed.), 73–4

275. CUCKOO VALLEY RAILWAY

This line is the Bodmin & Wadebridge in Cornwall; Tregarrick being Bodmin and Ponteglos Wadebridge. The Cuckoo River is the Camel.

This century was still young and ardent when ruin fell upon Cuckoo Valley. Its head rested on the slope of a high and sombre moorland, scattered with granite and china-clay; and by the small town of Ponteglos, where it widened out into arable and grey pasture-land, the Cuckoo River grew deep enough to float up vessels of small tonnage from the coast at the spring tides. I have seen there the boom of a trading schooner brush the grasses on the river-bank as she came before a westerly wind, and the haymakers stop and almost crick their necks staring up at her top-sails. But between the moors and Ponteglos the valley wound for fourteen miles or so between secular woods, so steeply converging that for the most part no more room was left at the bottom of the V than the river itself filled. The fisherman beside it trampled on pimpernels, sundew, water-mint, and asphodels, or pushed between clumps of *Osmundia regalis* that over-topped him by a couple of feet. If he took to wading, there was much ado to stand against the current. Only here and there it spread into a still black pool, greased with eddies; and beside such a pool it was odds that he found a diminutive meadow, green and flat as a billiard table, and edged with clumps of fern. To think of Cuckoo Valley is to call up the smell of that fern as it wrapped at the bottom of the creel the day's catch of salmon-peal and trout.

*

The town of Tregarrick (which possessed a gaol, a workhouse, and a lunatic asylum, and called itself the centre of the Duchy) stood three miles back from the lip of this happy valley, whither on summer evenings its burghers rambled to eat cream and junket at the Dairy Farm by the river bank, and afterwards sit to watch the fish rise, while the youngsters and maidens played at hide-and-seek in the woods. But there came a day when the names of Watt and Stephenson waxed great in the land, and these slow citizens caught the railway frenzy. They took it, however, in their own fashion. They never dreamed of connecting themselves with other towns and a larger world, but of aggrandisement by means of a railway that should run from Tregarrick to nowhere in particular, and bring the intervening wealth to their doors. They planned a railway that should join Tregarrick with Cuckoo Valley, and there divide into two branches, the one bringing ore and clay from the moors, the other fetching up sand and coal from the sea. Surveyors and engineers descended upon the woods; then a cloud of navvies. The days were filled with the crash of falling timber and the rush of emptied trucks. The stream was polluted, the fish died, the fairies were evicted from their rings beneath the oak, the morals of the junketing houses underwent change. The vale knew itself no longer; its smoke went up day by day, week by week, with the noise of pick-axes and oaths.

On August 13th, 1834, the Mayor of Tregarrick declared the new line open, and a locomotive was run along its rails to Dunford Bridge, at the foot of the moors. The engine was christened *The Wonder of the Age*; and I have before me a handbill of the festivities of that proud day, which tells me that the mayor himself rode in an open truck, "embellished with Union

Jacks, lions and unicorns, and other loyal devices". And then Nature settled down to heal her wounds, and the Cuckoo Valley Railway to pay no dividend to its promoters. ⟨1899⟩

Q (Sir Arthur Quiller-Couch), *The Delectable Duchy*
(1915 ed.), 56–8

276. AN INTRODUCTION TO THE WELSH LANGUAGE

The King's Heath [Birmingham] house backed on to a railway line, and life was punctuated by the roar of trains and the shunting of trucks in the nearby coal-yard. Yet the railway cutting had grass slopes, and here he discovered flowers and plants. And something else attracted his attention: the curious names on the coal trucks in the sidings below, odd names which he did not know how to pronounce but which had a strange appeal to him. So it came about that by pondering over *Nantyglo, Senghenydd, Blaen-Rhondda, Penrhiwceiber*, and *Tredegar* he discovered the existence of the Welsh language.

Later in childhood he went on a railway journey to Wales and as the station names flashed past him he knew that here were words more appealing to him than any he had yet encountered, a language that was old and yet alive. ⟨c.1901⟩   Humphrey Carpenter, *J. R. R. Tolkien: a Biography*
(1977), 26

277. THE RAILWAY CHILDREN

They all looked at each other. Each of the three expressive countenances expressed the same thought. That thought was double, and consisted, like the bits of information in the *Child's Guide to Knowledge*, of a question and an answer.

Q. Where shall we go?
A. To the railway.

So to the railway they went, and as soon as they started for the railway they saw where the garden had hidden itself. It was right behind the stables, and it had a high wall all round.

"Oh, never mind about the garden now!" cried Peter. "Mother told me this morning where it was. It'll keep till tomorrow. Let's get to the railway."

The way to the railway was all downhill over smooth, short turf with here and there furze bushes and grey and yellow rocks sticking out like candied peel from the top of a cake.

The way ended in a steep run and a wooden fence – and there was the railway with the shining metals and the telegraph wires and posts and signals.

They all climbed on to the top of the fence, and then suddenly there was a rumbling sound that made them look along the line to the right, where the dark mouth of a tunnel opened itself in the face of a rocky cliff; next moment a train had rushed out of the tunnel with a shriek and a snort, and had slid noisily past them. They felt the rush of its passing, and the pebbles on the line jumped and rattled under it as it went by.

"Oh!" said Roberta, drawing a long breath; "it was like a great dragon tearing by. Did you feel it fan us with its hot wings?"

"I suppose a dragon's lair might look very like that tunnel from the outside", said Phyllis.

But Peter said:

"I never thought we should ever get so near to a train as this. It's the most ripping sport."

"Better than toy-engines, isn't it?" said Roberta.

(I am tired of calling Roberta by her name. No one else did. Everyone else called her Bobbie, and I don't see why I shouldn't.)

"I don't know; it's different", said Peter. "It seems so odd to see *all* of a train. It's awfully tall, isn't it?"

"We've always seen them cut in half by platforms", said Phyllis.

"I wonder if that train was going to London", Bobbie said. "London's where Father is."

"Let's go down to the station and find out", said Peter.

So they went.

⟨1906⟩   E. Nesbit, *The Railway Children* (Puffin ed.), 30–4

278.   ADLESTROP

Yes. I remember Adlestrop –
The name, because one afternoon
Of heat, the express-train drew up there
Unwontedly. It was late June.

The steam hissed. Someone cleared his throat.
No one left and no one came
On the bare platform. What I saw
Was Adlestrop – only the name

And willows, willow-herb, and grass,
And meadowsweet, and haycocks dry,
No whit less still and lonely fair
Than the high cloudlets in the sky.

And for that minute a blackbird sang
Close by, and round him, mistier,
Farther and farther, all the birds
Of Oxfordshire and Gloucestershire.
⟨1915⟩ Edward Thomas, *Collected Poems*
(1936 ed.), 73

279.   AT EUSTON STATION

Yon is the train I used to take
    In the good days of yore
When I went home for love's dear sake,
    I who go home no more.

The station lights flare in the wind,
    The night is blurred with rain,
And there was someone, old and kind,
    Who will not come again.

Oh, that's an Irish voice I hear,
    And that's an Irish face,
And these will come when dawn is near
    To the belovèd place.

And these will see when day is grey
    And lightest winds are still
The long coast-line by Dublin Bay
    With exquisite hill on hill.

I would not follow if I might,
    Who came so oft of old;
No window-pane holds me a light,
    The warm hearth-fire is cold.

There is the train I used to take.
    Be blest from shore to shore,
O land of love and of heart-break!
    But I go home no more.

                        Katharine Tynan, *Collected Poems*
                        (1930), 23–4

280.   A LOCAL TRAIN OF THOUGHT

Alone, in silence, at a certain time of night,
Listening, and looking up from what I'm trying to write,
I hear a local train along the Valley. And "There
Goes the one-fifty", think I to myself; aware
That somehow its habitual travelling comforts me,
Making my world seem safer, homelier, sure to be
The same tomorrow; and the same, one hopes, next year.
"There's peacetime in that train." One hears it disappear
With needless warning whistle and rail-resounding wheels.
"That train's quite like an old familiar friend", one feels.
⟨1939⟩   Siegfried Sassoon, *Collected Poems, 1908–56*
                (1961), 240

281.   SKIMBLESHANKS: THE RAILWAY CAT

There's a whisper down the line at 11.39
When the Night Mail's ready to depart,
Saying "Skimble where is Skimble has he gone to hunt the thimble?
We must find him or the train can't start."
All the guards and all the porters and the stationmaster's daughters
They are searching high and low,
Saying, "Skimble where is Skimble for unless he's very nimble
Then the Night Mail just can't go."
At 11.42 then the signal's nearly due
And the passengers are frantic to a man –
Then Skimble will appear and he'll saunter to the rear:
He's been busy in the luggage van!
        He gives one flash of his glass-green eyes
            And the signal goes "All clear!"
        And we're off at last for the northern part
            Of the Northern hemisphere!

You may say that by and large it is Skimble who's in charge
Of the Sleeping Car Express.
From the driver and the guards to the bagmen playing cards
He will supervise them all, more or less.
Down the corridor he paces and examines all the faces
Of the travellers in the First and in the Third;
He establishes control by a regular patrol
And he'd know at once if anything occurred.

He will watch you without winking and he sees what you are thinking
And it's certain that he doesn't approve
Of hilarity and riot, so the folk are very quiet
When Skimble is about and on the move.
        You can play no pranks with Skimbleshanks!
          He's a cat that cannot be ignored;
        So nothing goes wrong on the Northern Mail
          When Skimbleshanks is aboard.

Oh! it's very pleasant when you have found your little den
With your name written up on the door.
And the berth is very neat with a newly folded sheet
And there's not a speck of dust on the floor.
There is every sort of light – you can make it dark or bright;
There's a handle that you turn to make a breeze.
There's a funny little basin you're supposed to wash your face in
And a crank to shut the window if you sneeze.
Then the guard looks in politely and will ask you very brightly
"Do you like your morning tea weak or strong?"
But Skimble's just behind him and was ready to remind him,
For Skimble won't let anything go wrong.
        And when you creep into your cosy berth
          And pull up the counterpane,
        You ought to reflect that it's very nice
        To know that you won't be bothered by mice –
        You can leave all that to the Railway Cat,
          The Cat of the Railway Train!

In the watches of the night he is always fresh and bright;
Every now and then he has a cup of tea
With perhaps a drop of Scotch while he's keeping on the watch,
Only stopping here and there to catch a flea.
You were fast asleep at Crewe and so you never knew
That he was walking up and down the station;
You were sleeping all the while he was busy at Carlisle,
Where he greets the stationmaster with elation.
But you saw him at Dumfries, where he speaks to the police
If there's anything they ought to know about:
When you get to Gallowgate there you do not have to wait –
For Skimbleshanks will help you to get out!
        He gives you a wave of his long brown tail
          Which says: "I'll see you again!
        You'll meet without fail on the Midnight Mail
          The Cat of the Railway Train."

⟨1939⟩   T. S. Eliot, *Old Possum's Book of Practical Cats*
                                 (1939), 40–1

282.   HOME-COMING TO CORNWALL

A landslide on the line, the train diverted
Back up the valley of the red Exe in spate
Rich with Devonshire soil, flooding the green
Meadows, swirling round the wooded bends,
The December quality of light on boles of trees,
Black and shining out of the gathering dark,
The sepia brushwork against the western skies
Filtering the last watercolour light.
(Why should the eyes fill with tears, as if
One should not look upon the like again?
So many eyes have seen that coign of wood,
That curve of river, the pencil screen of trees.)
I fall asleep; the train feels slowly round
The unfamiliar northern edge of Dartmoor.
It is night and we are entering Cornwall strangely:
The sense of excitement wakens me, to see
Launceston perched on a shoulder like Liège,
The young moon white above the moving clouds.
The train halts in the valley where monks prayed,
Under the castle-keep the Normans ruled
And Edward the Black Prince visited. We stop
At every wayside halt, a signal-box,
An open waiting shed, a shrub or two,
A friendly voice out of the night, a lamp –
Egloskerry, Tresmeer and Otterham –
And out upon the shaven moonlit moor.

⟨1942⟩   A. L. Rowse, *Poems Chiefly Cornish*
                     (1944), 56

283.   THE METROPOLITAN RAILWAY

BAKER STREET STATION BUFFET

Early Electric! with what radiant hope
   Men formed this many-branched electrolier,
Twisted the flex around the iron rope
   And let the dazzling vacuum globes hang clear,
And then with hearts the rich contrivance filled
Of copper, beaten by the Bromsgrove Guild.

Early Electric! Sit you down and see,
  'Mid this fine woodwork and a smell of dinner,
A stained-glass window and a pot of tea,
  And sepia views of leafy lanes in PINNER, –
Then visualize, far down the shining lines,
Your parents' homestead set in murmuring pines.

Smoothly from HARROW, passing PRESTON ROAD,
  They saw the last green fields and misty sky,
At NEASDEN watched a workman's train unload,
  And, with the morning villas sliding by,
They felt so sure on their electric trip
That Youth and Progress were in partnership.

And all that day in murky London Wall
  The thought of RUISLIP kept him warm inside;
At FARRINGDON that lunch hour at a stall
  He bought a dozen plants of London Pride;
While she, in arc-lit Oxford Street adrift,
Soared through the sales by safe hydraulic lift.

Early Electric! Maybe even here
  They met that evening at six-fifteen
Beneath the hearts of this electrolier
  And caught the first non-stop to WILLESDEN GREEN,
Then out and on, through rural RAYNER'S LANE
To autumn-scented Middlesex again.

Cancer has killed him. Heart is killing her.
  The trees are down. An Odeon flashes fire
Where stood their villa by the murmuring fir
  When "they would for their children's good conspire".
Of their loves and hopes on hurrying feet
Thou art the worn memorial, Baker Street.

⟨c.1950?⟩   John Betjeman, *A Few Late Chrysanthemums*
                          (1954), 38–40

284. ON THE ROOF
OF PADDINGTON STATION

Arthur Geary leaves his work as a scientist, his wife and his family, to go and live by himself in the Great Western Hotel at Paddington station. His one desire is to be alone; but the mechanism of modern public inquiry is employed to hunt him down, directed by a journalist, Adrian Swarthmore.

As he crossed the bridge, Geary slowed down to a firm walk. He had decided what to do. During his many hours of strolling about the station, he had become very well acquainted with its physical construction, and he knew that it was an easy matter, even for a middle-aged man, to lower himself from the bridge on to the roof of Platform Two. The high domes of the main glass roof come to an end about two-thirds of the way along the platforms, which are sheltered for their remaining length by ordinary curving metal roofs like those at any country station. Geary calculated that if he could get on to the roof of Platform Two, the easiest one to reach, he could leave Swarthmore safely behind. Swarthmore would be out of voice-range, and he could scarcely bellow questions at him through a megaphone.

Firm in his decision, Geary walked sedately to the point at which he intended to leave the bridge. . . . Then, with deliberate and economical movements, he reached up, grasped a conveniently situated iron lamp-bracket that curved down to meet him, put his other hand on the broad steel parapet of the bridge, and pulled himself up.

Steadying himself with one hand against a roof-pillar which soared up beside him, Geary climbed down on to a flat girder, moved easily along it, skirted another pillar, and dropped lightly on to the roof of Platform Two.

Adrian Swarthmore, following behind him, was nonplussed when he saw Geary climb up on to the parapet. A stifled exclamation escaped him. . . . Swarthmore, seeing Geary move purposefully out along the girder, broke into a run. "Here, come back", he said. For some reason he did not want to shout. He had an obscure feeling that if he could keep the whole scene quiet, prevent Geary from attracting a crowd, everything would remain under control. As Geary dropped down on to the roof of Platform Two, Swarthmore hurried up to the point at which Geary had climbed over the parapet, and leaned over. Above him was the end *façade* of the great glass roof; below, the long platforms with their snow-covered Dutch-barn lids. Geary was under the open sky; snow had already begun to speckle his overcoat and his dark hat.

"Geary", Swarthmore called, his voice urgent but cautious. "Come back. You'll kill yourself."

Geary stood impassively looking at him from a distance of some twenty yards. Swarthmore felt utterly impotent. He had no intention of climbing after Geary; for one thing it was dangerous, and for another he was sure there must be a law against it. If the man had run mad and decided to go clambering about the roofs, let the police get him down.

Geary could not be seen from the platform below him, but people on the other platforms were beginning to notice him and to move up to positions where they had a better view. Suddenly Swarthmore noticed that the chief cameraman was among them. He was setting up his camera, and as Swarthmore watched he focused it and began to film. At the same instant, the two young men with the second camera came hurrying up beside

Swarthmore, and without waiting for instructions balanced their camera on the parapet of the bridge and began filming also. Geary was caught and held in the sight-beams of the two contrivances.

Without hesitation he turned and walked along the centre of the platform roof, out towards the end, with his back to the station. The cameras followed him: the one on the platform swivelled its square black head, the one on the parapet merely lifted its snout a little. Geary walked fast amid the thick-falling snowflakes. His feet left tracks which immediately began to be covered up.

Reaching the end, he stood for a moment outlined against the open sky. The small crowds on the two adjacent platforms had moved along with him step by step, and now they halted with him. There seemed nowhere to go, and Geary began to hear the drums more loudly than ever, so that their thundering seemed to shake his chest inside its coating of plaster. The plaster was due to come off in three days' time, and Geary found himself wondering what would happen between now and then. It was Wednesday: how would he get through till Saturday? How would he come down off this roof? He looked forward very much to getting the plaster off, but he could not imagine Saturday. Would it still be morning then?

A policeman had appeared among the crowd on his left, and people were pointing up at Geary and explaining. He wondered what reasons they were giving for his being on the roof. The policeman began to call to him in a stern voice, but Geary paid no attention. He stood looking out along the snow-covered lines for a minute and then turned and began to walk back towards the great glass arches. As he walked, a train going to some unremarkable place pulled out along the line from Platform Five. It was full of people opening newspapers and settling where to put their feet. That evening, perhaps, they would read in the papers that a man had walked along a platform roof at Paddington, and would think how they had just missed seeing him, and for a moment they would feel important, brushed by the sleeve of great events.

The cameras followed Geary as he went back along the platform roof. Adrian Swarthmore was still staring incredulously at him from the bridge. The situation had left Swarthmore behind. He had no idea what to do. Events would carry him along and he was content that they should. And beneath his contentment was a shocked pity for Geary: and beneath the pity a dark, wild joy. Geary had done what was necessary, he had justified the whole expedition, the chief cameraman would not despise him any-more and Sir Ben would agree to take him on. He would be a success. Geary would make a success of him.

Geary's face was closed and preoccupied as he came back down the platform roof. At first, Swarthmore thought he intended to go back over the parapet on to the bridge. He looked at the two young men beside him, serious in their thick sweaters, intent on nothing but tending their cruel, impersonal instrument. Their presence reassured Swarthmore. With their aid, it should not be difficult to hold Geary until a policeman could take him in charge. Perhaps it would be worth trying to hold him without their help: they could go on filming and it would make a wonderful shot. TV Personality Grapples with Mad Scientist. See it actually happening on your screen. He slipped off his overcoat ready for the struggle.

Geary, however, did not come back to the bridge. When he reached the end of the platform roof, he pulled himself up till he was level with the point where Swarthmore stood, watching. But instead of coming back along the girder that led to the parapet of the bridge, he suddenly swung himself up on to the narrow strip of metal running along the front of the main *façade* of the station roof with its metal-and-glass arches. Then, deliberately, he moved on to the narrow passage between the two main arches, in the very centre of the roof.

What Geary had in mind was to walk along this central path until he reached the foyer end of the station. Then, somehow or other, he would make his way down, and peaceably give himself up. He had no objection to being interviewed by a policeman, even arrested. He knew it was illegal to clamber about on the station roof, that it created a disturbance and set a bad example to young people. He was quite willing to be summoned to a magistrate's court and fined five or ten pounds. He could come back to the station afterwards and all would be well and he would be safe from the drums. It was the cameras that made the drums beat so loudly. He had to get away from the cameras because of the way they stared at him and drew human eyes after him, so that he was being questioned, questioned, questioned all the time.

Geary climbed on to the central metal strip, between the two arches, on his hands and knees. Then he stood upright and began to walk, without haste, back down the length of the roof. But only for a couple of steps. With the drums thundering, he halted. His memory had been at fault. After all those hundreds of hours of strolling about the station, observing its features, he had still not grasped – not until this dreadful moment – that the arches forming the roof are not continuous. They are interrupted at two points by steel columns and high glass domes. It is not possible to walk along the whole length of the roof, even on the secure footing of the cat-walk between the central arches. For this, too, is twice interrupted by the high glass domes.

Geary stood absolutely still. No one could see him. The arches of Paddington station are made of glass only above a certain point. Up to that point, they are made of metal. A man standing between the arches cannot be seen from below, and if he keeps away from the far end he cannot be seen from any angle. So Geary stood, breathing quietly, the snow falling on to him from a softly luminous sky. He looked up at the sky, relishing its pearliness. It seemed bigger, more welcoming, than it had ever been before. All at once he felt that the station had outlived its usefulness to him. He wanted to walk freely under this vast open sky, to look up into it, to receive its blessings. The station had been essential to him when he needed a smaller sky, one that would fit over his world like a protecting lid. But now he needed the real sky, the immeasurable generosity of space.

He kept still, no longer willing to give himself up, but also no longer afraid. He decided that if he kept quite still for a sufficient length of time, the cameras would go away, the crowds would disperse, and he could make his way down and leave the station quietly. . . . Then the loudspeakers started.

"THIS IS A MESSAGE TO THE MAN WHO IS AT PRESENT ON THE MAIN ROOF OF THE STATION. IN THE INTERESTS OF YOUR OWN AND OTHER PEOPLE'S SAFETY WE ASK YOU TO COME DOWN AT ONCE."

It was a good idea on someone's part to use the public address system of the station to get in touch with the unclassifiable man, who was not a traveller, not a train-spotter, not waiting, but simply standing on the roof, and by that simple act challenging the whole sane and sturdy world of trains, timetables, business journeys and news-stands. The self-assured voice went on, in a matter-of-fact sub-Cockney intonation, to reassure the public. There was no danger. No one had any reason to believe that the man on the roof was a criminal, or that he was armed or in any way dangerous. Several police officers were standing by just in case, but as far as anyone knew he was just a member of the public who had taken it into his head to go climbing.

Then the voice turned back to Geary: "ONCE AGAIN WE ADDRESS THE MAN WHO IS AT PRESENT SOMEWHERE BETWEEN THE TWO CENTRAL ARCHES OF THE MAIN ROOF. PLEASE COME DOWN OR YOU WILL HAVE TO BE FETCHED DOWN."

The loudspeakers clicked off, and the station was held in a tense silence. Not even a diesel purred, not even a trolley clanked. Everyone was listening and watching for Geary. He understood this, but he did not know what to do. He could not come down, into reach of all the cameras and all the eyes. He needed to get away by himself, to some place where the sky was big and the drums would never be heard.

The silence was good, but he knew that at any moment the public address system would begin calling to him again, and the only way to go was up. He suddenly launched himself forward, climbing steeply, clawing at the tiles. There was just enough purchase for his feet and hands to thrust him upward, and as he climbed higher the slope grew less acute and he was able to let go with his hands and straighten up. He moved on: the tiles gave way to glass, but he did not falter. A great crack appeared under his feet: he shifted his weight on to a fresh pane just in time, but there was another crack, another, another, and as Geary reached the highest point and put his weight squarely on the glass, it gave way with a splintering sound that echoed in every corner of the station. There was nothing to hold Geary and he fell, turning over on to his back as he made a last effort to hold on.

It seemed to Geary that he fell for a long time. Landing on his back on the metals, he broke his spine and fractured his skull in the same instant. His body made one great writhing movement, as if he were trying to get up, but this must have been nothing more than a reflex on the part of the already dead nerves. As he fell back across the lines, his dark felt hat rolled off and lay beside him, open to the sky like a begging-bowl.

As Geary died, two good things happened. The drums ceased, and the snow went on falling. ⟨1967⟩

John Wain, *The Smaller Sky* (Penguin ed.), 136–42

285. SOME CLOSING WORDS

(a)

Her Majesty travels at the rate of forty miles an hour.

General Grey, Queen Victoria's private secretary, arranging a journey to Scotland with the secretary of the Great Northern Railway, 30 August 1854: Public Record Office, RAIL 236/606/1

(b)

The railways are the wonder of the age;
It was our fools who chiefly paid for them,
And everybody rides at their expense.

James Hurnard, *The Setting Sun*,
(1870), 249–50

(c)

Will alight precipitately at 5.38 from the deliberate 1.50

Telegram from Henry James: Simon Nowell Smith, *The Legend of the Master* (1947), 21

(d)

No liver can get in at Putney and remain sluggish beyond Walham Green.

Owen Seaman, commenting on the motion of the trains on the District line in London when it was first electrified: *Punch*, 131 (1906), 136. Walham Green (now called Fulham Broadway) is two stations from Putney Bridge

(e)

A railway station is, after all, significant of half life's pleasures, of its memories and anticipations, and some of its sorrows.

A. G. Bradley, *Exmoor Memories* (1926), 16

(f)

Accidents do not happen by accident.

Sir Herbert Walker of the Southern Railway, in a discussion with his senior officers on the Sevenoaks disaster, 1927: Sir John Elliot, *On and Off the Rails* (1982), 119

(g)

Trains sum up, to my mind, all the fogs and muddled misery of the nineteenth century. They constitute, in fact, so many slums on wheels.

Sir Osbert Sitwell, *Penny Foolish* (1935), 232

(h)

BEECHING IS FAB

Graffito on disused station in Suffolk, 1960s

(i)

TO THE DUNGEONS

Graffito on door at the north-eastern corner of St Pancras station, 1967

(j)

The clamorous confusion of parochial loyalties that enliven but muddy railway history.

Charles Wilson, *First with the News* (1985), 125

(k)

The railways were the great connecter, linking up the furthest corners of the country, and making one England out of many.

Harold Perkin, *The Age of the Railway* (1971), 101

INDEX

The references are to the numbered items,
except where "p" indicates a page.